Nineteenth-Century
American Plays

Nineteenth-Century American Plays

Edited by

Myron Matlaw

APPLAUSE
THEATRE BOOK PUBLISHERS
100 West 67 St. • New York, N.Y. 10023 • (212) 595 4735

NINETEENTH-CENTURY AMERICAN PLAYS

First Published by Applause Theatre Book Publishers, 1985

Grateful acknowledgment is made to John T. Herne for permis-
sion to publish in this anthology *Margaret Fleming* by his late
father James A. Herne.

This material originally appeared in, and is reprinted from, *The Black Crook*
(1967).

Library of Congress Cataloging in Publication Data
Main entry under title:

Nineteenth century American plays.

Bibliography: p.
Contents: Fashion/Anna Cora Mowatt—The Octoroon/Dion Bouci-
cault—Rip Van Winkle/Joseph Jefferson—[etc.]
1. American drama—19th century.   I. Matlaw, Myron, 1924–
PS632.N56   1985   812'.3'08   84-24289
ISBN 0-87910-228-4
ISBN 0-87910-227-6 (pbk.)

Applause Theatre Book Publishers
100 West 67th Street
New York, NY 10023
(212) 595-4735

First Applause Printing, 1985

For Sarah

Contents

Introduction

American drama began in the last years of the eighteenth century. In 1798 William Dunlap (1766–1839), "the Father of the American Drama," opened the Park Theatre in New York. Philadelphia was then still the theatre center of the young nation, although Baltimore, Annapolis, and even Boston, despite strong Puritanical opposition, each had at least one playhouse. The Park, however, was the most architecturally advanced theatre of its time. New York, then a city of 60,000, thus set out on its bid for the theatrical supremacy that it achieved some time before 1825 and that it has maintained, on Broadway and off, to this day.

Two plays by Americans had been performed before Dunlap's career started: Thomas Godfrey's romantic verse tragedy *The Prince of Parthia* (1767), and Royall Tyler's comedy *The Contrast* (1787). Dunlap, however, was the first professional native-born dramatist. Of his more than fifty plays, the best ones are *The Father* (1789), a comedy that became a theatrical success immediately, and *André* (1798), a poetic tragedy based on the famous Revolutionary spy story; this latter play became a hit only when Dunlap vulgarized it into a patriotic spectacle, *The Glory of Columbia* (1803). His most popular plays, however, were his adaptations of the sentimental dramas and melodramas of August von Kotzebue (1761–1819), the German playwright whose works dominated European and English stages at the turn of the century. In his *History of the American Theatre* (1832), the first record of its kind, Dunlap remarks that despite his grave financial difficulties, the successful adaptation of one of Kotzebue's many plays, *The Stranger*, "alone enabled the author to keep open the theatre." It is interesting to note the parallel with Richard Brinsley Sheridan, who at that time had the identical experience with his adaptations of Kotzebue during his management of the Drury Lane in London.

Indeed, much of the history of American drama and theatre—and written drama and living theatre were particularly interdependent in the nineteenth century, when star

9

rather than playwright predominated—is closely related to
English drama and London theatres. It is not surprising that
the first acting companies in America were organized by
English entrepreneurs and consisted of English actors, and
that their repertoire consisted of English drama: plays by
Shakespeare, and popular Restoration and eighteenth-century
dramas like Otway's *Venice Preserved*, Farquhar's *The Beaux'
Stratagem*, Addison's *Cato*, Steele's *The Conscious Lovers*,
Lillo's *The London Merchant*, Home's *Douglas*, and the two
English comic masterpieces of the eighteenth century, Gold-
smith's *She Stoops to Conquer* and Sheridan's *The School
for Scandal*. These plays, as well as Kotzebue's, retained their
popularity in this country throughout much of the nineteenth
century, and early American plays, such as Dunlap's and the
two that preceded his—not to mention much of the drama
that was written later—were modeled on them. It is not until
well into the nineteenth century that distinct American
characteristics, although germinal in individual early plays,
begin to predominate in our drama.

By the same token, although Americans at the beginning
of the nineteenth century were fiercely independent of
England politically, they felt very dependent culturally.
Audiences were more secure with plays that, as Dunlap puts
it in his *History*, "had been sanctioned by a London audience." A record of a successful London performance consti-
tuted a seal of approval, and some early American
playwrights, including Dunlap, were willing to have their
works advertised as having been written by Englishmen in
order to assure successful runs for them here. That audiences
persisted for many years in their defensive scorn of native
productions is evidenced by the opening lines of the Prologue
to *Fashion* (page 31).

Because of Dunlap's encouragement and the example he
provided with his own plays, however, the early years of the
century saw the composition and production of plays by
native playwrights, some of which dealt with native themes.
This trend continued after Dunlap's management of the Park
ended in 1805. Among the more successful of those plays
were Mordecai Manuel Noah's *She Would Be a Soldier*
(1819), a historic drama dealing with the War of 1812, and
a farce on the American Exchange (anticipating a topic that
would interest later playwrights), *Wall Street; or, Ten Min-*

utes Before Three (1819), probably written by Richard W. Mead. Aside from Dunlap, however, the only important playwrights born before the nineteenth century were John Howard Payne (1791–1852) and James Nelson Barker (1784–1858). Payne's immortality rests on "Home, Sweet Home," one of America's most popular songs, which he wrote for his otherwise unnotable operatic drama *Clari* (1823). Yet he was an immensely popular actor, both here and in England, and he wrote (and, even more frequently, adapted) a total of over fifty plays. Among them were heroic and romantic treatments of Roman history, and these started a vogue that resulted in the production of a host of minor historical dramas. Payne's best plays are a poetic tragedy written for and acted by Edmund Kean, *Brutus; or, The Fall of Tarquin* (1818), and a comedy written in collaboration with Washington Irving, *Charles the Second* (1824). Most of Payne's other works, although highly successful because of their great theatricality, are of no literary value; they are by and large melodramas based on contemporary German, French, and English plays. James Nelson Barker, unlike Payne, was neither a professional theatre man nor very prolific. His plays, considerably superior to the many others written at the time, deal with native themes. The best one, *Superstition* (1824)—a precursor of Arthur Miller's *The Crucible* (1953)—is based on seventeenth-century Colonial history. His *The Indian Princess* (1808), the first produced American play on an Indian theme, is a dramatization of the Pocahontas story.

Over fifty such "Indian" plays appeared before the Civil War, and the Indian character continued to remain popular for some time in minor roles, such as that of Wahnotee in *The Octoroon*. The most successful play in that genre, John Augustus Stone's *Metamora* (1829), portrayed the defeat of the Indian King Philip by the New England settlers in 1676. It was written especially for Edwin Forrest (1806–1872), who had offered a prize of $500 for the best five-act tragedy featuring an "aboriginal hero." Along with his Shakespearean and other roles, Forrest, one of America's great actors, played *Metamora* continually throughout his long stage career, and made a fortune on the play. (Stone, however, received nothing beyond his prize money; in financial despair, he eventually committed suicide.) Forrest scaled

ever greater heights of popularity. An exponent of the ranting
school of acting, he was at one time very popular with
fashionable audiences. But he lost their support after his feud
with the gentlemanly English actor William Charles
Macready erupted into the Astor Place Riot—a notorious
catastrophe (1849) that endeared him the more to the gallery
crowds at the Bowery.

In his quest for strong parts for himself, however, Forrest
helped to further the cause of native drama. He made prominent the work of a Philadelphia physician who became an
important playwright, Robert Montgomery Bird (1806–
1854). Partial to the type of romantic drama in which Forrest
excelled, Bird conceived for him the heroic part of the
Thracian leader of gladiator-slaves in *The Gladiator* (1831),
and Spartacus became another role Forrest played with
immense success in England and in America throughout
his career. Bird's best play was *The Broker of Bogota* (1834),
a domestic prose tragedy set in eighteenth-century Colombia;
Forrest (and later John McCullough) played the part of the
middle-class protagonist, whose tragedy occurs when he is
betrayed by the son he loves. Bird also rewrote *Metamora*
for Forrest in 1836, but Forrest was as niggardly about paying for the plays written for him by Bird, his personal friend
(who received but $1,000 for *The Gladiator*), as he had
been with Stone. Bird gave up a successful, but unlucrative,
playwriting career; the absence of copyright laws left him
powerless against Forrest. But there were other native playwrights and works that became and remained popular because
of Forrest. *Caius Marius* (1831), a historical verse tragedy
on the Roman rebellion against political oppression, provided
him with an excellent part; its author, Richard Penn Smith
(1799–1854), wrote twenty plays, some of which dealt with
American history. In 1852 Robert T. Conrad rewrote his
Jack Cade (1835), whose title character led the 1450 Kentish
serf rebellion; as *Aylmere*, the play provided Forrest with
another favorite role.

Forrest had made his debut as Young Norval in John
Home's long-popular Scottish tragedy *Douglas* (1756), in
Philadelphia in 1820. Other great actors began to gain recog-
nition in this early period: Charlotte Cushman (1816–1876),
Mrs. John Drew (1820–1897), and such prominent actor
families as the Booths, the Jeffersons, and the Wallacks. It

was for James William Wallack that Nathaniel Parker Willis (1806–1867) wrote *Tortesa the Usurer* (1839), a poetic drama; he had won a prize two years earlier from Josephine Clifton with another poetic drama, *Bianca Visconti*, which was written for this actress. The effect on our drama by James H. Hackett (1800–1871) was more distinctively American. Although Hackett was successful as a Shakespearean actor, of greater importance to our drama were his portrayals and popularization of Yankee types. Hackett played Rip Van Winkle for years before Jefferson made that role world famous, and he rewrote the part of Solomon Gundy (in Colman's *Who Wants a Guinea?*) into that of the Yankee Solomon Swap, a part he performed in England as well as America. His best and most successful role was that of Nimrod Wildfire the frontiersman, an offshoot of the Yankee type, in James Paulding's *The Lion of the West* (1830), one of the prize plays written for him. Other famous and color-fully named Yankee characters were Lot Sap Sago in *Yankee Land* (1834) and Deuteronomy Dutiful in *The Vermont Wool Dealer* (1840), both by Cornelius A. Logan, and, of course, Adam Trueman in *Fashion*. Plays like Samuel Wood-worth's *The Forest Rose* (1825) and Joseph S. Jones's *The People's Lawyer* (1839) remained popular for many years because their stage Yankees, Jonathan Ploughboy and Solon Shingle, were performed by such once-famous comedians as George Handel Hill, Danforth Marble, John E. Owens, and Joshua Silsbee.

Apart from the Indian and rural Yankee, there were two other distinctly American stage types that gained prominence in the first half of the century. Neither gave rise to drama that can make much claim to literary pretensions, but both were so popular that no account of nineteenth-century drama can disregard them. As is true of the other stage types, actors in their performances made a great deal more of these parts than may appear from a reading of the plays.

The first of these types was the tough city lad. The B'hoy, or volunteer New York fireman (fireboy), was the most popular representative of the type. As Mose, he first appeared in Benjamin A. Baker's *A Glance at New York* (1848). F.S. Chanfrau, who was to be identified with that character until his death in 1884, was wildly cheered by audiences that consisted of many of Mose's living prototypes. The play—an

almost plotless affair that existed only to enable Mose to
swagger, fight, and drag a firehose across the stage—became
so successful that many sequels followed soon and remained
popular for years: *Mose in California, Mose in France, A
Glance at Philadelphia*, and so on. The growth of urban life
was also reflected in the increasingly frequent portrayal of
the city merchant, in plays like *Fashion* and popular deriva-
tives of this play, like Mrs. Sidney F. Bateman's *Self* (1856).
Growing urbanization in the latter part of the century, of
course, saw city types much more frequently represented in
later American drama.

The final peculiarly American stage type to be noted is the
most indigenous one of all. Negro minstrelsy probably began
in the 1820's with T.D. Rice and his "Jim Crow" song-and-
shuffle routine in which the infant Joseph Jefferson III had
made one of his first stage appearances. By the 1840's, such
blackface troupes as those of Dan Emmett and E.P. Christy
offered full evening entertainments in major theatres. Later
in the century came such famous minstrels as McIntyre and
Heath, and Lew Dockstader, in whose troupe Al Jolson began
his career. In the first part of the minstrel show the enter-
tainers, grouped in a semicircular lineup, featured singing and
a comic repartee among the two end men (Tambo and
Bones) and the Interlocutor; the second part, the olio, was
somewhat like the old vaudeville finales, and concluded with
a travesty (called "burlesque") of one of the currently
popular plays, including the Shakespearean and other pre-
nineteenth-century drama that provided most of the theatrical
staple. Scripts of such burlesques are still extant, and they
furnish an interesting glimpse into the theatre of the age.
The minstrel, played by white actors in blackface, was a
native stage character as romantically (or unrealistically)
conceived as other type characters—shiftless but jolly and
good-natured. He is the only native nineteenth-century stage
character, however, who remained theatrically intact well
into our century. He found his way into much nineteenth-
century drama, including *The Octoroon* and the readily avail-
able and most popular of all American plays, George L.
Aiken's 1852 dramatization of *Uncle Tom's Cabin*.[1]

[1] This play's remarkable history may be pursued in Harry
Birdoff's *The World's Greatest Hit: Uncle Tom's Cabin* (New
York, 1947).

American drama and theatre before the Civil War, then, manifested considerable vitality, as it was to continue to do until the early twentieth century. However, there were few playwrights of even minor literary stature. Robert Montgomery Bird had turned away from playwriting because it was financially unrewarding at a time when stars could simply expropriate popular plays for their own sole profit. He might well have become a dramatist of note, for his few plays showed much promise. The best dramatist of the age was George Henry Boker. His *Francesca da Rimini* ranks as the finest play of the century, despite derivative poetic and dramatic conventions. Similarly *Fashion*, the best comedy of the century, was derivative of *The School for Scandal*, as Edgar Allan Poe noted in the first of his reviews of Mrs. Mowatt's popular play. In that review Poe also wrote: "We must discard all models. The Elizabethan theatre should be abandoned. We need thought of our own—principles of dramatic action drawn not from the 'old dramatists' but from the fountain of a Nature that can never grow old." These comments were to the point, but they remained unheeded for decades to come—on both sides of the Atlantic. The dominant figure in the American theatre of the 1850's, Dion Boucicault (pp. 203–256), used European models for most of his popular melodramas, although *The Octoroon* (his outstanding work) and *The Poor of New York* dealt with native themes. Ultimately of even greater importance to our drama was his work on behalf of the American copyright law of 1856, the first of its kind. It gave to dramatists some control, at least, over their own work, and paved the way for the later development of native drama.

Theatre conditions had greatly changed since Dunlap's day. The Park, periodically destroyed by fire and then rebuilt, like so many nineteenth-century theatres, dominated the American scene in the early decades. George Frederick Cooke had been the first great English star to begin his American tour there, in 1810, and he was followed at the Park by almost every contemporary star of importance, English and American. Other flourishing showplaces were Philadelphia's Chestnut Street, Washington's National, and Boston's Federal Street. By 1860, New York had many theatres, including the Bowery, the Chatham, the Olympic, and Wallack's Lyceum. Theatres had sprung up in every American city, spreading to the South, Midwest, and, beginning in the 1850's, California and other areas of the growing West. Showboats featured legitimate drama and reached areas that were otherwise difficult of access, around the Mississippi River and elsewhere. The second half of the century, of course, saw the rise of more theatres—such famous houses as the Ford in Washington, McVicker's in Chicago, and, in New York, the Fourteenth Street, Daly's Fifth Avenue, Hammerstein's Olympia, and many others.

Even before Dunlap's time, most cities had their own stock companies. The nineteenth century, however, was the century of the star system, when performers with phenomenal public followings were of far greater importance than the plays in which they were featured. Although individual stars could (and occasionally did) popularize the better plays of contemporary dramatists, the star system had distinct drawbacks as far as the drama—as well as the theatre—were concerned. Walt Whitman was but one of many observers who lamented the situation. He wrote in the Brooklyn *Eagle* (February 8, 1847): "One of the curses of the Park, and indeed of nearly all theatres now, is the *star* system. Some actor or actress flits about the country, playing a week here and a week there, bringing as his or her greatest recommendation, that of *novelty*—and very often indeed having no other. In all the intervals between the appearance of these much trumpeted people, the theatre is quite deserted, though the plays and playing are often far better than during some star engagements." Stock companies, Whitman complained, would put on excellent plays, well acted—but to empty houses, "while the next week crowds would crush each other to get a sight of some flippant well-puffed star, of no real merit, and playing a character written (for the play consists of nothing but *one* in such cases) by nobody knows whom. . . ." As the century wore on, stock companies were more and more relegated to the position of supporting local companies for touring stars, until Boucicault's (and later other) traveling companies, on tour with one New York hit, displaced them almost everywhere but in New York.

New York became the undisputed theatrical center after the Civil War. The community drama, which for so long has formed the staple of the many nonprofessional Little Theatres across the country, is indeed of great importance. Its influence, however, was not really felt before the work of Percy MacKaye in the first decades of this century. Among its early practitioners was George Melville Barker (1832–1890), who in the latter part of the nineteenth century wrote hundreds of community dramas: comedies, farces, and skits on various native topics.

The post-Civil War history of American drama, then, is largely the history of the New York stage. Paramount in the early part of this history is the career of Augustin Daly (1838–1899), its outstanding stage manager. Originally a drama critic for a number of newspapers, Daly began his career as a playwright with adaptations of French and German melodramas and popular English novels, such as those of Charles Reade and Wilkie Collins. Among the most successful of his early adaptations was his first one, *Leah the Forsaken* (1862). Based on Salomon von Mosenthal's *Deborah* (1849), a drama of eighteenth-century Austrian anti-Semitism, it was greeted with particular enthusiasm because of the timely analogy that Northerners made with anti-Negro prejudice in the South. In 1867 Daly produced his first original play, *Under the Gaslight*. Its name, like that of *Uncle Tom's Cabin*, is still a byword for nineteenth-century melodrama, and rightly so. The climax occurs at night in an almost deserted countryside. The heroine, Laura, attempts to axe her way out of a locked railway shanty to rescue Snorkey, a one-armed Civil War veteran who was tied to the tracks by the villain Byke. Tension builds up as the express train is heard in the distance, but the rescue comes in the nick of time, of course:

> SNORKEY: Cut the woodwork! Don't mind the lock—cut round it! How my neck tingles! (*A blow at door is heard.*) Courage! (*Another.*) Courage! (*The steam whistle heard again—nearer, and rumble of train on track. Another blow.*) That's a true woman! Courage! (*Noise of locomotive heard—with whistle. A last blow; the door swings open, mutilated—the lock hanging—and* LAURA *appears, axe in hand.*) Here—quick! (*She runs and unfastens him. The locomotive lights glare on scene.*) Victory! Saved! Hooray! (LAURA *leans exhausted against switch.*) And these are the women who aint to have a vote! (*As* LAURA *takes his head from the*

*track, the train of cars rushes past with roar and whistle
from left to right.*)

CURTAIN

What is particularly noteworthy in these stage directions
is the setting. In the beginning of the century stage settings
consisted mainly of painted backdrops. Gradually these gave
way to box sets and stage properties that, as the century
progressed, became increasingly more realistic—and important. The dramatist Steele MacKaye (1842–1894) was to
develop many technical inventions in lighting and scenic
effects, and the elevator (or double) stage, which greatly
accelerated and smoothed scene changes. In time came such
further discoveries as hydraulic lifts and various uses of
electricity that made possible even greater theatrical effects.
In fact, as a scene such as the one above suggests, props
themselves were often the main attraction: an actual train
roaring across the stage, elaborate pyrotechnics (as in *The
Octoroon* and other Boucicault plays), and so on. However
misplaced, this emphasis was nonetheless a step in the direction of realism, which was carried further by Bronson Howard
whose first plays were produced by Daly and whom Daly
greatly encouraged and supported in his career as one of America's foremost early dramatists.

Among Daly's greatest contributions to American drama
were the shows he produced in his Fifth Avenue Theatre. He
disliked the star system, and insisted that his company per-
form as an ensemble, with no one actor ever gaining special
prominence. When Fanny Davenport, John Drew, Clara
Morris, and Ada Rehan reached stellar positions, they left his
company. He rigorously controlled every element of the
production, and his dictatorial but sensitive directing became
proverbial.[2] Daly succeeded also in effecting a new style,
which dispensed at least partially with the hitherto-fashion-
able histrionics. Though ridiculed by some for being "under-
played," his productions gained critical acclaim and popular

[2] Eyewitness accounts of these, and, for comparison, the older
slapdash rehearsals, may be found in, respectively, Clara Morris's
Life on the Stage (New York, 1901) and Anna Cora Mowatt's
Autobiography of an Actress; or, Eight Years on the Stage (Boston,
1854).

support. The popularity of his company, of course, increased when he took it on national tour with his great individual hits, *Frou-Frou* (1870) and *Divorce* (1871).

Although Daly adapted many foreign plays and was also a frequent and prominent producer of Shakespeare, both here and in his London theatre, he also encouraged native dramatists and favored plays with American plots. Among his own plays (nearly one hundred) were a number of "frontier" dramas, of which *Horizon* (1871) was typical of Daly's kind of realistic setting and his attempts at emotional restraint. Dramas set—and featuring the life—in various areas removed from urban or semiurban civilization ("frontier drama"), increasingly popular in the latter part of the century, found expression also in such hits and long stock favorites as *My Partner* (1879) and *The White Slave* (1882), both by Bartley Campbell (1843–1888). The most popular of all "frontier" dramas was F.H. Murdoch's *Davy Crockett* (1872). Until his death in 1896, Frank Mayo played the part of this hero of fact and fiction with enormous success. The climax of the play occurs when Davy rescues the heroine during a blizzard and bars the cabin door with his arm all night, holding off the howling wolves. ("What can save us now?" "The strong arm of a Backwoodsman.") Major literary names are associated with other "frontier" plays, but none of these achieved any real success in the theatre. Bret Harte dramatized some of his stories: with Boucicault, *The Two Men of Sandy Bar* (1876), and with T. Edgar Pemberton, *Sue* (1896). He also collaborated with Mark Twain on *Ah Sin* (1877). Mark Twain's dramatization of *The Gilded Age* (1874) was fairly successful, but a second attempt at a play with the character of Colonel Mulberry Sellers failed.

William Dean Howells collaborated with Mark Twain on this second play, *The American Claimant* (1887). As America's most distinguished champion of nineteenth-century realism, Howells encouraged "realistic" drama and wrote over thirty plays himself, ranging from farces to heroic drama. Two notable farces, *The Mouse Trap* and *The Garroters* (also produced as *A Dangerous Ruffian*), were repeatedly performed both in America and in London in the 1880's and 1890's; the latter was praised by many, including Bernard Shaw. Among Howells's other works are two comedies: *A Counterfeit Presentment* (1877), successfully produced by

Lawrence Barrett, and *The Sleeping Car* (1883). Most of
his plays were one-act farces, popular with amateur companies and readers of the magazines in which they were
published. Despite the skill of their composition, however,
none of his dramatic works achieved the popularity of
Howells's other works.

In the same genre as Howells's farces, but immensely
popular, were the Harrigan and Hart productions of the
1870's and 1880's. Edward Harrigan (1845–1911) wrote and
acted in over eighty vaudeville sketches, some of which were
developed into full-length plays. His partnership with Tony
Hart, the female impersonator of the team, produced the
famous Mulligan plays.[3] *The Mulligan Guard* (1873) was
the first in this series, which featured city types like the Irish,
Negro, Italian, and German, and sharp partisan satires of
city politics and military organizations. Some of the routines
and characters in Harrigan's works are reminiscent of minstrelsy, and the Irish are urban transpositions of Boucicault's
Irish characters. In their focus on low-life, these plays also
follow directly in the footsteps of the Mose plays, which
Chanfrau was then still playing. However, Harrigan strove
for a truer picture of contemporary life and he avoided his
predecessors' romantic characterizations. He wrote in *Harper's Weekly* (February 2, 1889): "Though I use type and
never individuals, I try to be as realistic as possible"—at
least in dress and accouterments. Also of a farcical nature and
as popular as Harrigan's plays were those of Charles Hoyt
(1860–1900). His works too are episodic in format and contemporary in content: politics, sports, women's rights, the
militia, and so on. His most popular play, *A Trip to Chinatown* (1891), holds the nineteenth-century record of a run
of 657 continuous performances; it deals with the escapades
of an assorted group of characters in San Francisco—but
mostly outside of Chinatown.

There were other plays that qualify perhaps only margin-
ally as drama but that found immense favor with theatregoers
in the late decades of the century. No account of the
American drama can ignore the musical comedy, our most
notable contribution to world theatre. *The Black Crook*,

---

[3]See E. J. Kahn, Jr.'s *The Merry Partners: The Age and Stage of Harrigan and Hart*
(New York, 1955) and Richard Moody's *Ned Harrigan* (Chicago, 1980).

which still holds the record for its long and extravagant run, has been acclaimed the first "musical comedy," the precursor of the present-day genre. In another genre, what began as a vaudeville sketch for Denman Thompson in 1875, developed by 1886 into a four-act drama, *The Old Homestead*. Until his death in 1911, Thomas played Joshua Whitcomb, the kindly old New England farmer who goes to find and save his city-corrupted son. *The Great Diamond Robbery* (1895), a six-act detective thriller by Edward M. Alfriend and A.C. Wheeler, was one of the great hits for a decade. In the same romantic genre were the plays of the actor–dramatist William Gillette (1855–1937): *Held by the Enemy* (1886), *Secret Service* (1895), and *Sherlock Holmes* (1899). Immensely popular and frequently revived by Gillette, who played the dashing leads, these plays are among the best melodramas written after those of Boucicault; all the same, in accord with the spirit of the times, Gillette stressed the realism of his characters' actions and thoughts by inserting a profusion of details in his stage directions. Then, of course, there was *The Count of Monte Cristo*. James O'Neill began to act the Count in 1883, and eventually decided to confine his considerable acting talents to this great money-maker—a step whose agonizing consequences to himself and his family were immortalized by his son Eugene O'Neill in his masterpiece, *Long Day's Journey Into Night* (1955).

The outstanding power and personality in the theatre after Daly was David Belasco (1859–1931). He too exerted complete control over all phases of his productions and wrote and adapted plays, often with collaborators. He began his career in the 1870's and continued his professional activities until shortly before his death; his career thus spans the mid-nineteenth-century drama of Boucicault—whom he met and by whom he was greatly influenced—and the drama of the 1920's. Belasco was primarily interested in "show business," often in spectacular productions that aimed at incredible scenic realism: he went as far as reproducing, for example, a complete replica of a Childs restaurant on his stage. The scripts of the plays he wrote with Henry C. DeMille—hits like *The Wife* (1887), *Lord Chumley* (1888), and *Men and Women* (1890)—were often worked out during the production and in strict accord with effective theatre. If his nineteenth-century drama is of little permanent significance (his later dramas are historically more important, particularly because of Giacomo Puccini's use of Belasco's scripts for *Madame Butterfly* and *The Girl of the Golden West* as the librettos of his operas), he contributed considerably to the birth of modern drama by his development of realistic scenic and lighting display and, even more important, his ultimately successful struggle with the powerful Klaw-Erlanger Syndicate. In control of most of the theatres across the country, and running a central booking office that decided what productions and actors would play when and where, the Syndicate effectually dominated most of the theatrical activity for a decade at the turn of the century. The only opposition to its stranglehold came from Belasco and a few independent stars, including Sarah Bernhardt, James O'Neill, and Richard Mansfield.

It was Mansfield (who was to introduce Shaw to America in 1894 with *Arms and the Man*) who in 1889 engaged Clyde Fitch (1865–1909) to write for him *Beau Brummell*, a dramatization of the life of the famous Regency dandy who died in poverty. This play launched the career of the most popular turn-of-the-century dramatist, whose great successes came in the next century. But his *The Masked Ball*, a comedy in which John Drew and Maude Adams starred, and two historical plays, *Nathan Hale* and *Barbara Frietchie* (one of Julia Marlowe's early successes), were popular in the 1890's. In subject matter and form these typify the drama in which Fitch was to excel: comedy and history, with an emphasis on human relations but with resolutions that were constructed with a view toward audience approval and theatrical effect rather than historical fact, probability, or what is now called "psychological realism."

Augustus Thomas (1857—1934), the most distinguished playwright at the turn of the century, did most of his best work in the first two decades of this century. Although he occupied Boucicault's one-time post as adapter of foreign plays for the Madison Square Theatre, the very names of his early plays already point to the strongly American character of his works. *Alabama* (1891) deals with reconciliation after the Civil War; *In Mizzoura* (1893), an early "Western" with a love triangle, was written for Nat C. Goodwin, who played the sheriff; *The Capitol* (1895) is a deft mixture of political, economic, and love conflicts; and *Arizona* (1899) deals with the amatory intrigues of various Cavalry officers and their wives. Like Fitch, Thomas focused on human relations within his broad settings. But unlike Fitch, Thomas, despite his propensity for pseudoscience, superficiality, and melodrama, strove for truthful story and character development. He has been credited with being the first dramatist who successfully introduced New York audiences to the "drama of ideas."

"The drama of ideas," "realistic drama," and similar terms have been applied, perhaps wishfully, to various plays written before the end of the century. One of these was the domestic drama *Hazel Kirke* (1880), the most famous of some twenty plays by the stage innovator Steele MacKaye. This play was so great a hit that by 1882–83 fourteen *Hazel Kirke* road companies were touring the country. While the play is a melodrama whose main claim to realism rests on the absence of the old-fashioned villain, the dialogue is relatively constrained, reflecting the change in tastes. As has been seen, realism in scenery had begun even before the Civil War and was greatly developed by Daly and Belasco. The use of common folk like the B'hoys in place of the old-time larger-than-life heroes, and the detailed actions and gestures spelled out for the characters of Gillette's thrillers, carried realism a step further. Yet to be achieved was an inner realism that transcends the format of the "well-made play"—or its American equivalent, which Bronson Howard had defined and utilized so successfully in his dramas. It was James A. Herne— particularly in his *Margaret Fleming*—who for the first time staged drama that dispensed with the neat but conventionally contrived plot development and denouement that followed the theatrical laws of the past.

In *The Theatre Through Its Stage Door* (1919) Belasco described his own method of early scene construction as follows: "I seldom follow the stage directions on the printed page, either of my own plays or those of other dramatists. I prefer to plan the scenes myself with reference to stage values." Nothing contrasts more sharply with this method, particularly as specified in the last five words, than Herne's revision to achieve greater realism in the characters and situations of *Margaret Fleming*. Although our theatre subsequently lost the verve, buoyancy, and audience appeal it so remarkably displayed throughout the nineteenth century, it was this concern with what Herne called "Art for Truth's

Sake" that set the path American drama was to follow, and on which it was to develop and flourish in the twentieth century.

                                                    MYRON MATLAW

Queens College of the
City University of New York

FASHION

Preface to FASHION

Fashion; or, Life in New York, America's finest nineteenth-century comedy, is still fun to read—and to see. In a splendid revival in 1959 it was produced with period songs, and it became, in the words of one of the New York theatre critics, "the only successful off-Broadway musical show of the season." An even more successful revival had occurred in New York in 1924, when *Fashion* played for 235 consecutive performances.

The play's première took place at the Park Theatre on March 24, 1845, before an audience of New York's artistic, social, financial, and political *ee-light*, as the play's Mrs. Tiffany would say. In her *Autobiography*, Anna Cora Mowatt (1819–1870)—a lady with social position as well as some literary reputation—rightly alluded to the play as an "unequivocally brilliant success." The house remained packed for three weeks—an unprecedented run for a new play, and a long one for *any* play at the time; and it had equal success in other cities, here and in England. Edgar Allan Poe reviewed it in the *Broadway Journal* at great length on March 29, 1845—and then again a week later, when he had gone back to see the play every day for a total of eight times! Other New York newspapers also devoted more space to the play than they had ever devoted to drama before, rejoicing particularly in the play's American authorship.

Patriotic pride was heightened by the play's satire of affected foreign (French) manners and speech. A new idle wealthy class was rising in New York in the 1840's, and Mrs. Mowatt viewed many of its members' "parvenuisms," as she referred to them, with a mixture of irritation and humor. Both these attitudes may be seen in her characterization of Mrs. Tiffany, a composite of many people she saw about her. In the opening scene the foppish Negro servant Zeke foreshadows the pretentiousness of Mrs. Tiffany, as well as that of Augustus Fogg (the "drawing room appendage") and the daughter, Seraphina. Their model in manners and speech—

the putative French count, Jolimaitre—is, of course, the biggest impostor of them all.

Juxtaposed with this drawing-room mélange is the bluff but honest farmer, Adam Trueman. This stage Yankee is a character type that had been popular from its inception as Jonathan in Royall Tyler's *The Contrast*, an eighteenth-century precursor of *Fashion*. Trueman has the conventional attributes of this type: a way of forcefully expressing democratic principles at every opportunity, a natural but noble savagery combined with a heart of gold, New England peddler shrewdness, and a lack of education and manners. These attributes are not held up to ridicule; Trueman was, on the contrary, held up for admiration as an American ideal and the most appealing character in the play. He was the only one of the characters who was "sketched from life," Mrs. Mowatt relates in her *Autobiography*, and she notes that "the original was seen in the pit vociferously applauding Adam Trueman's strictures on fashionable society." His condemnations of the hypocrisy and affectation popularly believed to be among the characteristic evils of city life are echoed by Gertrude, who bitterly contrasts that life with rural life and the homely virtues that were thought to characterize it.

But edifying though all these sentiments may have been, it was not they that made this play a hit in the nineteenth century—and so superior to the many imitations that inevitably sprang up soon—or that make it good reading today. It is, rather, the vivacity and sureness of the comic touch, which is perceptible even in the portrayal of the minor and stock characters: the love-starved, husband-hunting spinster, Prudence; the poet manqué, T. Tennyson Twinkle, vainly trying to declaim over the distracting household bustle, finally blurting out his complete poem—two vapid lines; and the servants, Mrs. Tiffany's low-comic pendant, Zeke (the rechristened "A-dolph"), and her instructress in French, the soubrette Millinette. Even the various melodramatic parts, all deftly constructed, are entertaining.

Mrs. Mowatt wrote other plays, as well as poetry, stories, and articles; but *Fashion* (first published in 1850) is her best work. It greatly encouraged American writers by demonstrating the possibilities inherent in the hitherto despised native productions, and in native themes. Mrs. Mowatt's contribution to the American theatre does not end with her authorship of *Fashion*, however, important though that contribution may be. The success of the play and her consequent fame, as well as financial need occasioned by her husband's business failure, started her out on what became a distinguished career as an actress, here and in England—the first American society lady to embark on such a career. Her unexceptionable behavior as an actress, both on stage and off, as well as her energy, dignity, beauty, and charm, were all effective in raising and making respectable the status of what was still considered a fairly disreputable profession. Her importance in our theatrical annals, therefore, transcends her authorship of what is to this day a delightful comedy.

Fashion was first published in London, in 1850. Anna Cora Mowatt's *Autobiography of an Actress; or Eight Years on the Stage* (1854) is a charming reminiscence; her definitive biography—and also an excellent account of her theatre and milieu—is Eric Wollencott Barnes's *The Lady of Fashion* (1954).

M.M

FASHION;

or, LIFE IN NEW YORK. A Comedy in Five Acts
By Anna Cora Mowatt

Characters

ADAM TRUEMAN, a farmer from Catteraugus
COUNT JOLIMAITRE, a fashionable European importation
COLONEL HOWARD, an officer in the United States Army
MR. TIFFANY, a New York merchant
T. TENNYSON TWINKLE, a modern poet
AUGUSTUS FOGG, a drawing room appendage
SNOBSON, a rare species of confidential clerk
ZEKE, a colored servant
MRS. TIFFANY, a lady who imagines herself fashionable
PRUDENCE, a maiden lady of a certain age
MILLINETTE, a French lady's maid
GERTRUDE, a governess
SERAPHINA TIFFANY, a belle
LADIES and GENTLEMEN of the Ball-room

PROLOGUE[1]

(*Enter a Gentleman, reading a Newspaper.*)

" '*Fashion, a Comedy.*' I'll go; but stay—
Now I read farther, 'tis a native play!
Bah! homemade calicoes are well enough,
But homemade dramas *must* be stupid stuff.
Had it the *London* stamp, 'twould do—but then,
For plays, we lack the manners and the men!"
    Thus speaks one critic. Hear another's creed:—
" '*Fashion!*' What's here? (*Reads.*) It never can succeed!
What! from a woman's pen? It takes a man
To write a comedy—no woman can."
    Well, sir, and what say you, and why that frown?
His eyes uprolled, he lays the paper down:—
"Here! take," he says, "the unclean thing away!
'Tis tainted with the notice of a play!"
    But, sir!—but, gentlemen!—you, sir, who think
No comedy can flow from native ink,—
Are we such *perfect* monsters, or such *dull*,
That Wit no traits for ridicule can cull?
Have we no follies here to be redressed?
No vices gibbeted? no crimes confessed?
"But then a female hand can't lay the lash on!"
How know you that, sir, when the theme is FASHION?
    And now, come forth, thou man of sanctity!
How shall I venture a reply to thee?
The Stage—what is it, though beneath thy ban,
But a daguerreotype of life and man?
Arraign poor human nature, if you will,
But let the DRAMA have her mission still;
Let her, with honest purpose, still reflect
The faults which keeneyed Satire may detect.

---

[1] By Epes Sargent (1813–80), Boston author and journalist, and friend of the Mowatt family. He had suggested that she write the play, and later helped with some of the technical details of its composition.

For there *be* men who fear not an hereafter,
Yet tremble at the hell of public laughter!
    Friends, from these scoffers we appeal to you!
Condemn the false, but O, applaud the true.
Grant that *some* wit may grow on native soil,
And Art's fair fabric rise from woman's toil.
While we exhibit but to *reprehend*
The social voices, 'tis for *you* to mend!

ACT I

SCENE 1

A splendid Drawing Room in the House of MRS.
TIFFANY. *Open folding doors, discovering a Conservatory.
On either side glass windows down to the ground. Doors
on right and left. Mirror, couches, ottomans, a table with
albums, beside it an arm chair.* MILLINETTE *dusting furniture.* ZEKE *in a dashing livery, scarlet coat.*

ZEKE. Dere's a coat to take de eyes ob all Broadway! Ah!
Missy, it am de fixin's dat make de natural *born* gemman.
A libery for ever! Dere's a pair ob insuppressibles to
'stonish de colored population.
MILLINETTE. (*Very politely.*) Oh, *oui*, Monsieur Zeke.
(*Aside.*) I not *comprend* one word he say!
ZEKE. I tell 'ee what, Missy, I'm 'stordinary glad to find dis
a bery 'spectabul like situation! Now, as you've made de
acquaintance ob dis here family, and dere you've had a
supernumerary advantage ob me—seeing dat I only re-
ceibed my appointment dis morning. What I wants to know
is your publicated opinion, privately expressed, ob de
domestic circle.
MILLINETTE. You mean vat *espèce*, vat kind of *personnes* are
Monsieur and Madame Tiffany? Ah! Monsieur is not de
same ting as Madame—not at all.
ZEKE. Well, I s'pose he ain't altogether.
MILLINETTE. Monsieur is man of business, Madame is lady
of fashion. Monsieur make de money, Madame spend it.

Monsieur nobody at all, Madame everybody altogether. Ah! Monsieur Zeke, de money is all dat is *necessaire* in dis country to make one lady of fashion. Oh! it is quite anoder ting in *la belle France!*

ZEKE. A bery lucifer explanation. Well, now we've disposed ob de heads ob de family, who come next?

MILLINETTE. First, dere is Mademoiselle Seraphina Tiffany. Mademoiselle is not at all one proper *personne.* Mademoiselle Seraphina is one coquette. Dat is not de mode in *la belle France;* de ladies, dere, never learn *la coquetrie* until dey do get one husband.

ZEKE. I tell 'ee what, Missy, I disreprobate dat proceeding altogeder!

MILLINETTE. Vait! I have not tell you all *la famille* yet. Dere is Ma'mselle Prudence—Madame's sister, one very *bizarre personne.* Den dere is Ma'mselle Gertrude, but she not anybody at all; she only teach Mademoiselle Seraphina *la musique.*

ZEKE. Well now, Missy, what's your own special defunctions?

MILLINETTE. I not understand, Monsieur Zeke.

ZEKE. Den I'll amplify. What's de nature ob your exclusive services?

MILLINETTE. *Ah, oui! je comprend.* I am Madame's *femme de chambre*—her lady's maid, Monsieur Zeke. I teach Madame *les modes de Paris,* and Madame set de fashion for all New York. You see, Monsieur Zeke, dat it is me, *moi-même,* dat do lead de fashion for all de American *beau monde!*

ZEKE. Yah! yah! yah! I hab de idea by de heel. Well now, p'raps you can 'lustrify my officials?

MILLINETTE. Vat you will have to do? Oh! much tings, much tings. You vait on de table—you tend de door—you clean de boots—you run de errands—you drive de carriage—you rub de horses—you take care of de flowers—you carry de water—you help cook de dinner—you wash de dishes—and den you always remember to do everyting I tell you to!

ZEKE. Wheugh, am dat *all?*

MILLINETTE. All I can tink of now. To-day is Madame's day of reception, and all her grand friends do make her one *petite* visit. You mind run fast ven de bell do ring.

ZEKE. Run? If it wasn't for dese superfluminous trimmings, I tell 'ee what, Missy, I'd run—

MRS. TIFFANY. (*Outside.*) Millinette!

MILLINETTE. Here comes Madame! You better go, Monsieur Zeke.

ZEKE. (*Aside.*) Look ahea, Massa Zeke, doesn't dis open rich!   (*Exit* ZEKE.)

(*Enter* MRS. TIFFANY, *dressed in the most extravagant height of fashion.*)

MRS. TIFFANY. Is everything in order, Millinette? Ah! very elegant, very elegant, indeed! There is a *jenny-says-quoi*[1] look about this furniture—an air of fashion and gentility perfectly bewitching. Is there not, Millinette?

MILLINETTE. Oh, *oui*, Madame!

MRS. TIFFANY. But where is Miss Seraphina? It is twelve o'clock; our visitors will be pouring in, and she has not made her appearance. But I hear that nothing is more fashionable than to keep people waiting.—None but vulgar persons pay any attention to punctuality. Is it not so, Millinette?

MILLINETTE. Quite *comme il faut.*—Great *personnes* always do make little *personnes* wait, Madame.

MRS. TIFFANY. This mode of receiving visitors only upon one specified day of the week is a most convenient custom! It saves the trouble of keeping the house continually in order and of being always dressed. I flatter myself that *I* was the first to introduce it amongst the New York *ee-light.* You are quite sure that it is strictly a Parisian mode, Millinette?

MILLINETTE. Oh, *oui*, Madame; entirely *mode de Paris.*

MRS. TIFFANY. (*Aside.*) This girl is worth her weight in gold. Millinette, how do you say *arm-chair* in French?

MILLINETTE. *Fauteuil*, Madame.

MRS. TIFFANY. *Fo-tool!* That has a foreign—an out-of-the-wayish sound that is perfectly charming—and so genteel! There is something about our American words decidedly vulgar. *Fowtool!* how refined. *Fowtool! Arm-chair!* what a difference.

[1] *Je ne sais quoi*: I know not what; a certain something. The humor stemming from Mrs. Tiffany's consistent mispronunciation of French words is suggested in the spelling here and elsewhere. Another part of the comedy consists, of course, of her overuse—and occasional misuse—of common French expressions.

MILLINETTE. Madame have one charmante pronunciation. *Fowtool* (*Mimicking aside.*) charmante, Madame!

MRS. TIFFANY. Do you think so, Millinette? Well, I believe I have. But a woman of refinement and of fashion can always accommodate herself to everything foreign! And a week's study of that invaluable work—*French Without a Master*, has made me quite at home in the court language of Europe! But where is the new valet? I'm rather sorry that he is black, but to obtain a white American for a domestic is almost impossible; and they call this a free country! What did you say was the name of this new servant, Millinette?

MILLINETTE. He do say his name is Monsieur Zeke.

MRS. TIFFANY. Ezekiel, I suppose. Zeke! Dear me, such a vulgar name will compromise the dignity of the whole family. Can you not suggest something more aristocratic, Millinette? Something *French!*

MILLINETTE. *Oh, oui,* Madame; *Adolph* is one very fine name.

MRS. TIFFANY. A-dolph! Charming! Ring the bell, Millinette! (MILLINETTE *rings the bell.*) I will change his name immediately, besides giving him a few directions.

(*Enter* ZEKE. MRS. TIFFANY *addresses him with great dignity.*)

Your name, I hear, is *Ezekiel.*—I consider it too plebeian an appellation to be uttered in my presence. In future you are called A-dolph. Don't reply—never interrupt me when I am speaking. A-dolph, as my guests arrive, I desire that you will inquire the name of every person, and then announce it in a loud, clear tone. That is the fashion in Paris. (MILLINETTE *retires up the stage.*)

ZEKE. (*Speaking very loudly.*) Consider de officer discharged, Missus.

MRS. TIFFANY. Silence! Your business is to obey and not to talk.

ZEKE. I'm dumb, Missus!

MRS. TIFFANY. (*Pointing up stage*). A-dolph, place that *fowtool* behind me.

ZEKE. (*Looking about him.*) I habn't got dat far in de dictionary yet. No matter, a genus gets his learning by nature. (*Takes up the table and places it behind* Mrs. Tiffany, *then expresses in dumb show great satisfaction.* Mrs. Tiffany, *as she goes to sit, discovers the mistake.*)

MRS. TIFFANY. You dolt! Where have you lived not to know that *fow-tool* is the French for *arm-chair?* What ignorance! Leave the room this instant.

(Mrs. Tiffany *draws forward an arm-chair and sits.* Millinette *comes forward suppressing her merriment at* Zeke's *mistake and removes the table.*)

ZEKE. Dem's de defects ob not having a libery education. (*Exit.*)

(Prudence *peeps in.*)

PRUDENCE. I wonder if any of the fine folks have come yet. Not a soul—I knew they hadn't. There's Betsy all alone. (*Walks in.*) Sister Betsy!

MRS. TIFFANY. Prudence! how many times have I desired you to call me *Elizabeth?* Betsy is the height of vulgarity.

PRUDENCE. Oh! I forgot. Dear me, how spruce we do look here, to be sure—everything in first rate style now, Betsy. (Mrs. Tiffany *looks at her angrily.*)
Elizabeth, I mean. Who would have thought, when you and I were sitting behind that little mahogany-colored counter, in Canal Street, making up flashy hats and caps—

MRS. TIFFANY. Prudence, *what do* you mean? Millinette, leave the room.

MILLINETTE. *Oui,* Madame. (Millinette *pretends to arrange the books upon a side table, but lingers to listen.*)

PRUDENCE. But I always predicted it—I always told you so, Betsy—I always said you were destined to rise above your station!

MRS. TIFFANY. Prudence! Prudence! have I not told you that—

PRUDENCE. No, Betsy, it was *I* that told *you,* when we used to buy our silks and ribbons of Mr. Anthony Tiffany— "talking Tony," you know we used to call him, and when you always put on the finest bonnet in our shop to go to his—and when you stayed so long smiling and chattering with him, I always told you that *something* would grow out of it—and didn't it?

MRS. TIFFANY. Millinette, send Seraphina here instantly. Leave the room.

MILLINETTE. *Oui*, Madame. (*Aside.*) So dis Americaine ladi of fashion vas one *milliner?* Oh, vat a fine country for *les marchandes des modes!* I shall send for all my relation by de next packet!

(*Exit* MILLINETTE.)

MRS. TIFFANY. Prudence! never let me hear you mention this subject again. Forget what we *have* been, it is enough to remember that we *are* of the *upper ten thousand!*

(PRUDENCE *goes up and sits down.*)

(*Enter* SERAPHINA, *very extravagantly dressed.*)

MRS. TIFFANY. How bewitchingly you look, my dear! Does Millinette say that that head dress is strictly Parisian?

SERAPHINA. Oh, yes, Mamma, all the rage! They call it a *lady's tarpaulin*, and it is the exact pattern of one worn by the Princess Clementina at the last court ball.

MRS. TIFFANY. Now, Seraphina, my dear, don't be too particular in your attentions to gentlemen not eligible. There is Count Jolimaitre, decidedly the most fashionable foreigner in town—and so refined—so much accustomed to associate with the first nobility in his own country that he can hardly tolerate the vulgarity of Americans in general. You may devote yourself to him. Mrs. Proudacre is dying to become acquainted with him. By the by, if she or her daughters should happen to drop in, be sure you don't introduce them to the Count. It is not the fashion in Paris to introduce—Millinette told me so.

(*Enter* ZEKE.)

ZEKE. (*In a very loud voice.*) Mister T. Tennyson Twinkle!

MRS. TIFFANY. Show him up.

(*Exit* ZEKE.)

PRUDENCE. I must be running away! (*Going.*)

MRS. TIFFANY. Mr. T. Tennyson Twinkle—a very literary young man and a sweet poet! It is all the rage to patronize poets! Quick, Seraphina, hand me that magazine.—Mr. Twinkle writes for it.

(SERAPHINA *hands the magazine,* MRS. TIFFANY *seats herself in an arm-chair and opens the book.*)

PRUDENCE. (*Returning.*) There's Betsy trying to make out that reading without her spectacles. (*Takes a pair of spectacles out of her pocket and hands them to* MRS. TIFFANY.) There, Betsy, I knew you were going to ask for them. Ah! they're a blessing when one is growing old!

MRS. TIFFANY. What do you mean, Prudence? A woman of fashion *never* grows old! Age is always out of fashion.

PRUDENCE. Oh, dear! what a delightful thing it is to be fashionable.

(*Exit* PRUDENCE. MRS. TIFFANY *resumes her seat.*)

(*Enter* TWINKLE. *He salutes* SERAPHINA.)

TWINKLE. Fair Seraphina! the sun itself grows dim,
Unless you aid his light and shine on him!

SERAPHINA. Ah! Mr. Twinkle, there is no such thing as answering you.

TWINKLE. (*Looks around and perceives* MRS. TIFFANY.) (*Aside.*) The *New Monthly Vernal Galaxy.* Reading my verses by all that's charming! Sensible woman! I won't interrupt her.

MRS. TIFFANY. (*Rising and coming forward.*) Ah! Mr. Twinkle, is that you? I was perfectly *abimé* at the perusal of your very *distingué* verses.

TWINKLE. I am overwhelmed, Madam. Permit me. (*Taking the magazine.*) Yes, they do read tolerably. And you must take into consideration, ladies, the rapidity with which they were written. Four minutes and a half by the stop watch! The true test of a poet is the *velocity* with which he composes. Really they do look very prettily, and they read tolerably—*quite* tolerably—*very* tolerably,—especially the first verse. (*Reads.*) "To Seraphina T——."

SERAPHINA. Oh! Mr. Twinkle!

TWINKLE. (*Reads.*) "Around my heart"—

MRS. TIFFANY. How touching! Really, Mr. Twinkle, quite tender!

TWINKLE. (*Recommencing.*) "Around my heart"—

MRS. TIFFANY. Oh, I must tell you, Mr. Twinkle! I heard the other day that poets were the aristocrats of literature.

That's one reason I like them, for I do dote on all aristocracy!

TWINKLE. Oh, Madam, how flattering! Now pray lend me your ears! (*Reads.*) "Around my heart thou weavest"—

SERAPHINA. That is such a *sweet* commencement, Mr. Twinkle!

TWINKLE. (*Aside.*) I wish she wouldn't interrupt me! (*Reads.*) "Around my heart thou weavest a spell"—

MRS. TIFFANY. Beautiful! But excuse me one moment, while I say a word to Seraphina! (*Aside to* SERAPHINA.) Don't be too affable, my dear! Poets are very ornamental appendages to the drawing room, but they are always as poor as their own verses. They don't make eligible husbands!

TWINKLE. (*Aside.*) Confound their interruptions! My dear Madam, unless you pay the utmost attention you cannot catch the ideas. Are you ready? Well, now you shall hear it to the end! (*Reads.*)
"Around my heart thou weavest a spell
"Whose"—

(*Enter* ZEKE.)

ZEKE. Mister Augustus Fogg! (*Aside.*) A bery misty lookin young gemman.

MRS. TIFFANY. Show him up, Adolph!
(*Exit* ZEKE.)

TWINKLE. This is too much!

SERAPHINA. Exquisite verses, Mr. Twinkle—exquisite!

TWINKLE. Ah, lovely Seraphina! your smile of approval transports me to the summit of Olympus.

SERAPHINA. Then I must frown, for I would not send you so far away.

TWINKLE. Enchantress! (*Aside.*) It's all over with her.
(*Retire up and converse.*)

MRS. TIFFANY. Mr. Fogg belongs to one of our oldest families; to be sure, he is the most difficult person in the world to entertain, for he never takes the trouble to talk, and never notices anything or anybody—but then I hear that nothing is considered so vulgar as to betray any emotion, or to attempt to render oneself agreeable!

(*Enter* MR. FOGG, *fashionably attired but in very dark clothes.*)

FOGG. (*Bowing stiffly.*) Mrs. Tiffany, your most obedient. Miss Seraphina, yours. How d'ye do, Twinkle?

MRS. TIFFANY. Mr. Fogg, how do you do? Fine weather—delightful, isn't it?

FOGG. I am indifferent to weather, Madam.

MRS. TIFFANY. Been to the opera, Mr. Fogg? I hear that the *bow monde* make their *debutt* there every evening.

FOGG. I consider operas a bore, Madam.

SERAPHINA. (*Advancing.*) You must hear Mr. Twinkle's verses, Mr. Fogg!

FOGG. I am indifferent to verses, Miss Seraphina.

SERAPHINA. But Mr. Twinkle's verses are addressed to me!

TWINKLE. Now pay attention, Fogg! (*Reads*)—
"Around my heart thou weavest a spell
"Whose magic I"—

(*Enter* ZEKE.)

ZEKE. Mister—No, he say he ain't no Mister—

TWINKLE. "Around my heart thou weavest a spell
"Whose magic I can never tell!"

MRS. TIFFANY. Speak in a loud, clear tone, A-dolph!

TWINKLE. This is terrible!

ZEKE. Mister Count Jolly-made-her!

MRS. TIFFANY. Count Jolimaitre! Good gracious! Zeke, Zeke—A-dolph I mean. (*Aside.*) Dear me, what a mistake! Set that chair out of the way—put that table back. Seraphina, my dear, are you all in order? Dear me! dear me! Your dress is so tumbled! (*Arranges her dress.*) What are you grinning at? (*To* ZEKE.) Beg the Count to *honor* us by walking up!
(*Exit* ZEKE.)
Seraphina, my dear (*aside to her*), remember now what I told you about the Count. He is a man of the highest—good gracious! I am so flurried and nothing is so ungenteel as agitation! What will the Count think! Mr. Twinkle, pray stand out of the way! Seraphina, my dear, place yourself

on my right! Mr. Fogg, the conservatory—beautiful flowers
—pray amuse yourself in the conservatory.

FOGG. I am indifferent to flowers, Madam.

MRS. TIFFANY. (*Aside.*) Dear me! the man stands right in the
way—just where the Count must make his *entray!* Mr.
Fogg—pray—

(*Enter* COUNT JOLIMAITRE, *very dashingly dressed, wears
a moustache.*)

MRS. TIFFANY. Oh, Count, this unexpected honor—

SERAPHINA. Count, this inexpressible pleasure—

COUNT. Beg you won't mention it, Madam! Miss Seraphina,
your most devoted! (*Crosses.*)

MRS. TIFFANY. (*Aside.*) What condescension! Count, may I
take the liberty to introduce—(*Aside.*) Good gracious! I
forgot. Count, I was about to remark that we never introduce in America. All our fashions are foreign, Count.
(TWINKLE, *who has stepped forward to be introduced,
shows great indignation.*)

COUNT. Excuse me, Madame, our fashions have grown ante-
diluvian before you Americans discover their existence. You
are lamentably behind the age—lamentably! 'Pon my honor,
a foreigner of refinement finds great difficulty in existing in
this provincial atmosphere.

MRS. TIFFANY. How dreadful, Count! I am very much concerned. If there is anything which I can do, Count—

SERAPHINA. Or I, Count, to render your situation less de-
plorable—

COUNT. Ah! I find but one redeeming charm in America—the
superlative loveliness of the feminine portion of creation.
(*Aside.*) And the wealth of their obliging papas.

MRS. TIFFANY. How flattering! Ah! Count, I am afraid you
will turn the head of my simple girl here. She is a perfect
child of nature, Count.

COUNT. Very possibly, for though you American women are
quite charming, yet, demme, there's a deal of native rust
to rub off!

MRS. TIFFANY. *Rust?* Good gracious, Count! where do you
find any rust? (*Looking about the room.*)

COUNT. How very unsophisticated!

MRS. TIFFANY. Count, I am so much ashamed—pray excuse me! Although a lady of large fortune, and one, Count, who can boast of the highest connections, I blush to confess that I have never travelled, while you, Count, I presume are at home in all the courts of Europe.

COUNT. *Courts?* Eh? Oh, yes, Madam, very true. I believe I am pretty well known in some of the courts of Europe (*Aside, crossing.*)—*police courts.* In a word, Madam, I had seen enough of civilized life—wanted to refresh myself by a sight of barbarous countries and customs—had my choice between the Sandwich Islands and New York—chose New York!

MRS. TIFFANY. How complimentary to our country! And, Count, I have no doubt you speak every conceivable language? You talk English like a native.

COUNT. Eh, what? Like a native? Oh, ah, demme, yes, I am something of an Englishman. Passed one year and eight months with the Duke of Wellington, six months with Lord Brougham, two and a half with Count d'Orsay—knew them all more intimately than their best friends—no heroes to me—hadn't a secret from me, I assure you. (*Aside.*) *Especially of the toilet.*

MRS. TIFFANY. (*Aside to* SERAPHINA.) Think of that, my dear! Lord Wellington and Duke Broom!

SERAPHINA. (*Aside to* MRS. TIFFANY.) And only think of Count d'Orsay, Mamma! I am so wild to see Count d'Orsay!

COUNT. Oh! a mere man milliner. Very little refinement out of Paris! Why, at the very last dinner given at Lord—Lord Knowswho, would you believe it, Madam, there was an individual present who wore a *black* cravat and took *soup twice!*

MRS. TIFFANY. How shocking! The sight of him would have spoilt my appetite! (*Aside to* SERAPHINA.) Think what a great man he must be, my dear, to despise lords and counts in that way. (*Aside.*) I must leave them together. Mr. Twinkle, your arm. I have some really very *foreign exotics* to show you.

TWINKLE. I fly at your command. (*Aside, and glancing at the* COUNT.) I wish all her exotics were blooming in their native soil!

MRS. TIFFANY. Mr. Fogg, will you accompany us? My conservatory is well worthy a visit. It cost an immense sum of money.

FOGG. I am indifferent to conservatories, Madam; flowers are such a bore!

MRS. TIFFANY. I shall take no refusal. Conservatories are all the rage—I could not exist without mine! Let me show you —let me show you.

(Places her arm through MR. FOGG'S, *without his consent. Exeunt* MRS. TIFFANY, FOGG, *and* TWINKLE *into the conservatory, where they are seen walking about.)*

SERAPHINA. America, then, has no charms for you, Count?

COUNT. Excuse me, some exceptions. I find you, for instance, particularly charming! Can't say I admire your country. Ah! if you had ever breathed the exhilarating air of Paris, ate creams at Tortoni's, dined at the Café Royale, or if you had lived in London—felt at home at St. James's, and every afternoon driven a couple of Lords and a Duchess through Hyde Park, you would find America—where you have no kings, queens, lords, nor ladies—insupportable!

SERAPHINA. Not while there was a Count in it?

(Enter ZEKE, *very indignant.)*

ZEKE. Where's de Missus?

(Enter MRS. TIFFANY, FOGG, *and* TWINKLE, *from the conservatory.)*

MRS. TIFFANY. Whom do you come to announce, A-dolph?

ZEKE. He said he wouldn't trust me—no, not eben wid so much as his name; so I wouldn't trust him up stairs, den he ups wid *his stick* and I *cuts mine.*

MRS. TIFFANY. *(Aside.)* Some of Mr. Tiffany's vulgar acquaintances. I shall die with shame. A-dolph, inform him that I am *not at home.*

(Exit ZEKE.)

My nerves are so shattered, I am ready to sink. Mr. Twinkle, that *fow tool*, if you please!

TWINKLE. What? What do you wish, Madam?

MRS. TIFFANY. *(Aside.)* The ignorance of these Americans! Count, may I trouble you? That *fow tool*, if you please!

COUNT. (*Aside.*) She's not talking English, nor French, but I suppose it's American.

TRUEMAN. (*Outside.*) Not at home!

ZEKE. No, Sar—Missus say she's not at home.

TRUEMAN. Out of the way, you grinning nigger!

(*Enter* ADAM TRUEMAN, *dressed as a farmer, a stout cane in his hand, his boots covered with dust.* ZEKE *jumps out of his way as he enters.*)
(*Exit* ZEKE.)

TRUEMAN. Where's this woman that's not *at home* in her own house? May I be shot if I wonder at it! I shouldn't think she'd ever feel *at home* in such a show-box as this! (*Looking round.*)

MRS. TIFFANY. (*Aside.*) What a plebeian looking old farmer! I wonder who he is? Sir—(*Advancing very agitatedly.*) what do you mean, Sir, by this *ow*dacious conduct? How dare you intrude yourself into my parlor? Do you know who I am, Sir? (*With great dignity.*) You are in the presence of Mrs. Tiffany, Sir!

TRUEMAN. Antony's wife, eh? Well now, I might have guessed that—ha! ha! ha! for I see you make it a point to carry half your husband's shop upon your back! No matter; that's being a good helpmate, for he carried the whole of it once in a pack on his own shoulders; now you bear a share!

MRS. TIFFANY. How dare you, you impertinent, *ow*dacious, ignorant old man! It's all an invention. You're talking of somebody else. (*Aside.*) What will the Count think!

TRUEMAN. Why, I thought folks had better manners in the city! This is a civil welcome for your husband's old friend, and after my coming all the way from Catteraugus[1] to see you and yours! First a grinning nigger tricked out in scarlet regimentals—

MRS. TIFFANY. Let me tell you, Sir, that liveries are all the fashion!

TRUEMAN. The fashion, are they? To make men wear the *badge of servitude* in a free land, that's the fashion, is it?

[1] Catteraugus County is in the western part of the state of New York.

Hurrah for republican simplicity! I will venture to say now that you have your coat of arms too!

MRS. TIFFANY. Certainly, Sir; you can see it on the panels of my *voyture*.[1]

TRUEMAN. Oh! no need of that. I know what your escutcheon must be! A band-box *rampant* with a bonnet *couchant*, and a peddlar's pack *passant*! Ha, ha, ha! that shows both houses united!

MRS. TIFFANY. Sir! you are most profoundly ignorant—what do you mean by this insolence, Sir? (*Aside.*) How shall I get rid of him?

TRUEMAN. (*Looking at* SERAPHINA.) I hope that is not Gertrude!

MRS. TIFFANY. Sir, I'd have you know that—Seraphina, my child, walk with the gentlemen into the conservatory.

(*Exeunt* SERAPHINA, TWINKLE, FOGG *into conservatory.*)

Count Jolimaitre, pray make due allowances for the errors of this rustic! I do assure you, Count— (*Whispers to him.*)

TRUEMAN. (*Aside.*) "Count"! She calls that critter with a shoe brush over his mouth "Count"! To look at him, I should have thought he was a tailor's walking advertisement!

COUNT. (*Addressing* TRUEMAN *whom he has been inspecting through his eyeglass.*) Where did you say you belonged, my friend? Dug out of the ruins of Pompeii, eh?

TRUEMAN. I belong to a land in which I rejoice to find that you are a foreigner.

COUNT. What a barbarian! He doesn't see the honor I'm doing his country! Pray, Madam, is it one of the aboriginal inhabitants of the soil? To what tribe of Indians does he belong—the Pawnee or Choctaw? Does he carry a tomahawk?

TRUEMAN. Something quite as useful—do you see that? (*Shaking his stick.*)

(COUNT *runs behind* MRS. TIFFANY.)

MRS. TIFFANY. Oh, dear! I shall faint! Millinette! (*Approaching.*) Millinette!

(*Enter* MILLINETTE, *without advancing into the room.*)

[1] *Voiture*: carriage.

MILLINETTE. *Oui*, Madame.

MRS. TIFFANY. A glass of water!

(*Exit* MILLINETTE.)

Sir, (*Crossing to* TRUEMAN.) I am shocked at your plebeian conduct! Tis is a gentleman of the highest standing, Sir! He is a *Count*, Sir!

(*Enter* MILLINETTE, *bearing a salver with a glass of water. In advancing towards* MRS. TIFFANY, *she passes in front of the* COUNT, *starts and screams. The* COUNT, *after a start of surprise, regains his composure, plays with his eye glass, and looks perfectly unconcerned.*)

MRS. TIFFANY. What is the matter? What *is* the matter?

MILLINETTE. Noting, noting, only— (*Looks at* COUNT *and turns away her eyes again.*) only—noting at all!

TRUEMAN. Don't be afraid, girl! Why, did you never see a live Count before? He's tame—I dare say your mistress there leads him about by the ears.

MRS. TIFFANY. This is too much! Millinette, send for Mr. Tiffany instantly!

(*Crosses to* MILLINETTE, *who is going.*)

MILLINETTE. He just come in, Madame!

TRUEMAN. My old friend! Where is he? Take me to him; I long to have one more hearty shake of the hand!

MRS. TIFFANY. (*Crosses to him.*) Count, honor me by joining my daughter in the conservatory; I will return immediately. (COUNT *bows and walks towards conservatory,* MRS. TIFFANY *following part of the way and then returning to* TRUEMAN.)

TRUEMAN. What a Jezebel! These women always play the very devil with a man, and yet I don't believe such a damaged bale of goods as *that* (*Looking at* MRS. TIFFANY.) has smothered the heart of little Antony!

MRS. TIFFANY. This way, Sir, *sal vous plait*.

(*Exit with great dignity.*)

TRUEMAN. *Sal vous plait*. Ha, ha, ha! We'll see what Fashion has done for him. (*Exit.*)

ACT II

SCENE 1

Inner apartment of MR. TIFFANY'S *Counting House.* MR. TIFFANY, *seated at a desk looking over papers.* MR. SNOBSON, *on a high stool at another desk, with a pen behind his ear.*

SNOBSON. (*Rising, advances to the front of the stage, regards* TIFFANY *and shrugs his shoulders. Aside.*) How the old boy frets and fumes over those papers, to be sure! He's working himself into a perfect fever—ex-actly; therefore *bleeding's* the prescription! So here goes! Mr. Tiffany, a word with you, if you please, Sir?

TIFFANY. (*Sitting still.*) Speak on, Mr. Snobson, I attend.

SNOBSON. What I have to say, Sir, is a matter of the first importance to the credit of the concern—the *credit* of the concern, Mr. Tiffany!

TIFFANY. Proceed, Mr. Snobson.

SNOBSON. Sir, you've a handsome house—fine carriage—nigger in livery—feed on the fat of the land—everything first rate—

TIFFANY. Well, Sir?

SNOBSON. My salary, Mr. Tiffany!

TIFFANY. It has been raised three times within the last year.

SNOBSON. Still it is insufficient for the necessities of an honest man; mark me, an *honest* man, Mr. Tiffany.

TIFFANY. (*Crossing. Aside.*) What a weapon he has made of that word! Enough—another hundred shall be added. Does that content you?

SNOBSON. There is one other subject, which I have before mentioned, Mr. Tiffany: your daughter. What's the reason you can't let the folks at home know at once that I'm to be *the man*?

TIFFANY. (*Aside.*) Villain! And must the only seal upon this scoundrel's lips be placed there by the hand of my daughter? Well, Sir, it shall be as you desire.

SNOBSON. And Mrs. Tiffany shall be informed of your resolution?

TIFFANY. Yes.

SNOBSON. Enough said! That's the ticket! The CREDIT *of the concern's safe*, Sir! (*Returns to his seat.*)

TIFFANY. (*Aside.*) How low have I bowed to this insolent rascal! To rise himself he mounts upon my shoulders, and unless I can shake him off he must crush me!

(*Enter* TRUEMAN.)

TRUEMAN. Here I am, Antony, man! I told you I'd pay you a visit in your money-making quarters. (*Looks around.*) But it looks as dismal here as a cell in the States' prison!

TIFFANY. (*Forcing a laugh.*) Ha, ha, ha! States' prison! You are so facetious! Ha, ha, ha!

TRUEMAN. Well, for the life of me I can't see anything so amusing in that! I should think the States' prison plaguy uncomfortable lodgings. And you laugh, man, as though you fancied yourself there already.

TIFFANY. Ha, ha, ha!

TRUEMAN. (*Imitating him.*) Ha, ha, ha! What on earth do you mean by that ill-sounding laugh, that has nothing of a laugh about it! This *fashion*-worship has made heathens and hypocrites of you all! *Deception* is your household God! A man laughs as if he were crying, and cries as if he were laughing in his sleeve. Everything is something else from what it seems to be. I have lived in your house only three days, and I've heard more lies than were ever invented during a Presidential election! First your fine lady of a wife sends me word that she's not at home—I walk up stairs, and she takes good care that *I* shall not be *at home*—wants to turn me out of doors. Then *you* come in—take your old friend by the hand—whisper, the deuce knows what, in your wife's ear, and the tables are turned in a tangent! Madam curtsies—says she's enchanted to see me—and orders her grinning nigger to show me a room.

TIFFANY. We were exceedingly happy to welcome you as our guest!

TRUEMAN. Happy? *You* happy? Ah, Antony! Antony! that hatchet face of yours and those criss-cross furrows tell quite another story! It's many a long day since you were *happy* at anything! You look as if you'd melted down your flesh into dollars, and mortgaged your soul in the bargain!

Your warm heart has grown cold over your ledger—your light spirits heavy with calculation! You have traded away your youth—your hopes—your tastes, for wealth! and now you *have* the wealth you coveted, what does it profit you? Pleasure it cannot buy, for you have lost your *capacity* for enjoyment. Ease it will not bring, for the love of gain is never satisfied! It has made your counting-house a penitentiary, and your home a fashionable *museum* where there is no niche for you! You have spent so much time *ciphering* in the one, that you find yourself at last a very *cipher* in the other! See me, man! Seventy-two last August!—Strong as a hickory and every whit as sound!

TIFFANY. I take the greatest pleasure in remarking your superiority, Sir.

TRUEMAN. Bah! no man takes pleasure in remarking the superiority of another! Why the deuce can't you speak the truth, man? But it's not the *fashion*, I suppose! I have not seen one frank, open face since—no, no, I can't say that either, though lying *is* catching! There's that girl, Gertrude, who is trying to teach your daughter music—but Gertrude was bred in the country!

TIFFANY. A good girl; my wife and daughter find her very useful.

TRUEMAN. Useful? Well, I must say you have queer notions of *use!*—But come, cheer up, man! I'd rather see one of your old smiles than know you'd realized another thousand! I hear you are making money on the true, American, high pressure system! Better go slow and sure—the more steam, the greater danger of the boiler's bursting! All sound, I hope? Nothing rotten at the core?

TIFFANY. Oh, sound—quite sound!

TRUEMAN. Well, that's pleasant—though I must say you don't look very pleasant about it!

TIFFANY. My good friend, although I am solvent, I may say, perfectly solvent—yet you—the fact is, you can be of some assistance to me!

TRUEMAN. That's the *fact* is it? I'm glad we've hit upon one *fact* at last! Well—

(SNOBSON, *who during this conversation has been employed in writing, but stops occasionally to listen, now gives vent to a dry chuckling laugh.*)

TRUEMAN. Hey? What's that? Another of those deuced ill-

sounding city laughs! (*Sees* SNOBSON.) Who's that perched
up on the stool of repentance—eh, Antony?

SNOBSON. (*Aside and looking at* TIFFANY's *seat.*) The old
boy has missed his text there—*that's* the stool of repentance!

TIFFANY. One of my clerks—my confidential clerk.

TRUEMAN. Confidential? Why he looks for all the world like
a spy—the most inquisitorial, hang-dog face—ugh! The
sight of it makes my blood run cold! Come, (*Crosses.*) let
us talk over matters where this critter can't give us the
benefit of his opinion! Antony, the next time you choose a
confidential clerk, take one that carries his credentials in
his face—those in his pocket are not worth much without!
(*Exeunt* TRUEMAN *and* TIFFANY.)

SNOBSON. (*Jumping from his stool and advancing.*) The old
prig has got the tin, or Tiff would never be so civil! All
right—Tiff will work every shiner into the concern—all the
better for me! Now I'll go and make love to Seraphina.
The old woman needn't try to knock me down with any of
her French lingo! Six months from today if I ain't driving
my two footmen tandem, down Broadway—and as fashionable as Mrs. Tiffany herself—then I ain't the trump I
thought I was, that's all! (*Looks at his watch.*) Bless me!
eleven o'clock and I haven't had my julep yet! Snobson,
I'm ashamed of you! (*Exit.*)

SCENE 2

*The interior of a beautiful conservatory; walk through the
center; stands of flower pots in bloom; a couple of rustic seats.*
GERTRUDE, *attired in white, with a white rose in her hair,
watering the flowers.* COLONEL HOWARD *regarding her.*

HOWARD. I am afraid you lead a sad life here, Miss Gertrude?

GERTRUDE. (*Turning round gaily.*) What! amongst the flowers? (*Continues her occupation.*)

HOWARD. No, amongst the thistles, with which Mrs. Tiffany
surrounds you; the tempests, which her temper raises!

GERTRUDE. They never harm me. Flowers and herbs are excellent tutors. I learn prudence from the reed, and bend
until the storm has swept over me!

HOWARD. Admirable philosophy! But still, this frigid atmos-

phere of fashion must be uncongenial to you? Accustomed
to the pleasant companionship of your kind friends in
Geneva,[1] surely you must regret this cold exchange?

GERTRUDE. Do you think so? Can you suppose that I could
possibly prefer a ramble in the woods to a promenade in
Broadway? A wreath of scented wild flowers to a bouquet
of these sickly exotics? The odor of new-mown hay to the
heated air of this crowded conservatory? Or can you
imagine that I could enjoy the quiet conversation of my
Geneva friends more than the edifying chit-chat of a
fashionable drawing room? But I see you think me totally
destitute of taste?

HOWARD. You have a merry spirit to jest thus at your
grievances!

GERTRUDE. I have my *mania*—as some wise person declares
that all mankind have—and mine is a love of independence!
In Geneva, my wants were supplied by two kind old
maiden ladies, upon whom I know not that I have any
claim. I had abilities, and desired to use them. I came here
at my own request; for here I am no longer *dependent!*
Voila tout, as Mrs. Tiffany would say.

HOWARD. Believe me, I appreciate the confidence you repose
in me!

GERTRUDE. Confidence! Truly, Colonel Howard, the *confidence* is entirely on your part, in supposing that I confide
that which I have no reason to conceal! I think I informed
you that Mrs. Tiffany only received visitors on her reception
day; she is therefore not prepared to see you. Zeke—Oh!
I beg his pardon—Adolph, made some mistake in admitting
you.

HOWARD. Nay, Gertrude, it was not Mrs. Tiffany, nor Miss
Tiffany, whom I came to see; it—it was—

GERTRUDE. The conservatory perhaps? I will leave you to
examine the flowers at leisure! (*Crosses.*)

HOWARD. Gertrude—listen to me. (*Aside.*) If I only dared
to give utterance to what is hovering upon my lips! Gertrude!

GERTRUDE. Colonel Howard!

HOWARD. Gertrude, I must—must—

GERTRUDE. Yes, indeed you *must*, must leave me! I think I

[1] Geneva, New York.

hear somebody coming—Mrs. Tiffany would not be well
pleased to find you here—pray, pray leave me—that door
will lead you into the street.
(*Hurries him out through door; takes up her watering pot,
and commences watering flowers, tying up branches, etc.*)
What a strange being is man! Why should he hesitate to
say—nay, why should I prevent his saying, what I would
most delight to hear? Truly man *is* strange—but woman is
quite as incomprehensible! (*Walks about gathering
flowers.*)

(*Enter* COUNT JOLIMAITRE.)

COUNT. There she is—the bewitching little creature! Mrs.
Tiffany and her daughter are out of earshot. I caught a
glimpse of their feathers floating down Broadway, not ten
minutes ago. Just the opportunity I have been looking for!
Now for an engagement with this captivating little piece
of prudery! 'Pon honor, I am almost afraid she will not
resist a *Count* long enough to give value to the conquest.
(*Approaching her.*) *Ma belle petite*, were you gathering
roses for me?
GERTRUDE. (*Starts on first perceiving him, but instantly regains her self-possession.*) The roses here, Sir, are carefully
guarded with thorns—if you have the right to gather, pluck
for yourself!
COUNT. Sharp as ever, little Gertrude! But now that we are
alone, throw off this frigidity, and be at your ease.
GERTRUDE. Permit me to *be alone*, Sir, that I *may* be at my
ease!
COUNT. Very good, *ma belle*, well said! (*Applauding her with
his hands.*) Never yield too soon, even to a *title!* But as the
old girl may find her way back before long, we may as
well come to particulars at once. I love you; but that you
know already. (*Rubbing his eyeglass unconcernedly with
his handkerchief.*) Before long I shall make Mademoiselle
Seraphina my wife, and, of course, you shall remain in the
family!
GERTRUDE. (*Indignantly.*) Sir—
COUNT. 'Pon my honor you shall! In France we arrange these
little matters without difficulty!

GERTRUDE. But I am an *American!* Your conduct proves that you are not one! (*Going, crosses.*)

COUNT. (*Preventing her.*) Don't run away, my immaculate *petite Americaine!* Demme, you've quite overlooked my condescension—the difference of our stations—you a species of upper servant—an orphan—no friends.

(*Enter* TRUEMAN *unperceived.*)

GERTRUDE. And therefore more entitled to the respect and protection of every *true gentleman!* Had you been one, you would not have insulted me!

COUNT. My charming little orator, patriotism and declamation become you particularly! (*Approaches her.*) I feel quite tempted to taste—

TRUEMAN. (*Thrusting him aside.*) An American hickory-switch! (*Strikes him.*) Well, how do you like it?

COUNT. (*Aside.*) Old matter-of-fact! Sir, how dare you?

TRUEMAN. My stick has answered that question!

GERTRUDE. Oh! now I am quite safe!

TRUEMAN. Safe! not a bit safer than before! All women would be safe, if they knew how virtue became them! As for you, Mr. Count, what have you to say for yourself? Come, speak out!

COUNT. Sir,—aw—aw—you don't understand these matters!

TRUEMAN. That's a fact! Not having had *your* experience, I don't believe I *do* understand them!

COUNT. A piece of pleasantry—a mere joke—

TRUEMAN. A joke was it? I'll show you a joke worth two of that! I'll teach you the way we natives joke with a puppy who don't respect an honest woman! (*Seizing him.*)

COUNT. Oh! oh! demme—you old ruffian! let me go. What do you mean?

TRUEMAN. Oh! a piece of pleasantry—a mere joke—very pleasant isn't it?

(*Attempts to strike him again;* COUNT *struggles with him. Enter* MRS. TIFFANY *hastily, in her bonnet and shawl.*)

MRS. TIFFANY. What is the matter? I am perfectly *abimé* with terror. Mr. Trueman, what has happened?

TRUEMAN. Oh! we have been *joking!*

MRS. TIFFANY. (*To* COUNT, *who is re-arranging his dress.*) My dear Count, I did not expect to find you here—how kind of you!

TRUEMAN. Your *dear* Count has been showing his *kindness* in a very *foreign* manner. Too *foreign*, I think, he found it to be relished by an *unfashionable native!* What do you think of a puppy who insults an innocent girl all in the way of *kindness?* This Count of yours—this importation of—

COUNT. My dear Madam, demme, permit me to explain. It would be unbecoming—demme—particular unbecoming of you—aw—aw—to pay any attention to this ignorant person. (*Crosses to* TRUEMAN.) Anything that he says concerning a man of my standing—aw—the truth is, Madam—

TRUEMAN. Let us have the truth by all means—if it is only for novelty's sake!

COUNT. (*Turning his back to* TRUEMAN.) You see, Madam, hoping to obtain a few moments' private conversation with Miss Seraphina—with *Miss Seraphina* I say and—aw—and knowing her passion for flowers, I found my way to your very tasteful and *recherché* conservatory. (*Looks about him approvingly.*) *Very* beautifully arranged—does you great credit, Madame! Here I encountered this young person. She was inclined to be talkative; and I indulged her with—with a —aw—demme—a few *common places!* What passed between us was mere *harmless badinage*—on *my* part. You, Madame, you—so conversant with our European manners—you are aware that when a man of fashion—that is, when a woman—a man is bound—amongst noblemen, you know—

MRS. TIFFANY. I comprehend you perfectly—*parfittement*, my dear Count.

COUNT. (*Aside.*) 'Pon my honor, that's very obliging of her.

MRS. TIFFANY. I am shocked at the plebeian forwardness of this conceited girl!

TRUEMAN. (*Walking up to* COUNT.) Did you ever keep a reckoning of the lies you tell in an hour?

MRS. TIFFANY. Mr. Trueman, I blush for you! (*Crosses to* TRUEMAN.)

TRUEMAN. Don't do that—you have no blushes to spare!

MRS. TIFFANY. It is a man of rank whom you are addressing, Sir!

TRUEMAN. A rank villain, Mrs. Antony Tiffany! A *rich one* he would be, had he as much *gold* as *brass!*

MRS. TIFFANY. Pray pardon him, Count; he knows nothing of *how ton!*

COUNT. Demme, he's beneath my notice. I tell you what, old fellow—(TRUEMAN *raises his stick as* COUNT *approaches, the latter starts back.*) the sight of him discomposes me—aw—I feel quite uncomfortable—aw—let us join your charming daughter? (*To* TRUEMAN.) I can't do you the honor to shoot you, Sir—you are beneath me—a nobleman can't fight a commoner! Good bye, old Truepenny! I—aw—I'm insensible to your insolence!

(*Exeunt* COUNT *and* MRS. TIFFANY.)

TRUEMAN. You won't be insensible to a cowhide in spite of your nobility! The next time he practices any of his foreign fashions on you, Gertrude, you'll see how I'll wake up his sensibilities!

GERTRUDE. I do not know what I should have done without you, Sir.

TRUEMAN. Yes, you do—you know that you would have done well enough! Never tell a lie, girl! not even for the sake of pleasing an old man! When you open your lips let your heart speak. Never tell a lie! Let your face be the looking-glass of your soul—your heart its clock—while your tongue rings the hours! But the glass must be clear, the clock true, and then there's no fear but the tongue will do its duty in a woman's head!

GERTRUDE. You are very good, Sir!

TRUEMAN. That's as it may be!—(*Aside.*) How my heart warms towards her! Gertrude, I hear that you have no mother?

GERTRUDE. Ah! no, Sir; I wish I had.

TRUEMAN. (*Aside, and with emotion.*) So do I! Heaven knows, so do I! And you have no father, Gertrude?

GERTRUDE. No, Sir—I often wish I had!

TRUEMAN. (*Hurriedly.*) Don't do that, girl! don't do that! Wish you had a mother—but never wish that you had a father again! Perhaps the one you had did not deserve such a child!

(*Enter* PRUDENCE.)

PRUDENCE. Seraphina is looking for you, Gertrude.

GERTRUDE. I will go to her. (*Crosses.*) Mr. Trueman, you will

not permit me to thank you, but you cannot prevent my
gratitude! (*Exit.*)

TRUEMAN. (*Looking after her.*) If falsehood harbors there,
I'll give up searching after truth! (*Crosses, retires up the
stage musingly, and commences examining the flowers.*)

PRUDENCE. (*Aside.*) What a nice old man he is, to be sure! I
wish he would say something! (*Crosses, walks after him,
turning when he turns; after a pause.*)
Don't mind *me*, Mr. Trueman!

TRUEMAN. Mind you? Oh! no, don't be afraid (*Crosses.*)—I
wasn't minding you. Nobody seems to mind you much!
(*Continues walking and examining the flowers—*PRUDENCE
follows.)

PRUDENCE. Very pretty flowers, ain't they? Gertrude takes
care of them.

TRUEMAN. Gertrude? So I hear—(*advancing*) I suppose you
can tell me now who this Gertrude—

PRUDENCE. Who she's in love with? I *knew* you were going
to say that! I'll tell you all about it! Gertrude, she's in love
with—Mr. Twinkle! and he's in love with her. And Seraphina she's in love with Count Jolly—what-d'ye-call-it; but
Count Jolly don't take to her at all—but Colonel Howard—
he's the man—he's desperate about her!

TRUEMAN. Why you feminine newspaper! Howard in love
with that quintessence of affectation! Howard—the only
frank, straightforward fellow that I've met since—I'll tell
him my mind on the subject! And Gertrude hunting for
happiness in a rhyming dictionary! The girl's a greater
fool than I took her for! (*Crosses.*)

PRUDENCE. So she is; you see I know all about them!

TRUEMAN. I see you do! You've a wonderful knowledge—
wonderful—of *other people's concerns!* It may do here, but
take my word for it, in the county of Catteraugus you'd
get the name of a great *busybody*. But perhaps you know
that too?

PRUDENCE. Oh! I always know what's coming. I feel it before-
hand all over me. I knew something was going to happen
the day you came here—and what's more I can always tell
a married man from a single—I felt right off that you were
a bachelor!

TRUEMAN. Felt right off I was a bachelor did you? You were
sure of it—sure?—quite sure?

(*Prudence assents delightedly.*)

Then you felt wrong!—A bachelor and a widower are not the same thing!

PRUDENCE. Oh! but it all comes to the same thing—a widower's as good as a bachelor any day! And besides I knew that you were a farmer *right off*.

TRUEMAN. On the spot, eh? I suppose you saw cabbages and green peas growing out of my hat?

PRUDENCE. No, I didn't—but I knew all about you. And I knew—(*Looking down and fidgeting with her apron.*) I knew you were for getting married soon! For last night I dreamt I saw your funeral going along the streets, and the mourners all dressed in white. And a funeral is a sure sign of a wedding, you know! (*Nudging him with her elbow.*)

TRUEMAN. (*Imitating her voice.*) Well, I can't say that I *know* any such thing! you know! (*Nudging her back.*)

PRUDENCE. Oh! it does, and there's no getting over it! For my part, I like farmers—and I know all about setting hens and turkeys, and feeding chickens, and laying eggs, and all that sort of thing!

TRUEMAN. (*Aside.*) May I be shot if mistress newspaper is not putting in an advertisement for herself! This is your city mode of courting I suppose, ha, ha, ha!

PRUDENCE. I've been west, a little; but I never was in the county of Catteraugus, myself.

TRUEMAN. Oh! you were not? And you have taken a particular fancy to go there, eh?

PRUDENCE. Perhaps I shouldn't object—

TRUEMAN. Oh!—ah!—so I suppose. Now pay attention to what I am going to say, for it is a matter of great importance to yourself.

PRUDENCE. (*Aside.*) Now it's coming—I know what he's going to say!

TRUEMAN. The next time you want to tie a man for life to your apron-strings, pick out one that don't come from the county of Catteraugus—for greenhorns are scarce in those parts, and modest women plenty! (*Exit.*)

PRUDENCE. Now who'd have thought he was going to say that! But I won't give him up yet—I won't give him up. (*Exit.*)

ACT III

SCENE 1

MRS. TIFFANY'S *Parlor. Enter* MRS. TIFFANY, *followed by*
MR. TIFFANY.

TIFFANY. Your extravagance will ruin me, Mrs. Tiffany!

MRS. TIFFANY. And your stinginess will ruin me, Mr. Tiffany!
It is totally and *toot a fate* impossible to convince you of
the necessity of *keeping up appearances*. There is a certain
display which every woman of fashion is forced to make!

TIFFANY. And pray who made *you* a woman of fashion?

MRS. TIFFANY. What a vulgar question! All women of fashion,
Mr. Tiffany—

TIFFANY. In this land are *self-constituted*, like you, Madam—
and *fashion* is the cloak for more sins than charity ever
covered! It was for *fashion's* sake that you insisted upon
my purchasing this expensive house! It was for *fashion's*
sake that you ran me in debt at every exorbitant up-
holsterer's and extravagant furniture warehouse in the city!
It was for *fashion's* sake that you built that ruinous conservatory—hired more servants than they have persons to
wait upon—and dressed your footman like a harlequin!

MRS. TIFFANY. Mr. Tiffany, you are thoroughly plebeian, and
insufferably *American*, in your grovelling ideas! And, pray,
what was the occasion of these very *mal-ap-pro-pos* remarks? Merely because I requested a paltry fifty dollars to
purchase a new style of head-dress—a *bijou* of an article
just introduced in France.

TIFFANY. Time was, Mrs. Tiffany, when you manufactured
your own French headdresses—took off their first gloss at
the public balls, and then sold them to your shortest-
sighted customers. And all you knew about France, or
French either, was what you spelt out at the bottom of
your fashion plates; but now you have grown so fashionable, forsooth, that you have forgotten how to speak your
mother tongue!

MRS. TIFFANY. Mr. Tiffany, Mr. Tiffany! Nothing is more positively vulgarian—more *unaristocratic*—than any allusion to the past!

TIFFANY. Why I thought, my dear, that *aristocrats* lived principally upon the past—and traded in the market of fashion with the bones of their ancestors for capital?

MRS. TIFFANY. Mr. Tiffany, such vulgar remarks are only suitable to the counting house; in my drawing room you should—

TIFFANY. Vary my sentiments with my locality, as you change your *manners* with your *dress!*

MRS. TIFFANY. Mr. Tiffany, I desire that you will purchase Count d'Orsay's *Science of Etiquette*, and learn how to conduct yourself—especially before you appear at the grand ball, which I shall give on Friday!

TIFFANY. Confound your balls, Madam; they make *footballs* of my money, while you dance away all that I am worth! A pretty time to give a ball when you know that I am on the very brink of bankruptcy!

MRS. TIFFANY. So much the greater reason that nobody should suspect your circumstances, or you would lose your credit at once. Just at this crisis a ball is absolutely *necessary* to save your reputation! There is Mrs. Adolphus Dashaway—she gave the most splendid fête of the season—and I hear on very good authority that her husband has not paid his baker's bill in three months. Then there was Mrs. Honey-wood—

TIFFANY. Gave a ball the night before her husband shot himself; perhaps you wish to drive me to follow his example? (*Crosses.*)

MRS. TIFFANY. Good gracious! Mr. Tiffany, how you talk! I beg you won't mention anything of the kind. I consider black the most unbecoming color. I'm sure I've done all that I could to gratify you. There is that vulgar old torment, Trueman, who gives one the lie fifty times a day; haven't I been very civil to him?

TIFFANY. Civil to his *wealth*, Mrs. Tiffany! I told you that he was a rich, old farmer—the early friend of my father—my own benefactor—and that I had reason to think he might assist me in my present embarrassments. Your civility was *bought*, and like most of your *own* purchases has yet to be *paid* for. (*Crosses.*)

MRS. TIFFANY. And will be, no doubt! The condescension of a woman of fashion should command any price. Mr. Trueman is insupportably indecorous; he has insulted Count Jolimaitre in the most outrageous manner. If the Count was not so deeply interested, so *abimé* with Seraphina, I am sure he would never honor us by his visits again!

TIFFANY. So much the better; he shall never marry my daughter!—I am resolved on that. Why, Madam, I am told there is in Paris a regular matrimonial stock company, who fit out indigent dandies for this market. How do I know but this fellow is one of its creatures, and that he has come here to increase its dividends by marrying a fortune?

MRS. TIFFANY. Nonsense, Mr. Tiffany. The Count, the most fashionable young man in all New York—the intimate friend of all the dukes and lords in Europe—not marry my daughter? Not permit Seraphina to become a Countess? Mr. Tiffany, you are out of your senses!

TIFFANY. That would not be very wonderful, considering how many years I have been united to you, my dear. Modern physicians pronounce lunacy infectious!

MRS. TIFFANY. Mr. Tiffany, he is a man of fashion—

TIFFANY. Fashion makes fools, but cannot *feed* them. By the bye, I have a request. Since you are bent upon ruining me by this ball, and there is no help for it, I desire that you will send an invitation to my confidential clerk, Mr. Snobson.

MRS. TIFFANY. Mr. Snobson! Was there ever such an *you-nick* demand! Mr. Snobson would cut a pretty figure amongst my fashionable friends! I shall do no such thing, Mr. Tiffany.

TIFFANY. Then, Madam, the ball shall not take place. Have I not told you that I am in the power of this man? That there are circumstances which it is happy for you that you do not know, which you cannot comprehend, but which render it essential that you should be civil to Mr. Snobson? Not you merely, but Seraphina also? He is a more appropriate match for her than your foreign favorite.

MRS. TIFFANY. A match for Seraphina, indeed! (*Crosses.*) Mr. Tiffany, you are determined to make a *fow pas*.

TIFFANY. Mr. Snobson intends calling this morning. (*Crosses.*)

MRS. TIFFANY. But, Mr. Tiffany, this is not reception day— my drawing-rooms are in the most terrible disorder—

TIFFANY. Mr. Snobson is not particular; he must be admitted.

(*Enter* ZEKE.)

ZEKE. Mr. Snobson.

(*Enter* SNOBSON, *exit* ZEKE.)

SNOBSON. How dye do, Marm? (*Crosses.*) How are you? Mr. Tiffany, your most!—

MRS. TIFFANY. (*Formally.*) *Bung jure. Comment vow portè vow, Monsur Snobson?*

SNOBSON. Oh, to be sure—very good of you—fine day.

MRS. TIFFANY. (*Pointing to a chair with great dignity.*) *Sassoyez vow*, Monsur Snobson.

SNOBSON. (*Aside.*) I wonder what she's driving at? I ain't up to the fashionable lingo yet! Eh? What? Speak a little louder, Marm.

MRS. TIFFANY. (*Aside.*) What ignorance!

TIFFANY. I presume Mrs. Tiffany means that you are to take a seat.

SNOBSON. Ex-actly—very obliging of her—so I will. (*Sits.*) No ceremony amongst friends, you know, and likely to be nearer—you understand? *O.K.*, all correct. How *is* Seraphina?

MRS. TIFFANY. Miss Tiffany is not visible this morning. (*Retires up.*)

SNOBSON. (*Jumping up.*) Not visible? I suppose that's the English for can't see her? Mr. Tiffany, Sir—(*walking up to him*) what am I to understand by this *de-fal-ca-tion*, Sir? I expected your word to be as good as your bond—beg pardon, Sir—I mean *better*—considerably better—no humbug about it, Sir.

TIFFANY. Have patience, Mr. Snobson. (*Rings bell.*)

(*Enter* ZEKE.)

Zeke, desire my daughter to come here.

MRS. TIFFANY. (*Coming down.*) Adolph—I say, Adolph—
(ZEKE *straightens himself and assumes foppish airs, as he turns to* MRS. TIFFANY.)

TIFFANY. Zeke.

ZEKE. Don't know any such nigga, Boss.

TIFFANY. Do as I bid you instantly, or off with your livery and quit the house!

ZEKE. Wheugh! J'se all dismission!

(*Exit.*)

MRS. TIFFANY. A-dolph, A-dolph! (*Calling after him.*)

SNOBSON. (*Aside.*) I brought the old boy to his bearings, didn't I though! Pull that string, and he is sure to work right. Don't make any stranger of me, Marm—I'm quite at home. If you've got any odd jobs about the house to do up, I sha'n't miss you. I'll amuse myself with Seraphina when she comes; we'll get along very cosily by ourselves.

MRS. TIFFANY. Permit me to inform you, Mr. Snobson, that a French mother never leaves her daughter alone with a young man; she knows your sex too well for that!

SNOBSON. Very *dis*-obliging of her—but as we're none French—

MRS. TIFFANY. You have yet to learn, Mr. Snobson, that the American *ee-light*—the aristocracy—the *how-ton*—as a matter of conscience, scrupulously follow the foreign fashions.

SNOBSON. Not when they are foreign to their interests, Marm; for instance—

(*Enter* SERAPHINA.)

There you are at last, eh, Miss? How d'ye do? Ma said you weren't visible. Managed to get a peep at her, eh, Mr. Tiffany?

SERAPHINA. I heard you were here, Mr. Snobson, and came without even arranging my toilette; you will excuse my negligence?

SNOBSON. Of everything but *me*, Miss.

SERAPHINA. I shall never have to ask your pardon for *that*, Mr. Snobson.

MRS. TIFFANY. Seraphina—child—really—

(*As she is approaching* SERAPHINA, MR. TIFFANY *plants himself in front of his wife.*)

TIFFANY. Walk this way, Madam, if you please. (*Aside.*) To see that she fancies the surly fellow takes a weight from my heart.

MRS. TIFFANY. Mr. Tiffany, it is highly improper and not at all *distingué* to leave a young girl—

(*Enter* ZEKE.)

ZEKE. Mr. Count Jolly-made-her!

MRS. TIFFANY. Good gracious! The Count—Oh, dear!—Seraphina, run and change your dress—no there's not time!
A-dolph, admit him. (*Exit* ZEKE.) Mr. Snobson, get out
of the way, will you? Mr. Tiffany, what are you doing at
home at this hour?

(*Enter* COUNT JOLLIMAITRE, *ushered by* ZEKE.)

ZEKE. (*Aside.*) Dat's de genuine article ob a gemman. (*Exit.*)

MRS. TIFFANY. My dear Count, I am overjoyed at the very
sight of you.

COUNT. Flattered myself you'd be glad to see me, Madam—
knew it was not your *jour de reception.*

MRS. TIFFANY. But for you, Count, all days—

COUNT. I thought so. Ah, Miss Tiffany, on my honor, you're
looking beautiful. (*Crosses.*)

SERAPHINA. Count, flattery from you—

SNOBSON. What? Eh? What's that you say?

SERAPHINA. (*Aside to him.*) Nothing but what etiquette re-
quires.

COUNT. (*Regarding* MR. TIFFANY *through his eye glass.*) Your
worthy Papa, I believe? Sir, your most obedient.
(MR. TIFFANY *bows coldly;* COUNT *regards* SNOBSON *through
his glass, shrugs his shoulders and turns away.*)

SNOBSON. (*To* MRS. TIFFANY.) Introduce me, will you? I never
knew a Count in all my life—what a strange-looking
animal!

MRS. TIFFANY. Mr. Snobson, it is not the fashion to introduce
in France!

SNOBSON. But, Marm, we're in America. (MRS. TIFFANY
crosses to COUNT. *Aside.*) The woman thinks she's somewhere else than where she is; she wants to make an *alibi?*

MRS. TIFFANY. I hope that we shall have the pleasure of seeing
you on Friday evening, Count?

COUNT. Really, Madam, my invitations—my engagements—so
numerous—I can hardly answer for myself; and you Americans take offence so easily—

MRS. TIFFANY. But Count, everybody expects you at our ball—
you are the principal attraction—

SERAPHINA. Count, you *must* come!

COUNT. Since you insist—aw—aw—there's no resisting you,
Miss Tiffany

MRS. TIFFANY. I am so thankful. How can I repay your condescension! (COUNT *and* SERAPHINA *converse.*) Mr. Snobson, will you walk this way? I have *such* a cactus in full
bloom—remarkable flower! Mr. Tiffany, pray come here—I
have something particular to say.

TIFFANY. Then speak out, my dear. (*Aside to her.*) I thought
it was highly improper just now to leave a girl with a young
man?

MRS. TIFFANY. Oh, but the Count—that is different!

TIFFANY. I suppose you mean to say there's nothing of *the
man* about him?

(*Enter* MILLINETTE *with a scarf in her hand.*)

MILLINETTE. (*Aside.*) Adolph tell me he vas here. Pardon,
Madame, I bring dis scarf for Mademoiselle.

MRS. TIFFANY. Very well, Millinette; you know best what is
proper for her to wear.
    (MR. *and* MRS. TIFFANY *and* SNOBSON *retire up; she en-
gages the attention of both gentlemen.*)
    (MILLINETTE *crosses towards* SERAPHINA, *gives the* COUNT
a threatening look, and commences arranging the scarf over
SERAPHINA'S *shoulders.*)

MILLINETTE. Mademoiselle, *permettez-moi.* (*Aside to* COUNT.)
Perfide! (*To Seraphina.*) If Mademoiselle vil stand *tran-
quille* one *petit moment.* (*Turns* SERAPHINA'S *back to the*
COUNT, *and pretends to arrange the scarf. Aside to* COUNT.)
I must speak vid you to-day, or I tell all—you find me at
de foot of de stair ven you go. *Prends garde!*

SERAPHINA. What is that you say, Millinette?

MILLINETTE. Dis scarf make you so very beautiful, Mademoiselle—*Je vous salue mes dames.* (*Curtsies. Exit.*)

COUNT. (*Aside.*) Not a moment to lose! Miss Tiffany, I have
an unpleasant—a particularly unpleasant piece of intelli-
gence. You see, I have just received a letter from my
friend—the—aw—the Earl of Airshire; the truth is, the

Earl's daughter—beg you won't mention it—has distinguished me by a tender *penchant*.

SERAPHINA. I understand—and they wish you to return and marry the young lady; but surely you will not leave us, Count?

COUNT. If *you* bid me stay—I shouldn't have the conscience— I couldn't *afford* to tear myself away. (*Aside.*) I'm sure that's honest.

SERAPHINA. Oh, Count!

COUNT. Say but one word—say that you shouldn't mind being made a Countess—and I'll break with the Earl to-morrow.

SERAPHINA. Count, this surprise—but don't think of leaving the country, Count—we could not pass the time without you! I—yes—yes, Count—I do consent!

COUNT. (*Aside, while he embraces her.*) I thought she would! Enchanted, rapture, bliss, ecstasy, and all that sort of thing—words can't express it, but you understand. But it must be kept a secret—positively it *must!* If the rumor of our engagement were whispered abroad—the Earl's daughter—the delicacy of my situation, aw—you comprehend? It is even possible that our nuptials, my charming Miss Tiffany—*our nuptials*—must take place in private!

SERAPHINA. Oh, that is quite impossible!

COUNT. It's the latest fashion abroad—the very latest. Ah, I knew that would determine you. Can I depend on your secrecy?

SERAPHINA. Oh, yes! Believe me.

SNOBSON. (*Coming forward in spite of* MRS. TIFFANY's *efforts to detain him.*) Why, Seraphina, haven't you a word to throw to a dog?

TIFFANY. (*Aside.*) I shouldn't think she had after wasting so so many upon a puppy.

(*Enter* ZEKE, *wearing a three-cornered hat.*)

ZEKE. Missus, de bran new carriage am below.

MRS. TIFFANY. Show it up—I mean, very well, A-dolph.
(*Exit* ZEKE.)
Count, my daughter and I are about to take an airing in our new *voyture*—will you honor us with your company?

COUNT. Madam, I—I have a most *pressing* engagement. A

letter to write to the *Earl of Airshire*—who is at present
residing in the *Isle of Skye*. I must bid you good morning.

MRS. TIFFANY. Good morning, Count.

(*Exit* COUNT.)

SNOBSON. *I'm* quite at leisure, (*Crosses to* MRS. TIFFANY.)
Marm. Books balanced—ledger closed—nothing to do all
the afternoon; I'm for you.

MRS. TIFFANY. (*Without noticing him.*) Come, Seraphina,
come!

(*As they are going* SNOBSON *follows them.*)

SNOBSON. But, Marm—I was saying, Marm, I am quite at
leisure—not a thing to do; have I, Mr. Tiffany?

MRS. TIFFANY. Seraphina, child—your red shawl, remember!
Mr. Snobson, *bon swear!*

(*Exit, leading* SERAPHINA.)

SNOBSON. Swear! Mr. Tiffany, Sir, am I to be fobbed off with
a *bon swear?* D—n it, I will swear!

TIFFANY. Have patience, Mr. Snobson; if you will accompany
me to the counting house—

SNOBSON. Don't count too much on me, Sir. I'll make up no
more accounts until these are settled! I'll run down and
jump into the carriage in spite of her *bon swear.* (*Exit.*)

TIFFANY. You'll jump into a hornet's nest, if you do! Mr.
Snobson, Mr. Snobson! (*Exit after him.*)

SCENE 2

Housekeeper's room.

Enter MILLINETTE.

MILLINETTE. I have set dat bête, Adolph, to vatch for him.
He say he would come back so soon as Madame's voiture
drive from de door. If he not come—but he vill—he vill—he
bien étourdi, but he have *bon coeur.*

(*Enter* COUNT.)

COUNT. Ah! Millinette, my dear, you see what a good-natured
dog I am to fly at your bidding—

MILLINETTE. Fly? Ah! *trompeur!* Vat for you fly from Paris?

Vat for you leave me—and I love you so much? Ven you sick—you almost die—did I not stay by you—take care of you—and you have no else friend? Vat for you leave Paris?

COUNT. Never allude to disagreeable subjects, *mon enfant!* I was forced by uncontrollable circumstances to fly to the land of liberty—

MILLINETTE. Vat you do vid all de money I give you? The last sou I had—did I not give you?

COUNT. I dare say you did, ma petite—(*Aside.*) Wish you'd been better supplied! Don't ask any questions here—can't explain now—the next time we meet—

MILLINETTE. But, ah! ven shall ve meet—ven? You not deceive me, not any more.

COUNT. Deceive you! I'd rather deceive myself. (*Aside.*) I wish I could! I'd persuade myself you were once more washing linen in the Seine!

MILLINETTE. I vil tell you ven ve shall meet. On Friday night Madame give one grand ball—you come *sans doute*—den ven de supper is served—de Americans tink of noting else ven de supper come—den you steal out of de room, and you find me here—and you give me one grand *explanation!*

(*Enter* GERTRUDE, *unperceived.*)

COUNT. Friday night—while supper is serving—*parole d'honneur* I will be here—I will explain every thing—my sudden departure from Paris—my—demme, my countship—every thing! Now let me go—if any of the family should discover us—

GERTRUDE. (*Who during the last speech has gradually advanced.*) They might discover more than you think it advisable for them to know!

COUNT. The devil!

MILLINETTE. *Mon Dieu!* Mademoiselle Gertrude!

COUNT. (*Recovering himself.*) My dear Miss Gertrude, let me explain—aw—aw—nothing is more natural than the situation in which you find me—

GERTRUDE. I am inclined to believe that, Sir.

COUNT. Now—'pon my honor, that's not fair. Here is Millinette will bear witness to what I am about to say—

GERTRUDE. Oh, I have not the slightest doubt of that, Sir.

COUNT. You see, Millinette happened to be lady's-maid in the family of—of—the Duchess Chateau D'Espagne—and I chanced to be a particular friend of the Duchess—*very particular* I assure you! Of course I saw Millinette, and she, demme, she saw me! Didn't you, Millinette?

MILLINETTE. Oh! *oui*—Mademoiselle, I knew him ver vell.

COUNT. Well, it is a remarkable fact that—being in correspondence with this very Duchess—at this very time—

GERTRUDE. That is sufficient, Sir—I am already so well acquainted with your extraordinary talents for improvisation that I will not further tax your invention—

MILLINETTE. Ah! Mademoiselle Gertrude do not betray us—have pity!

COUNT. (*Assuming an air of dignity.*) Silence, Millinette! My word has been doubted—the word of a nobleman! I will inform my friend, Mrs. Tiffany, of this young person's audacity. (*Going.*)

GERTRUDE. (*Aside.*) His own weapons alone can foil this villain! Sir—Sir—Count!
    (*At the last word the* COUNT *turns.*) Perhaps, Sir, the least said about this matter the better!

COUNT. (*Delightedly.*) The least said? We won't say anything at all. (*Aside.*) She's coming round—couldn't resist me. Charming Gertrude—

MILLINETTE. *Quoi?* Vat that you say?

COUNT. (*Aside to her.*) My sweet, adorable Millinette, hold your tongue, will you?

MILLINETTE. (*Aloud.*) No, I vill not! If you do look so from out your eyes at her again, I vill tell all!

COUNT. (*Aside.*) Oh, I never could manage two women at once, jealousy makes the dear creatures so spiteful. The only valor is in flight! Miss Gertrude, I wish you good morning. Millinette, *mon enfant,* adieu. (*Exit.*)

MILLINETTE. But I have one word more to say. Stop, Stop! (*Exit after him.*)

GERTRUDE. (*Musingly.*) Friday night, while supper is serving, he is to meet Millinette here and explain—what? This man is an impostor! His insulting me—his familiarity with Millinette—his whole conduct—prove it. If I tell Mrs. Tiffany this she will disbelieve me, and one word may place this so-called Count on his guard. To convince Seraphina would be equally difficult, and her rashness and infatuation may render her miserable for life. No—she shall be saved! I must devise some plan for opening their eyes. Truly, if I *cannot* invent one, I shall be the first woman who was ever at a loss for a stratagem—especially to punish a villain or to shield a friend. (*Exit.*)

ACT IV

SCENE 1

Ball-room splendidly illuminated. A curtain hung at the further end. MR. *and* MRS. TIFFANY, SERAPHINA, GERTRUDE, FOGG, TWINKLE, COUNT, SNOBSON, COLONEL HOWARD, *a number of guests—some seated, some standing. As the curtain rises, a cotillion is danced;* GERTRUDE *dancing with* HOWARD, SERAPHINA *with* COUNT.

COUNT. (*Advancing with* SERAPHINA *to the front of the stage.*) To-morrow then—to-morrow—I may salute you as my bride—demme, my Countess!

(*Enter* ZEKE, *with refreshments.*)

SERAPHINA. Yes, to-morrow.
(*As the* COUNT *is about to reply,* SNOBSON *thrusts himself in front of* SERAPHINA.)
SNOBSON. You said you'd dance with me, Miss—now take my fin, and we'll walk about and see what's going on.
(COUNT *raises his eye-glass, regards* SNOBSON, *and leads* SERAPHINA *away;* SNOBSON *follows, endeavoring to attract her attention, but encountering* ZEKE, *bearing a waiter of refreshments; stops him, helps himself, and puts some in his pockets.*)
Here's the treat! get my to-morrow's luncheon out of Tiff.

(*Enter* TRUEMAN, *yawning and rubbing his eyes.*)

TRUEMAN. What a nap I've had, to be sure! (*Looks at his watch.*) Eleven o'clock, as I'm alive! (*To* TIFFANY, *who approaches.*) Just the time when country folks are comfortably *turned in*, and here your grand *turn-out* has hardly begun yet.

GERTRUDE. (*Advancing.*) I was just coming to look for you, Mr. Trueman. I began to fancy that you were paying a visit to dreamland.

TRUEMAN. So I was, child—so I was—and I saw a face—like yours—but brighter!—Even brighter. (*To* TIFFANY.) There's a smile for you, man! It makes one feel that the world has something worth living for in it yet! Do you remember a smile like that, Antony? Ah! I see you don't—but I do—I do! (*Much moved.*)

HOWARD. (*Advancing.*) Good evening, Mr. Trueman. (*Offers his hand.*)

TRUEMAN. That's right, man; give me your whole hand! When a man offers me the tips of his fingers, I know at once there's nothing in him worth seeking beyond his fingers' ends.

(TRUEMAN *and* HOWARD, GERTRUDE *and* TIFFANY *converse.*)

MRS. TIFFANY. (*Advancing.*) I'm in such a fidget lest that vulgar old fellow should disgrace us by some of his plebeian remarks! What it is to give a ball, when one is forced to invite vulgar people!

(MRS. TIFFANY *advances towards* TRUEMAN; SERAPHINA *stands conversing flippantly with the gentlemen who surround her; amongst them is* TWINKLE, *who, having taken a magazine from his pocket, is reading to her, much to the undisguised annoyance of* SNOBSON.)

Dear me, Mr. Trueman, you are very late—quite in the fashion, I declare!

TRUEMAN. Fashion! And pray what is *fashion*, madam? An agreement between certain persons to live without using their souls! To substitute etiquette for virtue—decorum for purity—manners for morals! To affect a shame for the works of their Creator! And expend all their rapture upon the works of their tailors and dressmakers!

MRS. TIFFANY. You have the most *ow-tray* ideas, Mr. Trueman—quite rustic, and deplorably *American!* But pray walk this way.

(MRS. TIFFANY *and* TRUEMAN *go up.*)

COUNT. (*Advancing to* GERTRUDE, HOWARD *a short distance behind her.*) Miss Gertrude—no opportunity of speaking to you before—in demand, you know!

GERTRUDE. (*Aside.*) I have no choice, I must be civil to him. What were you remarking, Sir?

COUNT. Miss Gertrude—charming Ger—aw—aw—(*Aside.*) I never found it so difficult to speak to a woman before.

GERTRUDE. Yes, a very charming ball—many beautiful faces here.

COUNT. Only one!—Aw—aw—one—the fact is—(*Talks to her in dumb show.*)

HOWARD. What could old Trueman have meant by saying she fancied that puppy of a Count—that paste jewel thrust upon the little finger of society.

COUNT. Miss Gertrude—aw—'pon my honor—you don't under-understand—really—aw—aw—will you dance the polka with me?

(GERTRUDE *bows and gives him her hand; he leads her to the set forming;* HOWARD *remains looking after them.*)

HOWARD. Going to dance with him, too! A few days ago she would hardly bow to him civilly—could old Trueman have had reasons for what he said? (*Retires up.*)

(*Dance, the polka;* SERAPHINA, *after having distributed her bouquet, vinaigrette and fan amongst the gentlemen, dances with* SNOBSON.)

PRUDENCE. (*Peeping in as dance concludes.*) I don't like dancing on Friday; something strange is always sure to happen! I'll be on the look out. (*Remains peeping and concealing herself when any of the company approach.*)

GERTRUDE. (*Advancing hastily.*) They are preparing the supper—now if I can only dispose of Millinette while I unmask this insolent pretender! (*Exit.*)

PRUDENCE. (*Peeping.*) What's that she said? It's coming!

(*Re-enter* GERTRUDE, *bearing a small basket filled with bouquets; approaches* MRS. TIFFANY; *they walk to the front of the stage.*)

GERTRUDE. Excuse me, Madam—I believe this is just the hour at which you ordered supper?

MRS. TIFFANY. Well, what's that to you! So you've been dancing with the Count—how dare you dance with a nobleman—*you?*

GERTRUDE. I will answer that question half an hour hence. At present I have something to propose, which I think will gratify you and please your guests. I have heard that at the most elegant balls in Paris, it is customary—

MRS. TIFFANY. What? What?

GERTRUDE. To station a servant at the door with a basket of flowers. A bouquet is then presented to every lady as she passes in. I prepared this basket a short time ago. As the company walk in to supper, might not the flowers be distributed to advantage?

MRS. TIFFANY. How *distingué!* You are a good creature, Gertrude—there, run and hand the *bokettes* to them yourself! You shall have the whole credit of the thing.

GERTRUDE. (*Aside.*) Caught in my own net! But, Madam, I know so little of fashions. Millinette, being French herself, will do it with so much more grace. I am sure Millinette—

MRS. TIFFANY. So am I. She will do it a thousand times better than you—there, go call her.

GERTRUDE. (*Giving basket.*) But, Madam, pray order Millinette not to leave her station till supper is ended; as the company pass out of the supper room she may find that some of the ladies have been overlooked.

MRS. TIFFANY. That is true—very thoughtful of you, Gertrude. (*Exit* GERTRUDE.)

What a *recherché* idea!

(*Enter* MILLINETTE.)

Here, Millinette, take this basket. Place yourself there, and distribute these *bokettes* as the company pass in to supper; but remember not to stir from the spot until supper is over. It is a French fashion you know, Millinette. I am so delighted to be the first to introduce it—it will be all the rage in the *bow-monde!*

MILLINETTE. (*Aside.*) Mon Dieu! dis vill ruin all! Madame, Madame, let me tell you, Madame, dat in France, in Paris, it is de custom to present *les* bouquets ven every body first come—long before de supper. Dis vould be *outré! barbare!* not at all la mode! Ven dey do come in—dat is de fashion in Paris!

MRS. TIFFANY. Dear me! Millinette, what is the difference? Besides I'd have you to know that Americans always improve upon French fashions! Here, take the basket, and let me see that you do it in the most *you-nick* and genteel manner.

(MILLINETTE *poutingly takes the basket and retires up stage. A march. Curtain hung at the further end of the room is drawn back, and discloses a room, in the center of which stands a supper table, beautifully decorated and illuminated; the company promenade two by two into the supper room;* MILLINETTE *presents bouquets as they pass;* COUNT *leads* MRS. TIFFANY.)

TRUEMAN. (*Encountering* FOGG, *who is hurrying alone to the supper room.*) Mr. Fogg, never mind the supper, man! Ha, ha, ha! Of course you are indifferent to suppers!

FOGG. Indifferent! Suppers—oh, ah—no, Sir—suppers? No—no—I'm not indifferent to suppers! (*Hurries away towards table.*)

TRUEMAN. Ha, ha, ha! Here's a new discovery I've made in the fashionable world! Fashion don't permit the critters to have *heads* or *hearts*, but it allows them stomachs! (*To* TIFFANY, *who advances.*) So it's not fashionable to *feel*, but it's fashionable to *feed*, eh, Antony? Ha, ha, ha!

(TRUEMAN *and* TIFFANY *retire towards supper room. Enter* GERTRUDE, *followed by* ZEKE.)

GERTRUDE. Zeke, go to the supper room instantly; whisper to Count Jolimaitre that all is ready, and that he must keep his appointment without delay. Then watch him, and as he passes out of the room, place yourself in front of Millinette in such a manner that the Count cannot see her nor she him. Be sure that they do not see each other—everything depends upon that. (*Crosses.*)

ZEKE. Missey, consider dat business brought to a scientific conclusion.

(*Exit into supper room. Exit* GERTRUDE.)

PRUDENCE. (*Who has been listening.*) What can she want of the Count? I always suspected that Gertrude, because she is so merry and busy! Mr. Trueman thinks so much of her too—I'll tell him this! There's something wrong—but it all comes of giving a ball on a Friday! How astonished the dear old man will be when he finds out how much I know! (*Advances timidly towards the supper room.*)

SCENE 2

Housekeeper's room; dark stage; table, two chairs.

Enter GERTRUDE, *with a lighted candle in her hand.*

GERTRUDE. So far the scheme prospers! And yet this imprudence. If I fail? Fail! To lack courage in a difficulty, or
ingenuity in a dilemma, are not woman's failings!

(*Enter* ZEKE, *with a napkin over his arm, and a bottle of
champagne in his hand.*)

Well, Zeke—Adolph!

ZEKE. Dat's right, Missey; I feels just now as if dat was my
legitimate title; dis here's de stuff to make a nigger feel
like a gemman!

GERTRUDE. But he is coming?

ZEKE. He's coming! (*Sound of a champagne cork heard.*) Do
you hear dat, Missey? Don't it put you all in a froth, and
make you feel as light as a cork? Dere's nothing like the
union brand, to wake up de harmonies ob de heart.
(*Drinks from bottle.*)

GERTRUDE. Remember to keep watch upon the outside—do
not stir from the spot; when I call you, come in quickly
with a light—now, will you be gone!

ZEKE. I'm off, Missey, like a champagne cork wid de strings
cut. (*Exit.*)

GERTRUDE. I think I hear the Count's step. (*Crosses, stage
dark; she blows out candle.*) Now if I can but disguise my
voice, and make the best of my French.

(*Enter* COUNT.)

COUNT. Millinette, where are you? How am I to see you in
the dark?

GERTRUDE. (*Imitating* MILLINETTE'S *voice in a whisper.*)
Hush! *parle bas.*

COUNT. Come here and give me a kiss.

GERTRUDE. Non—non—(*retreating alarmed,* COUNT *follows*) make haste, I must know all.

COUNT. You did not use to be so deuced particular.

ZEKE. (*Without.*) No admission, gemman! Box office closed, tickets stopped!

TRUEMAN. (*Without.*) Out of my way; do you want me to try if your head is as hard as my stick?

GERTRUDE. What shall I do? Ruined, ruined! (*She stands with her hands clasped in speechless despair.*)

COUNT. Halloa! they are coming here, Millinette! Millinette, why don't you speak? Where can I hide myself? (*Running about stage, feeling for a door.*) Where are all your closets? If I could only get out—or get in somewhere; may I be smothered in a clothes' basket if you ever catch me in such a scrape again! (*His hand accidentally touches the knob of a door opening into a closet.*) Fortune's favorite yet! I'm safe!

(*Gets into closet and closes door. Enter* PRUDENCE, TRUE-MAN, MRS. TIFFANY, *and* COLONEL HOWARD, *followed by* ZEKE, *bearing a light; lights up.*)

PRUDENCE. Here they are, the Count and Gertrude! I told you so! (*Stops in surprise on seeing only* GERTRUDE.)

TRUEMAN. And you see what a lie you told!

MRS. TIFFANY. Prudence, how dare you create this disturbance in my house? To suspect the Count, too—a nobleman!

HOWARD. My sweet Gertrude, this foolish old woman would—

PRUDENCE. Oh! you needn't talk—I heard her make the appointment—I know he's here—or he's been here. I wonder if she hasn't hid him away! (*Runs peeping about the room.*)

TRUEMAN. (*Following her angrily.*) You're what I call a confounded—troublesome—meddling—old—prying—

(*As he says the last word,* PRUDENCE *opens closet where the* COUNT *is concealed.*)

Thunder and lightning!

PRUDENCE. I told you so!

(*They all stand aghast;* MRS. TIFFANY, *with her hands lifted in surprise and anger;* TRUEMAN, *clutching his stick;* HOWARD, *looking with an expression of bewildered horror from the* COUNT *to* GERTRUDE.)

MRS. TIFFANY. (*Shaking her fist at* GERTRUDE.) You depraved little minx! this is the meaning of your dancing with the Count!

COUNT. (*Stepping from the closet and advancing. Aside.*) I don't know what to make of it! Millinette not here! Miss Gertrude. Oh! I see—a disguise—the girl's desperate about me—the way with them all.

TRUEMAN. I'm choking—I can't speak—Gertrude—no—no—it is some horrid mistake! (*Partly aside, changes his tone suddenly.*) The villain! I'll hunt the truth out of him, if there's any in—(*crosses, approaches* COUNT *threateningly.*) Do you see this stick? You made its first acquaintance a few days ago; it is time you were better known to each other.

(*As* TRUEMAN *attempts to seize him,* COUNT *escapes, and shields himself behind* MRS. TIFFANY, TRUEMAN *following.*)

COUNT. You ruffian! Would you strike a woman?—Madam—my dear Madam—keep off that barbarous old man, and I will explain! Madam, with—aw—your natural *bon gout*—aw—your fashionable refinement—aw—your—aw—your knowledge of *foreign customs*—

MRS. TIFFANY. Oh! Count, I hope it ain't a *foreign custom* for the nobility to shut themselves up in the dark with young women? We think such things *dreadful* in *America*.

COUNT. Demme—aw—hear what I have to say, Madam—I'll satisfy all sides—I am perfectly innocent in this affair—'pon my honor I am! That young lady shall inform you that I am so herself!—Can't help it, sorry for her. Old matter-of-fact won't be convinced any other way. (*Aside.*) That club of his is so particularly unpleasant! Madam, I was summoned here *malgré moi,* and not knowing whom I was to meet—Miss Gertrude, favor the company by saying whether or not you directed—that—aw—aw—that colored individual to conduct me here?

GERTRUDE. Sir, you well know—

COUNT. A simple yes or no will suffice.

MRS. TIFFANY. Answer the Count's question instantly, Miss.

GERTRUDE. I did—but—

COUNT. You hear, Madam—

TRUEMAN. I won't believe it—I can't! Here, you nigger, stop rolling up your eyes, and let us know whether she told you to bring that critter here?

ZEKE. I'se refuse to gib ebidence; dat's de device ob de

skilfullest counsels ob de day! Can't answer, Boss—neber git a word out ob dis child.—Yah! yah! (*Exit.*)

GERTRUDE. Mrs. Tiffany, Mr. Trueman, if you will but have patience—

TRUEMAN. Patience! Oh, Gertrude, you've taken from an old man something better and dearer than his patience—the one bright hope of nineteen years of self-denial—of nineteen years of—(*Throws himself upon a chair, his head leaning on table.*)

MRS. TIFFANY. Get out of my house, you *ow*dacious—you ruined—you *abimé* young woman! You will corrupt all my family. Good gracious! don't touch me,—don't come near me. Never let me see your face after to-morrow. Pack. (*Goes up.*)

HOWARD. Gertrude, I have striven to find some excuse for you—to doubt—to disbelieve—but this is beyond all endurance! (*Exit.*)

(*Enter* MILLINETTE *in haste.*)

MILLINETTE. I could not come before— (*Stops in surprise at seeing the persons assembled.*) Mon Dieu! vat does dis mean?

COUNT. (*Aside to her.*) Hold your tongue, fool! You will ruin everything, I will explain to-morrow. Mrs. Tiffany—Madam—my dear Madam, let me conduct you back to the ball-room. (*She takes his arm.*) You see I am quite innocent in this matter; a man of my standing, you know; aw—aw—you comprehend the whole affair.

(*Exit* COUNT *leading* MRS. TIFFANY.)

MILLINETTE. I will say to him von vord, I will! (*Exit.*)

GERTRUDE. Mr. Trueman, I beseech you—I insist upon being heard; I claim it as a right!

TRUEMAN. Right? How dare you have the face, girl, to talk of rights? (*Comes down.*) You had more rights than you thought, but you have forfeited them all! All rights to love, respect, protection, and to not a little else that you don't dream of. Go, go! I'll start for Catteraugus to-morrow; I've seen enough of what fashion can do! (*Exit.*)

PRUDENCE. (*Wiping her eyes.*) Dear old man, how he takes on! I'll go and console him! (*Exit.*)

GERTRUDE. This is too much! How heavy a penalty has my

imprudence cost me!—His esteem, and that of one dearer—
my home—my—
(*Burst of lively music from ball-room.*)
They are dancing, and I—I should be weeping, if pride
had not sealed up my tears.
(*She sinks into a chair. Band plays the polka behind till
Curtain falls.*)

ACT V

MRS. TIFFANY'S *Drawing Room—same Scene as Act I.*
GERTRUDE *seated at a table, with her head leaning on her
hand; in the other hand she holds a pen. A sheet of paper
and an ink-stand before her.*

GERTRUDE. How shall I write to them? What shall I say?
Prevaricate I cannot—(*rises and comes forward*) and yet
if I write the truth—simple souls! How can they comprehend the motives for my conduct? Nay—the truly pure see
no imaginary evil in others! It is only vice that, reflecting
its own image, suspects even the innocent. I have no time
to lose—I must prepare them for my return. (*Resumes her
seat and writes.*) What a true pleasure there is in daring
to be frank! (*After writing a few lines more pauses.*) Not
so frank either; there is one name that I cannot mention.
Ah! that he should suspect—should despise me. (*Writes.*)

(*Enter* TRUEMAN.)

TRUEMAN. There she is! If this girl's soul had only been as
fair as her face! Yet she dared to speak the truth; I'll not
forget that! A woman who refuses to tell a lie has one
spark of heaven in her still. (*Approaches her.*) Gertrude,
(GERTRUDE *starts and looks up.*)
What are you writing there? Plotting more mischief, eh,
girl?
GERTRUDE. I was writing a few lines to some friends in
Geneva.
TRUEMAN. The Wilsons, eh?

GERTRUDE. (*Surprised, rising.*) Are you acquainted with them, Sir?

TRUEMAN. I shouldn't wonder if I was. I suppose you have taken good care not to mention the dark room—that foreign puppy in the closet—the pleasant surprise—and all that sort of thing, eh?

GERTRUDE. I have no reason for concealment, Sir, for I have done nothing of which I am ashamed!

TRUEMAN. Then I can't say much for your modesty.

GERTRUDE. I should not wish you to say more than I deserve.

TRUEMAN. (*Aside.*) There's a bold minx!

GERTRUDE. Since my affairs seem to have excited your interest —I will not say *curiosity*—perhaps you even feel a desire to inspect my correspondence? There, (*Handing the letter.*) I pride myself upon my good nature; you may like to take advantage of it?

TRUEMAN. (*Aside.*) With what an air she carries it off! Take advantage of it? So I will. (*Reads.*) What's this? "French chambermaid — Count — impostor — infatuation — Seraphina — Millinette—disguised myself—expose him." Thunder and lightning! I see it all! Come and kiss me, girl!

(GERTRUDE *evinces surprise.*)

No, no—I forgot—it won't do to come to that yet! She's a rare girl! I'm out of my senses with joy! I don't know what to do with myself! Tol, de rol, de rol, de ra. (*Capers and sings.*)

GERTRUDE. (*Aside.*) What a remarkable old man! Then you do me justice, Mr. Trueman?

TRUEMAN. I say I don't! Justice? You're above all dependence upon justice! Hurrah! I've found one true woman at last! *True?* (*Pauses thoughtfully.*) Humph! I didn't think of that flaw! Plotting and maneuvering—not much truth in that! An honest girl should be above stratagems!

GERTRUDE. But my *motive*, Sir, was good.

TRUEMAN. That's not enough—your *actions* must be *good* as well as your *motives!* Why could you not tell the silly girl that man was an impostor?

GERTRUDE. I did inform her of my suspicions—she ridiculed them; the plan I chose was an imprudent one, but I could not devise—

TRUEMAN. I hate devising! Give me a woman with the *firmness* to be *frank!* But no matter—I had no right to look for an angel out of Paradise; and I am as happy—as happy as a Lord! that is, ten times happier than any Lord ever was! Tol, de rol, de rol! Oh! you—you—I'll thrash every fellow that says a word against you!

GERTRUDE. You will have plenty of employment then, Sir, for I do not know of one just now who would speak in my favor!

TRUEMAN. Not *one*, eh? Why, where's your dear Mr. Twinkle? I know all about it—can't say that I admire your choice of a husband! But there's no accounting for a girl's taste.

GERTRUDE. Mr. Twinkle! Indeed you are quite mistaken!

TRUEMAN. No—really? Then you're not taken with him, eh?

GERTRUDE. Not even with his rhymes.

TRUEMAN. Hang that old mother meddle-much! What a fool she has made of me. And so you're quite free, and I may choose a husband for you myself? Heart-whole, eh?

GERTRUDE. I—I—I trust there is nothing *unsound* about my heart.

TRUEMAN. There it is again. Don't prevaricate, girl! I tell you an *evasion* is a *lie in contemplation,* and I hate lying! Out with the truth! Is your heart *free* or not?

GERTRUDE. Nay, Sir, since you *demand* an answer, permit *me* to demand by what right you ask the question?

(*Enter* HOWARD.)

Colonel Howard here!

TRUEMAN. I'm out again! What's the Colonel to her? (*Retires up.*)

HOWARD. (*Crosses to her.*) I have come, Gertrude, to bid you farewell. To-morrow I resign my commission and leave this city, perhaps forever. You, Gertrude, it is you who have exiled me! After last evening—

TRUEMAN. (*Coming forward to* HOWARD.) What the plague have you got to say about last evening?

HOWARD. Mr. Trueman!

TRUEMAN. What have you got to say about last evening? And what have you to say to that little girl at all? It's Tiffany's precious daughter you're in love with.

HOWARD. Miss Tiffany? Never! I never had the slightest pretension—

TRUEMAN. That lying old woman! But I'm glad of it! Oh!

Ah! Um! (*Looking significantly at* GERTRUDE *and then at* HOWARD.) I see how it is. So you don't choose to marry Seraphina, eh? Well now, whom do you choose to marry? (*Glancing at* GERTRUDE.)

HOWARD. I shall not marry at all!

TRUEMAN. You won't? (*Looking at them both again.*) Why you don't mean to say that you don't like— (*Points with his thumb to* GERTRUDE.)

GERTRUDE. Mr. Trueman, I may have been wrong to boast of my good nature, but do not presume too far upon it.

HOWARD. You like frankness, Mr. Trueman, therefore I will speak plainly. I have long cherished a dream from which I was last night rudely awakened.

TRUEMAN. And that's what you call speaking plainly? Well, I differ with you! But I can guess what you mean. Last night you suspected Gertrude there of—(*Angrily.*) of what no man shall ever suspect her again while I'm above ground! You did her injustice; it was a mistake! There, now that matter's settled. Go, and ask her to forgive you— she's woman enough to do it! Go, go!

HOWARD. Mr. Trueman, you have forgotten to whom you dictate.

TRUEMAN. Then you won't do it? You won't ask her pardon?

HOWARD. Most undoubtedly I will not—not at any man's bidding. I must first know—

TRUEMAN. You won't do it? Then if I don't give you a lesson in politeness—

HOWARD. It will be because you find me your *tutor* in the same science. I am not a man to brook an insult, Mr. Trueman! But we'll not quarrel in presence of the lady.

TRUEMAN. Won't we? I don't know that—

GERTRUDE. Pray, Mr. Trueman—Colonel Howard, pray desist, Mr. Trueman, for my sake! (*Taking hold of his arm to hold him back.*) Colonel Howard, if you will read this letter it will explain everything.

(*Hands letter to* HOWARD, *who reads.*)

TRUEMAN. He don't deserve an explanation! Didn't I tell him that it was a mistake? Refuse to beg your pardon! I'll teach him, I'll teach him!

HOWARD. (*After reading.*) Gertrude, how have I wronged you!

TRUEMAN. Oh, you'll beg her pardon now?

(*Between them.*)

HOWARD. Hers, Sir, and yours! Gertrude, I fear—

TRUEMAN. You needn't, she'll forgive you. You don't know these women as well as I do: they're always ready to pardon; it's their nature, and they can't help it. Come along, I left Antony and his wife in the dining room; we'll go and find them. I've a story of my own to tell! As for you, Colonel, you may follow. Come along. Come along!

(*Leads out* GERTRUDE, *followed by* HOWARD.)

(*Enter* MR. *and* MRS. TIFFANY, MR. TIFFANY *with a bundle of bills in his hand.*)

MRS. TIFFANY. I beg you won't mention the subject again, Mr. Tiffany. Nothing is more plebeian than a discussion upon economy—nothing more *ungenteel* than looking over and fretting over one's bills!

TIFFANY. Then I suppose, my dear, it is quite as ungenteel to *pay* one's bills?

MRS. TIFFANY. Certainly! I hear the *ee-light* never condescend to do anything of the kind. The honor of their invaluable patronage is sufficient for the persons they employ!

TIFFANY. *Patronage* then is a newly invented food upon which the working classes fatten? What convenient appetites poor people must have! Now listen to what I am going to say. As soon as my daughter marries Mr. Snobson—

(*Enter* PRUDENCE, *a three-cornered note in her hand.*)

PRUDENCE. Oh, dear! Oh, dear! What shall we do! Such a misfortune! Such a disaster! Oh, dear! Oh, dear!

MRS. TIFFANY. Prudence, you are the most tiresome creature! What *is* the matter?

PRUDENCE (*Pacing up and down the stage.*) Such a disgrace to the whole family! But I always expected it. Oh, dear! Oh, dear!

MRS. TIFFANY. (*Following her up and down the stage.*) What are you talking about, Prudence? Will you tell me what has happened?

PRUDENCE. (*Still pacing,* MRS. TIFFANY *following.*) Oh! I can't, I can't! You'll feel so dreadfully! How could she do such a thing! But I expected nothing else! I never did, I never did!

MRS. TIFFANY. (*Still following.*) Good gracious! what do you mean, Prudence? Tell me, will you tell me? I shall get into such a passion! What *is* the matter?

PRUDENCE. (*Still pacing.*) Oh, Betsy, Betsy! That your daughter should have come to that! Dear me, dear me!

TIFFANY. Seraphina? Did you say Seraphina? What has happened to her? What has she done?

(*Following* PRUDENCE *up and down the stage on the opposite side from* MRS. TIFFANY.)

MRS. TIFFANY. (*Still following.*) What *has* she done? What *has* she done?

PRUDENCE. Oh! something dreadful—dreadful—shocking!

TIFFANY. (*Still following.*) Speak quickly and plainly—you torture me by this delay; Prudence, be calm, and speak! What is it?

PRUDENCE. (*Stopping.*) Zeke just told me—he carried her travelling trunk himself—she gave him a whole dollar! Oh, my!

TIFFANY. Her trunk? Where? Where?

PRUDENCE. Round the corner!

MRS. TIFFANY. What did she want with her trunk? You are the most vexatious creature, Prudence! There is no bearing your ridiculous conduct!

PRUDENCE. Oh, you will have worse to bear—worse! Seraphina's gone!

TIFFANY. Gone! Where?

PRUDENCE. Off!—Eloped—eloped with the Count! Dear me, dear me! I always told you she would!

TIFFANY. Then I am ruined! (*Stands with his face buried in his hands.*)

MRS. TIFFANY. Oh, what a ridiculous girl! And she might have had such a splendid wedding! What could have possessed her?

TIFFANY. The devil himself possessed her, for she has ruined me past all redemption! Gone, Prudence, did you say gone? Are you *sure* they are gone?

PRUDENCE. Didn't I tell you so! Just look at this note—one might know by the very fold of it—

TIFFANY. (*Snatching the note.*) Let me see it! (*Opens the note and reads.*) "My dear Ma,—When you receive this I shall be a *countess!* Isn't it a sweet title? The Count and I were forced to be married privately, for reasons which I will explain in my next. You must pacify Pa, and put him in a good humor before I come back, though now I'm to be a countess I suppose I shouldn't care!" Undutiful huzzy! "We are going to make a little excursion and will be back in a week

> Your dutiful daughter—Seraphina."

A man's curse is sure to spring up at his own hearth; here is mine! The sole curb upon that villain gone, I am wholly in his power! Oh! The first downward step from honor—he who takes it cannot pause in his mad descent and is sure to be hurried on to ruin!

MRS. TIFFANY. Why, Mr. Tiffany, how you do take on! And I dare say to elope was the most fashionable way after all!

(*Enter* TRUEMAN, *leading* GERTRUDE, *and followed by* HOWARD.)

TRUEMAN. Where are all the folks? Here, Antony, you are the man I want. We've been hunting for you all over the house. Why—what's the matter? There's a face for a thriving city merchant! Ah! Antony, you never wore such a hang-dog look as that when you trotted about the country with your pack upon your back! Your shoulders are no broader now—but they've a heavier load to carry—that's plain!

MRS. TIFFANY. Mr. Trueman, such allusions are highly improper! What would my daughter, *the Countess*, say!

GERTRUDE. The Countess? Oh! Madam!

MRS. TIFFANY. Yes, the Countess! My daughter Seraphina, the Countess *dee* Jolimaitre! What have you to say to that? No wonder you are surprised after your *recherché, abimé* conduct! I have told you already, Miss Gertrude, that you were not a proper person to enjoy the inestimable advantages of my patronage. You are dismissed—do you understand? Discharged!

TRUEMAN. Have you done? Very well, it's my turn now. Antony, perhaps what I have to say don't concern you as much as some others—but I want you to listen to me. You remember, Antony, (*His tone becomes serious.*) a blue-eyed, smiling girl—

TIFFANY. Your daughter, Sir? I remember her well.

TRUEMAN. None ever saw her to forget her! Give me your hand, man. There—that will do! Now let me go on. I never coveted wealth—yet twenty years ago I found myself the richest farmer in Catteraugus. This cursed money made my girl an object of speculation. Every idle fellow that wanted to feather his nest was sure to come courting Ruth. There was one—my heart misgave me the instant I laid eyes upon him—for he was a city chap, and not over fond of the truth. But Ruth—ah! She was too pure herself to look for guile! His fine words and his fair looks—the old story—she was taken with him. I said, "no"—but the girl liked her own way better than her old father's—girls always do! And one morning—the rascal robbed me; not of my money—he would have been welcome to that—but of the only treasure I cherished—my daughter!

TIFFANY. But you forgave her!

TRUEMAN. I did! I knew she would never forgive herself— that was punishment enough! The scoundrel thought he was marrying my gold with my daughter—he was mistaken! I took care that they should never want; but that was all. She loved him—what will not woman love? The villain broke her heart—mine was tougher, or it wouldn't have stood what it did. A year after they were married, he forsook her! She came back to her old home—her old father! It couldn't last long—she pined—and pined—and—then—she died! Don't think me an old fool—though I am one—for grieving won't bring her back. (*Bursts into tears.*)

TIFFANY. It was a heavy loss!

TRUEMAN. So heavy, that I should not have cared how soon I followed her, but for the child she left! As I pressed that child in my arms, I swore that my unlucky wealth should never curse it, as it had cursed its mother! It was all I had to love—but I sent it away—and the neighbors thought it was dead. The girl was brought up tenderly but humbly by my wife's relatives in Geneva. I had her taught true independence—she had hands—capacities—and should use them! Money should never buy her a husband! For I resolved not to claim her until she had made her choice, and found the man who was willing to take her for herself alone. She turned out a rare girl! And it's time her old grandfather claimed her. Here he is to do it! And there

stands Ruth's child! Old Adam's heiress! Gertrude, Gertrude!—My child!

(GERTRUDE *rushes into his arms.*)

PRUDENCE. (*After a pause.*) Do tell; I want to know! But I
knew it! I always said Gertrude would turn out somebody,
after all!

MRS. TIFFANY. Dear me! Gertrude an heiress! My dear Gertrude, I always thought you a very charming girl—quite
YOU-NICK—an heiress! (*Aside.*) I must give her a ball! I'll
introduce her into society myself—of course an heiress must
make a sensation!

HOWARD. (*Aside.*) I am too bewildered even to wish her joy.
Ah! there will be plenty to do that now—but the gulf
between us is wider than ever.

TRUEMAN. Step forward, young man, and let us know what
you are muttering about. I said I would never claim her
until she had found the man who loved her for herself. I
have claimed her—yet I never break my word—I think I
have found that man! and here he is. (*Strikes* HOWARD *on
the shoulder.*) Gertrude's yours! There—never say a word,
man—don't bore me with your thanks—you can cancel all
obligations by making that child happy! There—take her!—
Well, girl, and what do you say?

GERTRUDE. That I rejoice too much at having found a parent
for my first act to be one of disobedience! (*Gives her hand
to* HOWARD.)

(TIFFANY *retires up—and paces the stage, exhibiting great
agitation.*)

PRUDENCE. (*To* TRUEMAN). All the *single folks* are getting
married!

TRUEMAN. No they are not. You and I are single folks, and
we're not likely to get married.

MRS. TIFFANY. My dear Mr. Trueman—my sweet Gertrude,
when my daughter, the Countess, returns, she will be
delighted to hear of this *deenooment!* I assure you that the
countess will be quite charmed!

GERTRUDE. The Countess? Pray, Madam, where *is* Seraphina?

MRS. TIFFANY. The Countess *dee* Jolimaitre, my dear, is at
this moment on her way to—to Washington! Where after
visiting all the fashionable curiosities of the day—including
the President—she will return to grace her native city!

GERTRUDE. I hope you are only jesting, Madam? Seraphina is not married?

MRS. TIFFANY. Excuse me, my dear, my daughter had this morning the honor of being united to the Count *dee* Jolimaitre!

GERTRUDE. Madam! He is an impostor!

MRS. TIFFANY. Good gracious! Gertrude, how can you talk in that disrespectful way of a man of rank? An heiress, my dear, should have better manners! The Count—

(*Enter* MILLINETTE, *crying.*)

MILLINETTE. Oh! Madame! I will tell everyting—oh! dat monstre! He break my heart!

MRS. TIFFANY. Millinette, what is the matter?

MILLINETTE. Oh! he promise to marry me—I love him much—and now Zeke say he run away vid Mademoiselle Seraphina!

MRS. TIFFANY. What insolence! The girl is mad! Count Jolimaitre marry my *femmy de chamber!*

MILLINETTE. Oh! Madame, he is not one Count, not at all! Dat is only de title he go by in dis country. De foreigners always take de large title ven dey do come here. His name *à Paris* vas Gustave Treadmill. But he not one Frenchman at all, but he do live one long time *à Paris.* First he live vid Monsieur Vermicelle—dere he vas de head cook! Den he live vid Monsieur Tire-nez, de barber! After dat he live wid Monsieur le Comte Frippon-fin—and dere he vas le Comte's valet! Dere, now I tell everyting I feel one great deal better!

MRS. TIFFANY. Oh! Good gracious! I shall faint! Not a Count! What will everybody say? It's no such thing! I say he *is* a Count! One can see the foreign *jenny says quoi* in his face! Don't you think I can tell a Count when I see one? I say he *is* a Count!

(*Enter* SNOBSON, *his hat on, his hands thrust in his pocket, evidently a little intoxicated.*)

SNOBSON. I won't stand it! I say I won't!

TIFFANY. (*Rushing up to him. Aside.*) Mr. Snobson, for heaven's sake—

SNOBSON. Keep off! I'm a hard customer to get the better of!
You'll see if I don't come out strong!

TRUEMAN. (*Quietly knocking off* SNOBSON's *hat with his stick.*)
Where are your manners, man?

SNOBSON. My business ain't with you, Catteraugus; you've
waked up the wrong passenger! (*Aside.*) Now the way
I'll put it into Tiff will be a caution. I'll make him wince!
That extra mint julep has put the true pluck in me. Now
for it! —Mr. Tiffany, Sir—you needn't think to come over
me, Sir—you'll have to get up a little earlier in the morning
before you do *that*, Sir! I'd like to know, Sir, how you came
to assist your daughter in running away with that foreign
loafer? It was a downright swindle, Sir. After the conversation I and you had on that subject she wasn't your property, Sir.

TRUEMAN. What, Antony, is that the way your city clerk
bullies his boss?

SNOBSON. You're drunk, Catteraugus—don't expose your-self—
you're drunk! Taken a little too much toddy, my old boy!
Be quiet! I'll look after you, and they won't find it out. If
you want to be busy, you may take care of my *hat*—I feel
so deuced weak in the chest, I don't think I *could* pick it
up myself. (*Aside.*) Now to put the screws to Tiff. Mr.
Tiffany, Sir—you have broken your word, as no virtuous
individual—no honorable member—of—the—com—mu—ni—
ty—

TIFFANY. (*Aside to him.*) Have some pity, Mr. Snobson, I
beseech you! I had nothing to do with my daughter's
elopement! I will agree to anything you desire—your salary
shall be doubled—trebled—

SNOBSON. (*Aloud.*) No you don't. No bribery and corruption.

TIFFANY. (*Aside to him.*) I implore you to be silent. You shall
become partner of the concern, if you please—only do not
speak. You are not yourself at this moment.

SNOBSON. Ain't I, though? I feel *twice* myself. I feel like two
Snobsons rolled into one, and I'm chock full of the spunk
of a dozen! Now Mr. Tiffany, Sir—

TIFFANY. (*Aside to him.*) I shall go distracted! Mr. Snobson,
if you have one spark of manly feeling—

TRUEMAN. Antony, why do you stand disputing with that
drunken jackass? Where's your nigger? Let him kick the
critter out, and be of use for once in his life.

SNOBSON. Better be quiet, Catteraugus. This ain't your hash, so keep your spoon out of the dish. Don't expose yourself, old boy.

TRUEMAN. Turn him out, Antony!

SNOBSON. He daren't do it! Ain't I up to him? Ain't he in my power? Can't I knock him into a cocked hat with a word? And now he's got my steam up—I *will* do it!

TIFFANY. (*Beseechingly.*) Mr. Snobson—my friend—

SNOBSON. It's no go—steam's up—and I don't stand at anything!

TRUEMAN. You won't *stand* here long unless you mend your manners—you're not the first man I've *upset* because he didn't know his place.

SNOBSON. I know where Tiff's place is, and that's in the *States' Prison!* It's bespoke already. He would have it! He wouldn't take pattern of me, and behave like a gentleman! He's a *forger*, Sir!

(TIFFANY *throws himself into a chair in an attitude of despair; the others stand transfixed with astonishment.*)

He's been forging Dick Anderson's endorsements of his notes these ten months. He's got a couple in the bank that will send him to the wall anyhow—if he can't make a raise. I took them there myself! Now you know what he's worth. I said I'd expose him, and I have done it!

MRS. TIFFANY. Get out of the house! You ugly, little, drunken brute, get out! It's not true. Mr. Trueman, put him out; you have got a stick—put him out!

(*Enter* SERAPHINA, *in her bonnet and shawl—a parasol in her hand.*)

SERAPHINA. I hope Zeke hasn't delivered my note. (*Stops in surprise at seeing the persons assembled.*)

MRS. TIFFANY. Oh, here is the Countess! (*Advances to embrace her.*)

TIFFANY. (*Starting from his seat, and seizing* SERAPHINA *violently by the arm.*) Are—you—married?

SERAPHINA. Goodness, Pa, how you frighten me! No, I'm not married, *quite.*

TIFFANY. Thank heaven.

MRS. TIFFANY. (*Drawing* SERAPHINA *aside.*) What's the matter? Why did you come back?

SERAPHINA. The clergyman wasn't at home—I came back for my jewels—the Count said nobility couldn't get on without them.

TIFFANY. I may be saved yet! Seraphina, my child, you will not see me disgraced—ruined! I have been a kind father to you—at least I have tried to be one—although your mother's extravagance made a *madman* of me! The Count is an impostor—you seemed to like him—(*pointing to* SNOBSON.) (*Aside.*) Heaven forgive me!—Marry *him* and save *me.* You, Mr. Trueman, you will be my friend in this hour of extreme need—you will advance the sum which I require— I pledge myself to return it. My wife—my child—who will support them were I—the thought makes me frantic! You will aid me? You had a child yourself.

TRUEMAN. But I did not *sell* her—it was her own doings. Shame on you, Antony! Put a price on your own flesh and blood! Shame on such foul traffic!

TIFFANY. Save me—I conjure you—for my father's sake.

TRUEMAN. For your *father's* SON's sake I will *not* aid you in becoming a greater villain than you are!

GERTRUDE. Mr. Trueman—Father, I should say—save him— do not embitter our happiness by permitting this calamity to fall upon another—

TRUEMAN. Enough—I did not need your voice, child. I am going to settle this matter my own way.
    (*Goes up to* SNOBSON—*who has seated himself and fallen asleep—tilts him out of the chair.*)

SNOBSON. (*Waking up.*) Eh? Where's the fire? Oh! it's you, Catteraugus.

TRUEMAN. If I comprehend aright, you have been for some time aware of your principal's forgeries?
    (*As he says this, he beckons to* HOWARD, *who advances as witness.*)

SNOBSON. You've hit the nail, Catteraugus! Old chap saw that I was up to him six months ago; left off throwing dust into my eyes—

TRUEMAN. Oh, he did!

SNOBSON. Made no bones of forging Anderson's name at my elbow.

TRUEMAN. Forged at your elbow? You saw him do it?

SNOBSON. I did.

TRUEMAN. Repeatedly.

SNOBSON. Re—pea—ted—ly.

TRUEMAN. Then you, Rattlesnake, if he goes to the States' Prison, you'll take up your quarters there too. You are an accomplice, an *accessory!*

(TRUEMAN *walks away and seats himself,* HOWARD *rejoins* GERTRUDE. SNOBSON *stands for some time bewildered.*)

SNOBSON. The deuce, so I am! I never thought of that! I must make myself scarce. I'll be off! Tif, I say, Tif! (*Going up to him and speaking confidentially*) That drunken old rip has got us in his power. Let's give him the slip and be off. They want men of genius at the West—we're sure to get on! You—you can set up for a writing master, and teach copying *signatures;* and I—I'll give lectures on *temperance!* You won't come, eh? Then I'm off without you. Good bye, Catteraugus! Which is the way to California? (*Steals off.*)

TRUEMAN. There's one debt your city owes me. And now let us see what other nuisances we can abate. Antony, I'm not given to preaching; therefore I shall not say much about what you have done. Your face speaks for itself—the crime has brought its punishment along with it.

TIFFANY. Indeed it has, Sir! In *one year* I have lived a *century* of misery.

TRUEMAN. I believe you, and upon one condition I will assist you—

TIFFANY. My friend—my first, ever kind friend—only name it!

TRUEMAN. You must sell your house and all these gew-gaws, and bundle your wife and daughter off to the country. There let them learn economy, true independence, and home virtues, instead of foreign follies. As for yourself, continue your business—but let moderation, in future, be your counsellor, and let *honesty* be your confidential clerk.

TIFFANY. Mr. Trueman, you have made existence once more precious to me! My wife and daughter shall quit the city tomorrow, and—

PRUDENCE. It's all coming right! It's all coming right! We'll go to the county of Catteraugus. (*Walking up to* TRUEMAN.)

TRUEMAN. No, you won't—I make that a stipulation, Antony; keep clear of Catteraugus. None of your fashionable examples there!

(JOLIMAITRE *appears in the Conservatory and peeps into the room unperceived.*)

COUNT. What can detain Seraphina? We ought to be off!

MILLINETTE. (*Turns round, perceives him, runs and forces him into the room.*) Here he is! Ah, Gustave, mon cher Gustave! I have you now and we never part no more. Don't frown, Gustave, don't frown—

TRUEMAN. Come forward, Mr. Count! and for the edification of fashionable society confess that you're an impostor.

COUNT. An impostor? Why, you abominable old—

TRUEMAN. Oh, your feminine friend has told us all about it, the cook—the valet—barber and all that sort of thing. Come, confess, and something may be done for you.

COUNT. Well, then, I do confess I am no count; but really, ladies and gentlemen, I may recommend myself as the most capital cook.

MRS. TIFFANY. Oh, Seraphina!

SERAPHINA. Oh, Ma!

(*They embrace and retire up.*)

TRUEMAN. Promise me to call upon the whole circle of your fashionable acquaintances with your own advertisements and in your cook's attire, and I will set you up in business tomorrow. Better turn stomachs than turn heads!

MILLINETTE. But you will marry me?

COUNT. Give us your hand, Millinette! Sir, command me for the most delicate *paté*—the daintiest *croquette à la royale* —the most transcendent *omelette soufflée* that ever issued from a French pastry-cook's oven. I hope you will pardon my conduct, but I heard that in America, where you pay homage to titles while you profess to scorn them—where *Fashion* makes the basest coin current—where you have no kings, no princes, no *nobility*—

TRUEMAN. Stop there! I object to your use of that word. When justice is found only among lawyers, health among physicians, and patriotism among politicians, *then* may you say that there is no *nobility* where there are no titles! But we *have* kings, princes, and nobles in abundance—of *Nature's stamp*, if not of *Fashion's*; we have honest men, warm hearted and brave, and we have women—gentle, fair, and true, to whom no *title* could add *nobility*.

EPILOGUE

PRUDENCE. I told you so! And now you hear and see.
   I told you *Fashion* would the fashion be!
TRUEMAN. Then both its point and moral I distrust.
COUNT. Sir, is that liberal?
HOWARD.   Or is it just?
TRUEMAN. The guilty have escaped!
TIFFANY.   Is, therefore, sin
   Made charming? Ah! There's punishment within!
   Guilt ever carries his own scourge along.
GERTRUDE. Virtue her own reward!
TRUEMAN.   You're right, I'm wrong.
MRS. TIFFANY. How we have been deceived!
PRUDENCE.   I told you so.
SERAPHINA. To lose at once a title and a beau!
COUNT. A count no more, I'm no more of *account*.
TRUEMAN. But to a nobler title you may mount,
   And be in time—who knows?—an honest man!
COUNT. Eh, Millinette?
MILLINETT.   Oh, *oui*—I know you can!
GERTRUDE. (*To audience.*) But ere we close the scene, a
     word with you,—
   We charge you answer: Is this picture true?
   Some little mercy to our efforts show,
   Then let the world your honest verdict know.
   Here let it see portrayed its ruling passion,
   And learn to prize at its just value—*Fashion*.

THE OCTOROON

Preface to THE OCTOROON

The Octoroon was one of the most successful melodramas of the last half of the nineteenth century and one of the few plays that ventured to deal with the explosive subject of slavery. Its overall effect was not the same as the one Lincoln attributed to the author of its famous and oft-reprinted prototype, *Uncle Tom's Cabin*: "So this is the little woman who brought on this great war." Nonetheless, the atmosphere was charged when the New York première of *The Octoroon* took place at the packed Winter Garden on December 6, 1859, only a few days after the execution of John Brown. Referring to the slave auction scene, Agnes Robertson (Mrs. Boucicault, who had the part of Zoe) wrote: "I was solemnly warned that if I attempted to play this scene I should be shot as I stood on the table to be sold." But instead of shots and riots, there were shouts and applause for the play. The Boucicaults left the cast a week later, but the play continued to draw large audiences in American and English theatres, and it was frequently revived for over forty years.

The success of the play was in part due to Boucicault's astuteness in capitalizing on a controversial subject that would attract large crowds, and his adeptness in presenting such a subject without offending even pro-slavery partisans. As Joseph Jefferson, who played Salem Scudder, said of the play in his *Autobiography*: "The truth of the matter is, it was noncommittal. The dialogue and characters of the play made one feel for the South, but the action proclaimed against slavery, and called loudly for its abolition." *The Octoroon* also reflects its author's showmanship. The plot moves swiftly, and there is much violent action, including a chase and a bowie-knife fight, as well as a pyrotechnic spectacle when the steamer explodes. Furthermore, Boucicault artfully utilized for theatrical purposes the recently-invented camera, which he employed to unmask the villain. Accompanying these and other scenes was suitable music, which helped create suspense and set the mood. Acts ended with the tableaux so dear to audiences of the nineteenth century: groupings of actors, frozen silent and motionless in their climactic curtain positions. There were also such familiar stage characters as the Indian (played by Boucicault himself), the Yankee (a whimsical one, played by Jefferson), the hero (played by A.H. Davenport), the villain (whom Boucicault shrewdly also made a Yankee), and the loyal Negro slave "Ole Uncle" Pete. The language, too, was suitable to the genre. It strikes the modern reader as being particularly amusing when it voices now-discarded superstitions. In the love scene, for example, Zoe agonizingly reveals her Negro "taint," "the ineffaceable curse of Cain": a "bluish tinge" in the fingernails, eyewhites, and hair roots! She will not marry her still-undaunted lover, much as she loves him, for it would break the heart of his aunt, who is also her benefactress:

GEORGE: Zoe, must we immolate our lives on her prejudice?
ZOE: Yes, for I'd rather be black than ungrateful!

All these actions and speeches are, of course, characteristic of melodrama. But the story of the love of a white man and a free southern mulatto girl was deeply affecting in the theatre. A six-week revival in 1961 at the Phoenix Theatre in New York again demonstrated the theatricality of the play, which a reading can only suggest. Melodrama in a nineteenth-century format usually appears jaded to today's more sophisticated theatre audiences. But this recent performance of *The Octoroon* (which was played straight, unlike a brief burlesque revival on Broadway in 1924) proved quite successful. For, however melodramatically, Boucicault's play may still have things to say to us in our age. "The vestigial bitterness [of slavery] remains with us to be read in the daily papers," T. Edward Hambleton commented in his "Program Note" in the *Playbill*; "its remains are a part of our heritage. 'The Octoroon' is a living picture of a part of our country's past. We believe it retains today what made it significant, moving, entertaining and above all, theatrical to its first audience in 1859."

Its author, Dion Boucicault (1822?–1890), was one of the most important figures in the nineteenth-century American (as well as English) theatre. Born in Ireland, he achieved prominence in England with a comedy, *London Assurance*, in 1841. He married Agnes Robertson, who was to star in many of his plays. When he first came to this country in 1853, he was well acquainted with English novels and French drama, whose plots he freely used for his own plays. *The Octoroon*, for example, was an adaptation of an English novel, Mayne Reid's *The Quadroon* (1856). As he did with many of his other plays, however, he skilfully reshaped his source and transformed it into a highly theatrical work. In all, he wrote and adapted close to 150 plays, the most popular of which were such "Irish life" productions as *The Colleen Bawn* (1860) and *The Shaughraun* (1874); an adaptation of Dickens's *Cricket on the Hearth, Dot* (1859), in which Jefferson created his important role of Caleb Plummer; the *Rip Van Winkle* (1865) that Jefferson eventually altered into his own vehicle; and one of Boucicault's most sensational productions, *The Poor of New York* (1857), which dealt with financial panics and featured, as its *pièce de résistance*, a house going up in flames.

Boucicault was not only a prolific playwright. He was also an actor of no mean ability, whose Shaughraun, for example, was a unique creation. He was, as well, an important and influential experimenter in scenic effects and lighting, and the first entrepreneur to send a traveling company on national tour with a New York (or London) hit play. Beyond that, he succeeded, where others had failed, in securing passage of the first copyright law (1856), a law that afforded at least some protection to playwrights and generally helped raise their professional status.

There are variant acting versions of *The Octoroon*. One ends happily—in miscegenation (it was thus performed only in England), and another ends with the death of all the principal characters upon the explosion of the steamer. The text here printed was collated for this book from various acting editions and scripts, and follows the version most frequently used in American productions. For the biography of Boucicault see Townsend Walsh, *The Career of Dion Boucicault* (1915). The collection of Boucicault source material (including unproduced and unpublished scripts) was acquired by the University of South Florida Library in 1966.

M.M.

THE OCTOROON;

or, LIFE IN LOUISIANA

By Dion Boucicault

Characters

GEORGE PEYTON, Mrs. Peyton's Nephew, educated in Europe, and just returned home

JACOB M'CLOSKY, formerly Overseer of Terrebonne, but now Owner of one half of the Estate

SALEM SCUDDER, a Yankee from Massachusetts, now Overseer of Terrebonne, great on improvements and inventions, once a Photographic Operator, and been a little of everything generally

PETE, an "Ole Uncle," once the late Judge's body servant, but now "too ole to work, sa."

SUNNYSIDE, a Planter, Neighbor, and Old Friend of the Peytons

PAUL, a Yellow Boy, a favorite of the late Judge's, and so allowed to do much as he likes

RATTS, Captain of the Steamer *Magnolia*

LAFOUCHE, a Rich Planter

COLONEL POINTDEXTER, an Auctioneer and Slave Salesman

JULES THIBODEAUX
JUDGE CAILLOU ⎫ Prospective Buyers at the Auction
JACKSON

SOLON, a Slave

WAHNOTEE, an Indian Chief of the Lepan Tribe

MRS. PEYTON, of Terrebonne Plantation, in the Attakapas, Widow of the late Judge Peyton

ZOE, an Octoroon Girl, free, the Natural Child of the late Judge by a Quadroon Slave

DORA SUNNYSIDE, only Daughter and Heiress to Sunnyside, a Southern Belle

GRACE, a Yellow Girl, a Slave
DIDO, the Cook, a Slave
MINNIE, a Quadroon Slave

PLANTERS, SLAVES, DECK HANDS

ACT I

A view of the Plantation Terrebonne, in Louisiana. A branch of the Mississippi is seen winding through the Estate. A low built but extensive Planter's Dwelling, surrounded with a veranda, and raised a few feet from the ground, occupies the left side. On the right a table and chairs. GRACE *discovered sitting at breakfast-table with children.*

SOLON *enters, from the house.*

SOLON. Yah! You bomn'ble fry—git out—a gen'leman can't pass for you.

GRACE. (*Seizing a fly whisk.*) Hee!—Ha—git out!
(*Drives the children away: in escaping they tumble against* SOLON, *who falls with the tray; the children steal the bananas and rolls that fall about.*)
(*Enter* PETE, *who is lame; he carries a mop and pail.*)

PETE. Hey! Laws a massey! Why, clar out! drop dat banana! I'll murder this yer crowd.
(*Chases children about; they leap over railing at back. Exit* SOLON.)
Dem little niggers is a judgment upon dis generation.

(*Enter* GEORGE, *from the house.*)

GEORGE. What's the matter, Pete?

PETE. It's dem black trash, Mas'r George; dis ere property wants claring; dem's getting too numerous round: when I gets time I'll kill some on 'em, sure!

GEORGE. They don't seem to be scared by the threat.

PETE. Stop, you varmin! Stop till I get enough of you in one place!

GEORGE. Were they all born on this estate?

PETE. Guess they nebber was born—dem tings! What, dem?— Get away! Born here—dem darkies? What, on Terrebonne! Don't b'lieve it, Mas'r George; dem black tings never was born at all; dey swarmed one mornin' on a sassafras tree in the swamp; I cotched 'em; dey ain't no 'count. Don't believe dey'll turn out niggers when dey're growed; dey'll come out sunthin' else.

GRACE. Yes, Mas'r George, dey was born here; and old Pete is fonder on 'em dan he is of his fiddle on a Sunday.

PETE. What? Dem tings—dem?—Get away. (*Makes blow at the children.*) Born here! Dem darkies! What, on Terrebonne? Don't b'lieve it, Mas'r George,—no. One morning dey swarmed on a sassafras tree in de swamp, and I cotched 'em all in a sieve,—dat's how dey come on top of dis yearth—git out, you,—ya, ya! (*Laughs. Exit* GRACE.)

(*Enter* MRS. PEYTON, *from the house.*)

MRS. PEYTON. So, Pete, you are spoiling those children as usual!

PETE. Dat's right, missus! Gib it to ole Pete! He's allers in for it. Git away dere! Ya! if dey ain't all lighted, like coons, on dat snake fence, just out of shot. Look dar! Ya, ya! Dem debils. Ya!

MRS. PEYTON. Pete, do you hear?

PETE. Git down dar! I'm arter you! (*Hobbles off.*)

MRS. PEYTON. You are out early this morning, George.

GEORGE. I was up before daylight. We got the horses saddled, and galloped down the shell road over the Piney Patch; then coasting the Bayou Lake, we crossed the long swamps, by Paul's Path, and so came home again.

MRS. PEYTON. (*Laughing.*) You seem already familiar with the names of every spot on the estate.

(*Enter* PETE, *arranging breakfast.*)

GEORGE. Just one month ago I quitted Paris. I left that siren city as I would have left a beloved woman.

MRS. PEYTON. No wonder! I dare say you left at least a dozen beloved women there, at the same time.

GEORGE. I feel that I departed amid universal and sincere regret. I left my loves and my creditors equally inconsolable.

MRS. PEYTON. George, you are incorrigible. Ah! You remind me so much of your uncle, the judge.

GEORGE. Bless his dear old handwriting, it's all I ever saw of him. For ten years his letters came every quarter-day[1], with a remittance and a word of advice in his formal cavalier style; and then a joke in the postscript, that upset the dignity of the foregoing. Aunt, when he died, two years ago, I read over those letters of his, and if I didn't cry like a baby—

MRS. PEYTON. No, George; say you wept like a man. And so you really kept those foolish letters?

GEORGE. Yes; I kept the letters, and squandered the money.

MRS. PEYTON. (*Embracing him.*) Ah! Why were you not my son—you are so like my dear husband.

(*Enter* SALEM SCUDDER.)

SCUDDER. Ain't he! Yes—when I saw him and Miss Zoe galloping through the green sugar crop, and doing ten dollars' worth of damage at every stride, says I, how like his old uncle he do make the dirt fly.

GEORGE. O, aunt! What a bright, gay creature she is!

SCUDDER. What, Zoe! Guess that you didn't leave anything female in Europe that can lift an eyelash beside that gal. When she goes along, she just leaves a streak of love behind her. It's a good drink to see her come into the cotton fields—the niggers get fresh on the sight of her. If she ain't worth her weight in sunshine you may take one of my fingers off, and choose which you like.

MRS. PEYTON. She need not keep us waiting breakfast, though. Pete, tell Miss Zoe that we are waiting.

PETE. Yes, missus. Why, Minnie, why don't you run when you hear, you lazy crittur?
(*Minnie runs off.*)
Dat's de laziest nigger on dis yere property. (*Sits down.*) Don't do nuffin.

MRS. PEYTON. My dear George, you are left in your uncle's will heir to this estate.

GEORGE. Subject to your life interest and an annuity to Zoe, is it not so?

MRS. PEYTON. I fear that the property is so involved that the strictest economy will scarcely recover it. My dear husband

---

[1] I.e., four times a year.

never kept any accounts, and we scarcely know in what
condition the estate really is.

SCUDDER. Yes, we do, ma'am; it's in a darned bad condition.
Ten years ago the judge took as overseer a bit of Con-
necticut hardware called M'Closky. The judge didn't understand accounts—the overseer did. For a year or two all went
fine. The judge drew money like Bourbon whisky from a
barrel, and never turned off the tap. But out it flew, free
for everybody or anybody to beg, borrow, or steal. So it
went, till one day the judge found the tap wouldn't run.
He looked in to see what stopped it, and pulled out a big
mortgage. "Sign that," says the overseer; "it's only a
formality." "All right," says the judge, and away went a
thousand acres; so at the end of eight years, Jacob
M'Closky, Esquire, finds himself proprietor of the richest
half of Terrebonne—

GEORGE. But the other half is free.

SCUDDER. No, it ain't; because, just then, what does the judge
do, but hire another overseer—a Yankee—a Yankee named
Salem Scudder.

MRS. PEYTON. O, no, it was—

SCUDDER. Hold on, now! I'm going to straighten this account
clear out. What was this here Scudder? Well, he lived in
New York by sittin' with his heels up in front of French's
Hotel, and inventin'—

GEORGE. Inventing what?

SCUDDER. Improvements—anything, from a stay-lace to a fire-
engine. Well, he cut that for the photographing line. He
and his apparatus arrived here, took the judge's likeness
and his fancy, who made him overseer right off. Well, sir,
what does this Scudder do but introduces his inventions
and improvements on this estate. His new cotton gins
broke down, the steam sugar-mills burst up, until he
finished off with his folly what Mr. M'Closky with his
knavery began.

MRS. PEYTON. O, Salem! How can you say so? Haven't you
worked like a horse?

SCUDDER. No, ma'am, I worked like an ass—an honest one, and
that's all. Now, Mr. George, between the two overseers,
you and that good old lady have come to the ground; that
is the state of things, just as near as I can fix it.

(ZOE *sings outside.*)

GEORGE. 'T is Zoe.

SCUDDER. O, I have not spoiled that anyhow. I can't introduce any darned improvement there. Ain't that a cure for old age; it kinder lifts the heart up, don't it?

MRS. PEYTON. Poor child! What will become of her when I am gone? If you haven't spoiled her, I fear I have. She has had the education of a lady.

GEORGE. I have remarked that she is treated by the neighbors with a kind of familiar condescension that annoyed me.

SCUDDER. Don't you know that she is the natural daughter of the judge, your uncle, and that old lady thar just adored anything her husband cared for; and this girl, that another woman would 'a' hated, she loves as if she'd been her own child.

GEORGE. Aunt, I am prouder and happier to be your nephew and heir to the ruins of Terrebonne than I would have been to have had half Louisiana without you.

(*Enter* ZOE, *from the house.*)

ZOE. Am I late? Ah! Mr. Scudder, good morning.

SCUDDER. Thank'ye. I'm from fair to middlin', like a bamboo cane, much the same all the year round.

ZOE. No; like a sugar cane; so dry outside, one would never think there was so much sweetness within.

SCUDDER. Look here: I can't stand that gal! If I stop here, I shall hug her right off.
  (*Sees* PETE, *who has set his pail down up stage, and goes to sleep on it.*)
  If that old nigger ain't asleep, I'm blamed. Hillo!
  (*Kicks pail from under* PETE, *and lets him down. Exit.*)

PETE. Hi! Debbel's in de pail! Whar's breakfass?

(*Enter* SOLON *and* DIDO *with coffee-pot and dishes.*)

DIDO. Bless'ee, Missey Zoe, here it be. Dere's a dish of pompano—jess taste, Mas'r George—and here's fried bananas; smell 'em, do, sa glosh.

PETE. Hole yer tongue, Dido. Whar's de coffee? (*He pours it out.*) If it don't stain de cup, your wicked ole life's in danger, sure! Dat right! Black as nigger; clar as ice. You may drink dat, Mas'r George. (*Looks off.*) Yah! Here's

Mas'r Sunnyside, and Missey Dora, jist drove up. Some of you niggers run and hole de hosses; and take dis, Dido. (*Gives her coffee-pot to hold, and hobbles off, followed by* SOLON *and* DIDO.)

(*Enter* SUNNYSIDE *and* DORA.)

SUNNYSIDE. Good day, ma'am. (*Shakes hands with George.*) I see we are just in time for breakfast. (*Sits.*)

DORA. O, none for me; I never eat. (*Sits.*)

GEORGE. (*Aside.*) They do not notice Zoe.—(*Aloud.*) You don't see Zoe, Mr. Sunnyside.

SUNNYSIDE. Ah! Zoe, girl; are you there?

DORA. Take my shawl, Zoe.

(ZOE *helps her.*)

What a good creature she is.

SUNNYSIDE. I dare say, now, that in Europe you have never met any lady more beautiful in person, or more polished in manners, than that girl.

GEORGE. You are right, sir; though I shrank from expressing that opinion in her presence, so bluntly.

SUNNYSIDE. Why so?

GFORGE. It may be considered offensive.

SUNNYSIDE. (*Astonished.*) What? I say, Zoe, do you hear that?

DORA. Mr. Peyton is joking.

MRS. PEYTON. My nephew is not acquainted with our customs in Louisiana, but he will soon understand.

GEORGE. Never, aunt! I shall never understand how to wound the feelings of any lady; and, if that is the custom here, I shall never acquire it.

DORA. Zoe, my dear, what does he mean?

ZOE. I don't know.

GEORGE. Excuse me, I'll light a cigar. (*Goes up.*)

DORA. (*Aside to* ZOE). Isn't he sweet! O, dear, Zoe, is he in love with anybody?

ZOE. How can I tell?

DORA. Ask him, I want to know; don't say I told you to inquire, but find out. Minnie, fan me, it is so nice—and his clothes are French, ain't they?

ZOE. I think so; shall I ask him that too?

DORA. No, dear. I wish he would make love to me. When he speaks to one he does it so easy, so gentle; it isn't barroom

style; love lined with drinks, sighs tinged with tobacco—
and they say all the women in Paris were in love with him,
which I feel I shall be. Stop fanning me; what nice boots
he wears.

SUNNYSIDE. (*To* MRS. PEYTON.) Yes, ma'am, I hold a mortgage
over Terrebonne; mine's a ninth, and pretty near covers all
the property, except the slaves. I believe Mr. M'Closky has
a bill of sale on them. O, here he is.

(*Enter* M'CLOSKY.)

SUNNYSIDE. Good morning, Mr. M'Closky.

M'CLOSKY. Good morning, Mr. Sunnyside; Miss Dora, your
servant.

DORA. (*Seated.*) Fan me, Minnie.— (*Aside.*) I don't like that
man.

M'CLOSKY. (*Aside.*) Insolent as usual.—(*Aloud.*) You begged
me to call this morning. I hope I'm not intruding.

MRS. PEYTON. My nephew, Mr. Peyton.

M'CLOSKY. O, how d'ye do, sir?
(*Offers his hand,* GEORGE *bows coldly.*) (*Aside.*) A puppy—
if he brings any of his European airs here we'll fix him.—
(*Aloud.*) Zoe, tell Pete to give my mare a feed, will ye?

GEORGE. (*Angrily.*) Sir!

M'CLOSKY. Hillo! Did I tread on ye?

MRS. PEYTON. What is the matter with George?

ZOE. (*Takes fan from* MINNIE.) Go, Minnie, tell Pete; run!
(*Exit* MINNIE.)

MRS. PEYTON. Grace, attend to Mr. M'Closky.

M'CLOSKY. A julep, gal, that's my breakfast, and a bit of
cheese.

GEORGE. (*Aside to* MRS. PEYTON.) How can you ask that
vulgar ruffian to your table!

MRS. PEYTON. Hospitality in Europe is a courtesy; here, it is
an obligation. We tender food to a stranger, not because
he is a gentleman, but because he is hungry.

GEORGE. Aunt, I will take my rifle down to the Atchafalaya.
Paul has promised me a bear and a deer or two. I see my
little Nimrod yonder, with his Indian companion. Excuse
me, ladies. Ho! Paul! (*Enters house.*)

PAUL. (*Outside.*) I'ss, Mas'r George.

(*Enter* PAUL *with the Indian,* WAHNOTEE.)

SUNNYSIDE. It's a shame to allow that young cub to run over the swamps and woods, hunting and fishing his life away instead of hoeing cane.

MRS. PEYTON. The child was a favorite of the judge, who encouraged his gambols. I couldn't bear to see him put to work.

GEORGE. (*Returning with rifle.*) Come, Paul, are you ready?

PAUL. I'ss, Mas'r George. O, golly! Ain't that a pooty gun.

M'CLOSKY. See here, you imp; if I catch you, and your redskin yonder, gunning in my swamps, I'll give you rats, mind. Them vagabonds, when the game's about, shoot my pigs (*Exit* GEORGE *into house.*)

PAUL. You gib me rattan, Mas'r Clostry, but I guess you take a berry long stick to Wahnotee. Ugh, he make bacon of you.

M'CLOSKY. Make bacon of me, you young whelp! Do you mean that I'm a pig? Hold on a bit. (*Seizes whip, and holds* PAUL.)

ZOE. O, sir! Don't, pray, don't.

M'CLOSKY. (*Slowly lowering his whip.*) Darn you, redskin, I'll pay you off some day, both of ye. (*Returns to table and drinks.*)

SUNNYSIDE. That Indian is a nuisance. Why don't he return to his nation out West?

M'CLOSKY. He's too fond of thieving and whiskey.

ZOE. No; Wahnotee is a gentle, honest creature, and remains here because he loves that boy with the tenderness of a woman. When Paul was taken down with the swamp fever the Indian sat outside the hut, and neither ate, slept, nor spoke for five days, till the child could recognize and call him to his bedside. He who can love so well is honest— don't speak ill of poor Wahnotee.

MRS. PEYTON. Wahnotee, will you go back to your people?

WAHNOTEE. Sleugh.

PAUL. He don't understand; he speaks a mash-up of Indian and Mexican. Wahnotee Patira na sepau assa wigiran?

WAHNOTEE. Weal Omenee.

PAUL. Says he'll go if I'll go with him. He calls me Omenee, the Pigeon, and Miss Zoe is Ninemoosha, the Sweetheart.

WAHNOTEE. (*Pointing to* ZOE.) Ninemoosha.

ZOE. No, Wahnotee, we can't spare Paul.

PAUL. If Omenee remain, Wahnotee will die in Terrebonne.
(*During the dialogue,* WAHNOTEE *has taken* GEORGE's *gun.*)

(*Enter* GEORGE.)

GEORGE. Now I'm ready.
(GEORGE *tries to regain his gun;* WAHNOTEE *refuses to give
it up;* PAUL *quietly takes it from him and remonstrates with
him.*)

DORA. Zoe, he's going; I want him to stay and make love to
me; that's what I came for to-day.

MRS. PEYTON. George, I can't spare Paul for an hour or two;
he must run over to the landing; the steamer from New
Orleans passed up the river last night, and if there's a mail
they have thrown it ashore.

SUNNYSIDE. I saw the mail-bags lying in the shed this morning.

MRS. PEYTON. I expect an important letter from Liverpool;
away with you, Paul; bring the mail-bags here.

PAUL. I'm 'most afraid to take Wahnotee to the shed, there's
rum there.

WAHNOTEE. Rum!

PAUL. Come, then, but if I catch you drinkin', O, laws a
mussey, you'll get snakes! I'll gib it you! Now mind.
(*Exit with Indian.*)

GEORGE. Come, Miss Dora, let me offer you my arm.

DORA. Mr. George, I am afraid, if all we hear is true, you have
led a dreadful life in Europe.

GEORGE. That's a challenge to begin a description of my
feminine adventures.

DORA. You have been in love, then?

GEORGE. Two hundred and forty-nine times! Let me relate
you the worst cases.

DORA. No! No!

GEORGE. I'll put the naughty parts in French.

DORA. I won't hear a word! O, you horrible man! Go on.
(*Exit* GEORGE *and* DORA *to the house.*)

M'CLOSKY. Now, ma'am, I'd like a little business, if agreeable.
I bring you news; your banker, old Lafouche, of New
Orleans, is dead; the executors are winding up his affairs,
and have foreclosed on all overdue mortgages, so Terre-

bonne is for sale. Here's the *Picayune* (*Producing paper.*) with the advertisement.

ZOE. Terrebonne for sale!

MRS. PEYTON. Terrebonne for sale, and you, sir, will doubtless become its purchaser.

M'CLOSKY. Well, ma'am, I s'pose there's no law agin my bidding for it. The more bidders, the better for you. You'll take care, I guess, it don't go too cheap.

MRS. PEYTON. O, sir, I don't value the place for its price, but for the many happy days I've spent here; that landscape, flat and uninteresting though it may be, is full of charm for me; those poor people, born around me, growing up about my heart, have bounded my view of life; and now to lose that homely scene, lose their black, ungainly faces! O, sir, perhaps you should be as old as I am, to feel as I do, when my past life is torn away from me.

M'CLOSKY. I'd be darned glad if somebody would tear my past life away from *me*. Sorry I can't help you, but the fact is, you're in such an all-fired mess that you couldn't be pulled out without a derrick.

MRS. PEYTON. Yes, there is a hope left yet, and I cling to it. The house of Mason Brothers, of Liverpool, failed some twenty years ago in my husband's debt.

M'CLOSKY. They owed him over fifty thousand dollars.

MRS. PEYTON. I cannot find the entry in my husband's accounts; but you, Mr. M'Closky, can doubtless detect it. Zoe, bring here the judge's old desk; it is in the library.

(*Exit* ZOE *to the house.*)

M'CLOSKY. You don't expect to recover any of this old debt, do you?

MRS. PEYTON. Yes; the firm has recovered itself, and I received a notice two months ago that some settlement might be anticipated.

SUNNYSIDE. Why, with principal and interest this debt has been more than doubled in twenty years.

MRS. PEYTON. But it may be years yet before it will be paid off, if ever.

SUNNYSIDE. If there's a chance of it, there's not a planter round here who wouldn't lend you the whole cash, to keep your name and blood amongst us. Come, cheer up, old friend.

MRS. PEYTON. Ah! Sunnyside, how good you are; so like my poor Peyton.

(*Exit* MRS. PEYTON *and* SUNNYSIDE *to the house.*)

M'CLOSKY. Curse their old families—they cut me—a bilious, conceited, thin lot of dried up aristocracy. I hate 'em. Just because my grandfather wasn't some broken-down Virginia transplant, or a stingy old Creole, I ain't fit to sit down to the same meat with them. It makes my blood so hot I feel my heart hiss. I'll sweep these Peytons from this section of the country. Their presence keeps alive the reproach against me that I ruined them. Yet, if this money should come! Bah! There's no chance of it. Then, if they go, they'll take Zoe—she'll follow them. Darn that girl; she makes me quiver when I think of her; she's took me for all I'm worth. (*Enter* ZOE *from house, with the desk.*) O, here, do you know what the annuity the old judge left you is worth to-day? Not a picayune.

ZOE. It's surely worth the love that dictated it; here are the papers and accounts. (*Putting the desk on the table.*)

M'CLOSKY. Stop, Zoe; come here! How would you like to rule the house of the richest planter on Atchafalaya—eh? Or say the word, and I'll buy this old barrack, and you shall be mistress of Terrebonne.

ZOE. O, sir, do not speak so to me!

M'CLOSKY. Why not! Look here, these Peytons are bust; cut 'em; I am rich, jine me; I'll set you up grand, and we'll give these first families here our dust, until you'll see their white skins shrivel up with hate and rage; what d'ye say?

ZOE. Let me pass! O, pray, let me go!

M'CLOSKY. What, you won't, won't ye? If young George Peyton was to make you the same offer, you'd jump at it pretty darned quick, I guess. Come, Zoe, don't be a fool; I'd marry you if I could, but you know I can't; so just say what you want. Here, then, I'll put back these Peytons in Terrebonne, and they shall know you done it; yes, they'll have you to thank for saving them from ruin.

ZOE. Do you think they would live here on such terms?

M'CLOSKY. Why not? We'll hire out our slaves, and live on their wages.

ZOE. But I'm not a slave.

M'CLOSKY. No; if you were I'd buy you, if you cost all I'm worth.

ZOE. Let me pass!

M'CLOSKY. Stop.

(*Enter* SCUDDER.)

SCUDDER. Let her pass.

M'CLOSKY. Eh?

SCUDDER. Let her pass!

(*Takes out his knife. Exit* ZOE *to house.*)

M'CLOSKY. Is that you, Mr. Overseer? (*Examines paper.*)

SCUDDER. Yes, I'm here, somewhere, interferin'.

M'CLOSKY. (*Sitting.*) A pretty mess you've got this estate in—

SCUDDER. Yes—me and Co.—we done it; but, as you were senior partner in the concern, I reckon you got the big lick.

M'CLOSKY. What d'ye mean?

SCUDDER. Let me proceed by illustration. (*Sits.*) Look thar! (*Points with his knife off.*) D'ye see that tree?—It's called a live oak, and is a native here; beside it grows a creeper. Year after year that creeper twines its long arms round and round the tree—sucking the earth dry all about its roots— living on its life—overrunning its branches, until at last the live oak withers and dies out. Do you know what the niggers round here call that sight? They call it the Yankee hugging the Creole.

M'CLOSKY. Mr. Scudder, I've listened to a great many of your insinuations, and now I'd like to come to an understanding what they mean. If you want a quarrel—

SCUDDER. No, I'm the skurriest crittur at a fight you ever see; my legs have been too well brought up to stand and see my body abused; I take good care of myself, I can tell you.

M'CLOSKY. Because I heard that you had traduced my character.

SCUDDER. Traduced! Whoever said so lied. I always said you were the darndest thief that ever escaped a white jail to misrepresent the North to the South.

M'CLOSKY. (*Raises hand to back of his neck.*) What!

SCUDDER. Take your hand down—take it down.

(M'CLOSKY *lowers his hand.*)

Whenever I gets into company like yours, I always start with the advantage on my side.

M'CLOSKY. What d'ye mean?

SCUDDER. I mean that before you could draw that bowie-knife you wear down your back, I'd cut you into shingles. Keep quiet, and let's talk sense. You wanted to come to an understanding, and I'm coming thar as quick as I can. Now, Jacob M'Closky, you despise me because you think I'm a fool; I despise you because I know you to be a knave. Between us we've ruined these Peytons; you fired the judge, and I finished off the widow. Now, I feel bad about my share in the business. I'd give half the balance of my life to wipe out my part of the work. Many a night I've laid awake and thought how to pull them through, till I've cried like a child over the sum I couldn't do; and you know how darned hard 't is to make a Yankee cry.

M'CLOSKY. Well, what's that to me?

SCUDDER. Hold on, Jacob, I'm coming to that—I tell ye, I'm such a fool—I can't bear the feeling, it keeps at me like a skin complaint, and if this family is sold up—

M'CLOSKY. What then?

SCUDDER. (*Rising.*) I'd cut my throat—or yours—yours I'd prefer.

M'CLOSKY. Would you now? Why don't you do it?

SCUDDER. 'Cos I's skeered to try! I never killed a man in my life—and civilization is so strong in me I guess I couldn't do it—I'd like to, though!

M'CLOSKY. And all for the sake of that old woman and that young puppy—eh? No other cause to hate—to envy me—to be jealous of me—eh?

SCUDDER. Jealous? What for?

M'CLOSKY. Ask the color in your face: d'ye think I can't read you, like a book? With your New England hypocrisy, you would persuade yourself that it was this family alone you cared for; it ain't—you know it ain't—'t is the "Octoroon"; and you love her as I do; and you hate me because I'm your rival—that's where the tears come from, Salem Scudder, if you ever shed any—that's where the shoe pinches.

SCUDDER. Wal, I do like the gal; she's a—

M'CLOSKY. She's in love with young Peyton; it made me curse whar it made you cry, as it does now; I see the tears on your cheeks now.

SCUDDER. Look at 'em, Jacob, for they are honest water from the well of truth. I ain't ashamed of it—I do love the gal; but I ain't jealous of you, because I believe the only sincere feeling about you is your love for Zoe, and it does your heart good to have her image thar; but I believe you put it thar to spile. By fair means I don't think you can get her, and don't you try foul with her, 'cause if you do, Jacob, civilization be darned, I'm on you like a painter, and when I'm drawed out I'm pizin. (*Exit* SCUDDER *to house.*)

M'CLOSKY. Fair or foul, I'll have her—take that home with you! (*He opens desk.*) What's here—judgments? Yes, plenty of 'em; bill of costs, account with Citizens' Bank— what's this? "Judgment, $40,000, 'Thibodeaux against Peyton,'"—surely, that is the judgment under which this estate is now advertised for sale—(*Takes up paper and examines it*) yes, "Thibodeaux against Peyton, 1838." Hold on! Whew! This is worth taking to—in this desk the judge used to keep one paper I want—this should be it. (*Reads.*) "The free papers of my daughter Zoe, registered February 4th, 1841." Why, judge, wasn't you lawyer enough to know that while a judgment stood against you it was a lien on your slaves? Zoe is your child by a quadroon slave, and you didn't free her; blood! If this is so, she's mine! This old Liverpool debt—that may cross me—if it only arrive too late—if it don't come by this mail—Hold on! This letter the old lady expects—that's it; let me only head off that letter, and Terrebonne will be sold before they can recover it. That boy and the Indian have gone down to the landing for the post-bags; they'll idle on the way as usual; my mare will take me across the swamp, and before they can reach the shed, I'll have purified them bags—ne'er a letter shall show this mail. Ha, ha!—(*Calls.*) Pete, you old turkey-buzzard, saddle my mare. Then, if I sink every dollar I'm worth in her purchase, I'll own that Octoroon. (*Stands with his hand extended towards the house, and tableau.*)

ACT II

The Wharf with goods, boxes, and bales scattered about— a camera on a stand; DORA *being photographed by* SCUDDER, *who is arranging photographic apparatus,* GEORGE *and* PAUL *looking on at back.*

SCUDDER. Just turn your face a leetle this way—fix your—let's see—look here.

DORA. So?

SCUDDER. That's right. (*Putting his head under the darkening apron.*) It's such a long time since I did this sort of thing, and this old machine has got so dirty and stiff, I'm afraid it won't operate. That's about right. Now don't stir.

PAUL. Ugh! she looks as though she war gwine to have a tooth drawed!

SCUDDER. I've got four plates ready, in case we miss the first shot. One of them is prepared with a self-developing liquid that I've invented. I hope it will turn out better than most of my notions. Now fix yourself. Are you ready?

DORA. Ready!

SCUDDER. Fire!—One, two, three. (SCUDDER *takes out watch.*)

PAUL. Now it's cooking; laws mussey! I feel it all inside, as if I was at a lottery.

SCUDDER. So! (*Throws down apron.*) That's enough. (*Withdrawing slide, turns and sees* PAUL.) What! What are you doing there, you young varmint! Ain't you took them bags to the house yet?

PAUL. Now, it ain't no use trying to get mad, Mas'r Scudder. I'm gwine! I only come back to find Wahnotee; whar is dat ign'ant Injiun?

SCUDDER. You'll find him scenting round the rum store, hitched up by the nose. (*Exit into the room.*)

PAUL. (*Calling at the door.*) Say, Mas'r Scudder, take me in dat telescope?

SCUDDER. (*Inside the room.*) Get out, you cub! Clar out!

PAUL. You got four of dem dishes ready. Gosh, wouldn't I like to hab myself took! What's de charge, Mas'r Scudder? (*Runs off.*)

(*Enter* SCUDDER, *from the room.*)

SCUDDER. Job had none of them critters on his plantation, else he'd never ha' stood through so many chapters. Well, that has come out clear, ain't it? (*Showing the plate.*)

DORA. O, beautiful! Look, Mr. Peyton.

GEORGE. (*Looking.*) Yes, very fine!

SCUDDER. The apparatus can't mistake. When I travelled round with this machine, the homely folks used to sing out, "Hillo, mister, this ain't like me!" "Ma'am," says I, "the apparatus can't mistake." "But, mister, that ain't my nose." "Ma'am, your nose drawed it. The machine can't err—you mistake your phiz but the apparatus don't." "But, sir, it ain't agreeable." "No, ma'am, the truth seldom is."

(*Enter* PETE, *puffing.*)

PETE. Mas'r Scudder! Mas'r Scudder!

SCUDDER. Hillo! What are you blowing about like a steamboat with one wheel for?

PETE. *You* blow, Mas'r Scudder, when I tole you: dere's a man from Noo Aleens just arriv'd at de house, and he's stuck up two papers on de gates: "For sale—dis yer property," and a heap of oder tings—an he seen missus, and arter he shown some papers she burst out crying—I yelled; den de corious of little niggers dey set up, den de hull plantation children—de live stock reared up and created a purpiration of lamentation as did de ole heart good to har.

DORA. What's the matter?

SCUDDER. He's come.

PETE. Dass it—I saw'm!

SCUDDER. The sheriff from New Orleans has taken possession— Terrebonne is in the hands of the law.

(*Enter* ZOE.)

ZOE. O, Mr. Scudder! Dora! Mr. Peyton! Come home—there are strangers in the house.

DORA. Stay, Mr. Peyton: Zoe, a word! (*Leads her forward— aside.*) Zoe, the more I see of George Peyton the better I like him; but he is too modest—that is a very impertinent virtue in a man.

ZOE. I'm no judge, dear.

DORA. Of course not, you little fool; no one ever made love to you, and you can't understand; I mean, that George knows I am an heiress; my fortune would release this estate from debt.

ZOE. O, I see!

DORA. If he would only propose to marry me I would accept him, but he don't know that, and he will go on fooling, in his slow European way, until it is too late.

ZOE. What's to be done?

DORA. You tell him.

ZOE. What? That he isn't to go on fooling in his slow—

DORA. No, you goose! Twit him on his silence and abstraction
—I'm sure it's plain enough, for he has not spoken two
words to me all the day; then joke round the subject, and
at last speak out.

SCUDDER. Pete, as you came here, did you pass Paul and the
Indian with the letter-bags?

PETE. No, sar; but dem vagabonds neber take the 'specable
straight road, dey goes by de swamp. (*Exit up the path.*)

SCUDDER. Come, sir!

DORA. (*To* ZOE.) Now's your time.—(*Aloud.*) Mr. Scudder,
take us with you—Mr. Peyton is so slow, there's no getting
him on.

(*Exit* DORA *and* SCUDDER.)

ZOE. They are gone!—(*Glancing at* GEORGE.) Poor fellow, he
has lost all.

GEORGE. Poor child! How sad she looks now she has no
resource.

ZOE. How shall I ask him to stay?

GEORGE. Zoe, will you remain here? I wish to speak to you.

ZOE. (*Aside.*) Well, that saves trouble.

GEORGE. By our ruin you lose all.

ZOE. O, I'm nothing; think of yourself.

GEORGE. I can think of nothing but the image that remains
face to face with me; so beautiful, so simple, so confiding,
that I dare not express the feelings that have grown up so
rapidly in my heart.

ZOE. (*Aside.*) He means Dora.

GEORGE. If I dared to speak!

ZOE. That's just what you must do, and do it at once, or it
will be too late.

GEORGE. Has my love been divined?

ZOE. It has been more than suspected.

GEORGE. Zoe, listen to me, then. I shall see this estate pass
from me without a sigh, for it possesses no charm for me;
the wealth I covet is the love of those around me—eyes
that are rich in fond looks, lips that breathe endearing
words; the only estate I value is the heart of one true
woman, and the slaves I'd have are her thoughts.

ZOE. George, George, your words take away my breath!

GEORGE. The world, Zoe, the free struggle of minds and hands
is before me; the education bestowed on me by my dear

uncle is a noble heritage which no sheriff can seize; with that I can build up a fortune, spread a roof over the heads I love, and place before them the food I have earned; I will work—

ZOE. Work! I thought none but colored people worked.

GEORGE. Work, Zoe, is the salt that gives savor to life.

ZOE. Dora said you were slow; if she could hear you now—

GEORGE. Zoe, you are young; your mirror must have told you that you are beautiful. Is your heart free?

ZOE. Free? Of course it is!

GEORGE. We have known each other but a few days, but to me those days have been worth all the rest of my life. Zoe, you have suspected the feeling that now commands an utterance—you have seen that I love you.

ZOE. Me! You love *me?*

GEORGE. As my wife—the sharer of my hopes, my ambitions, and my sorrows; under the shelter of your love I could watch the storms of fortune pass unheeded by.

ZOE. *My* love! *My* love? George, you know not what you say! *I* the sharer of your sorrows—your wife! Do you know what I am?

GEORGE. Your birth—I know it. Has not my dear aunt forgotten it—she who had the most right to remember it? You are illegitimate, but love knows no prejudice.

ZOE. (*Aside.*) Alas! He does not know, he does not know! And will despise me, spurn me, loathe me, when he learns who, what, he has so loved.—(*Aloud.*) George, O, forgive me! Yes, I love you—I did not know it until your words showed me what has been in my heart; each of them awoke a new sense, and now I know how unhappy—how very unhappy I am.

GEORGE. Zoe, what have I said to wound you?

ZOE. Nothing; but you must learn what I thought you already knew. George, you cannot marry me; the laws forbid it!

GEORGE. Forbid it?

ZOE. There is a gulf between us, as wide as your love, as deep as my despair; but, O, tell me, say you will pity me! That you will not throw me from you like a poisoned thing!

GEORGE. Zoe, explain yourself—your language fills me with shapeless fears.

ZOE. And what shall I say? I—my mother was—no, no—not her! Why should I refer the blame to her? George, do you see that hand you hold? Look at these fingers; do you see the nails are of a bluish tinge?

GEORGE. Yes, near the quick there is a faint blue mark.

ZOE. Look in my eyes; is not the same color in the white?

GEORGE. It is their beauty.

ZOE. Could you see the roots of my hair you would see the same dark, fatal mark. Do you know what that is?

GEORGE. No.

ZOE. That is the ineffaceable curse of Cain. Of the blood that feeds my heart, one drop in eight is black—bright red as the rest may be, that one drop poisons all the flood; those seven bright drops give me love like yours—hope like yours—ambition like yours—life hung with passions like dewdrops on the morning flowers; but the one black drop gives me despair, for I'm an unclean thing—forbidden by the laws—I'm an Octoroon!

GEORGE. Zoe, I love you none the less; this knowledge brings no revolt to my heart, and I can overcome the obstacle.

ZOE. But *I* cannot.

GEORGE. We can leave this country, and go far away where none can know.

ZOE. And your aunt, she who from infancy treated me with such fondness, she who, as you said, has most reason to spurn me, can she forget what I am? Will she gladly see you wedded to the child of her husband's slave? No! She would revolt from it, as all but you would; and if I consented to hear the cries of my heart, if I did not crush out my infant love, what would she say to the poor girl on whom she had bestowed so much? No, no!

GEORGE. Zoe, must we immolate our lives on her prejudice?

ZOE. Yes, for I'd rather be black than ungrateful! Ah, George, our race has at least one virtue—it knows how to suffer!

GEORGE. Each word you utter makes my love sink deeper into my heart.

ZOE. And I remained here to induce you to offer that heart to Dora!

GEORGE. If you bid me do so I will obey you—

ZOE. No, no! If you cannot be mine, O, let me not blush when I think of you.

GEORGE. Dearest Zoe!

(*Exit* GEORGE *and* ZOE. *As they exit,* M'CLOSKY *rises from behind a rock and looks after them.*)

M'CLOSKY. She loves him! I felt it—and how she can love! (*Advances.*) That one black drop of blood burns in her veins and lights up her heart like a foggy sun. O, how I lapped up her words, like a thirsty bloodhound! I'll have her, if it costs me my life! Yonder the boy still lurks with those mail-bags; the devil still keeps him here to tempt me, darn his yellow skin! I arrived just too late, he had grabbed the prize as I came up. Hillo! He's coming this way, fighting with his Injiun. (*Conceals himself.*)

(*Enter* PAUL, *wrestling with* WAHNOTEE.)

PAUL. It ain't no use now: you got to gib it up!

WAHNOTEE. Ugh!

PAUL. It won't do! You got dat bottle of rum hid under your blanket—gib it up now, you—. Yar! (*Wrenching it from him.*) You nasty, lying Injiun! It's no use you putting on airs; I ain't gwine to sit up wid you all night and you drunk. Hillo! War's de crowd gone? And dar's de 'paratus— O, gosh, if I could take a likeness ob dis child! Uh—uh, let's have a peep. (*Looking through camera.*) O, golly! Yar, you Wahnotee! You stan' dar, I see you. Ta demine usti.

(*Looks at* WAHNOTEE *through the camera;* WAHNOTEE *springs back with an expression of alarm.*)

WAHNOTEE. No tue Wahnotee.

PAUL. Ha, ha! He tinks it's a gun. You ign'ant Injiun, it can't hurt you! Stop, here's dem dishes—plates—dat's what he call 'em, all fix: I see Mas'r Scudder do it often—tink I can take likeness—stay dere, Wahnotee.

WAHNOTEE. No, carabine tue.

PAUL. I must operate and take my own likeness too—how debbel I do dat? Can't be ober dar an' here too—I ain't twins. Ugh. Ach! 'Top; you look, you Wahnotee; you see dis rag, eh? Well when I say go, den lift dis rag like dis, see! den run to dat pine tree up dar (*Points.*) and back ag'in, and den pull down de rag so, d'ye see?

WAHNOTEE. Hugh!

PAUL. Den you hab glass ob rum.

WAHNOTEE. Rum!

PAUL. Dat wakes him up. Coute, Wahnotee in omenee dit go Wahnotee, poina la fa, comb a pine tree, la revieut sala, la fa.

WAHNOTEE. Fire-water!

PAUL. Yes, den a glass ob fire-water; now den. (*Throwing mail-bags down and sitting on them.*) Pret, now den go.

(WAHNOTEE *raises the apron and runs off.* PAUL *sits for his picture*—M'CLOSKY *appears.*)

M'CLOSKY. Where are they? Ah, yonder goes the Indian!

PAUL. De time he gone just 'bout enough to cook dat dish plate.

M'CLOSKY. Yonder is the boy—now is my time! What's he doing; is he asleep? (*Advancing.*) He is sitting on my prize! darn his carcass! I'll clear him off there—he'll never know what stunned him. (*Takes Indian's tomahawk and steals to* PAUL.)

PAUL. Dam dat Injiun! Is dat him creeping dar? I darn't move fear to spile myself.

(M'CLOSKY *strikes him on the head—he falls dead.*)

M'CLOSKY. Hooraw; the bags are mine—now for it!—(*Opening the mail-bags.*) What's here? Sunnyside, Pointdexter, Jackson, Peyton; here it is—the Liverpool postmark, sure enough!—(*Opening letter—reads.*) "Madam, we are instructed by the firm of Mason and Co., to inform you that a dividend of forty per cent. is payable on the 1st proximo, this amount in consideration of position, they send herewith, and you will find enclosed by draft to your order, on the Bank of Louisiana, which please acknowledge—the balance will be paid in full, with interest, in three, six, and nine months—your drafts on Mason Brothers at those dates will be accepted by La Palisse and Compagnie, N. O., so that you may command immediate use of the whole amount at once, if required. Yours, etc., James Brown." What a find! This infernal letter would have saved all. (*During the reading of letter he remains nearly motionless under the focus of the camera.*) But now I guess it will arrive too late—these darned U.S. mails are to blame. The Injiun! He must not see me. (*Exit rapidly.*)

(WAHNOTEE *runs on, and pulls down the apron. He sees* PAUL, *lying on the ground and speaks to him, thinking that he is shamming sleep. He gesticulates and jabbers to him and moves him with his feet, then kneels down to rouse him. To his horror he finds him dead. Expressing great grief he raises his eyes and they fall upon the camera. Rising with a savage growl, he seizes the tomahawk and smashes the camera to pieces. Going to* PAUL *he expresses in pantomime grief, sorrow, and fondness, and takes him in his arms to carry him away. Tableau.)*

ACT III

A Room in MRS. PEYTON's *house showing the entrance on which an auction bill is pasted.* SOLON *and* GRACE *are there.*

PETE. (*Outside.*) Dis way—dis way.

(*Enter* PETE, POINTDEXTER, JACKSON, LAFOUCHE *and* CAILLOU.)

PETE. Dis way, gen'l'men; now, Solon—Grace—dey's hot and tirsty—sangaree, brandy, rum.
JACKSON. Well, what d'ye say, Lafouche—d'ye smile?

(*Enter* THIBODEAUX *and* SUNNYSIDE.)

THIBODEAUX. I hope we don't intrude on the family.
PETE. You see dat hole in dar, sar? I was raised on dis yar plantation—nebber see no door in it—always open, sar, for stranger to walk in.
SUNNYSIDE. And for substance to walk out.

(*Enter* RATTS.)

RATTS. Fine southern style that, eh!
LAFOUCHE. (*Reading the bill.*) "A fine, well-built old family mansion, replete with every comfort."
RATTS. There's one name on the list of slaves scratched, I see.
LAFOUCHE. Yes; No. 49, Paul, a quadroon boy, aged thirteen.
SUNNYSIDE. He's missing.
POINTDEXTER. Run away, I suppose.
PETE. (*Indignantly.*) No, sar; nigger nebber cut stick on Terrebonne; dat boy's dead, sure.
RATTS. What, Picayune Paul, as we called him, that used to come aboard my boat?—Poor little darkey, I hope not; many a picayune he picked up for his dance and nigger songs,

and he supplied our table with fish and game from the Bayous.

PETE. Nebber supply no more, sar—nebber dance again. Mas'r Ratts, you hard him sing about de place where de good niggers go, de last time.

RATTS. Well!

PETE. Well, he gone dar hisself; why I tink so—'cause we missed Paul for some days, but nebber tout nothin' till one night dat Injiun Wahnotee suddenly stood right dar 'mongst us—was in his war paint, and mighty cold and grave—he sit down by de fire. "Whar's Paul?" I say—he smoke and smoke, but nebber look out ob de fire; well knowing dem critters, I wait a long time—den he say, "Wahnotee great chief"; den I say nothing—smoke anoder time—last, rising to go, he turn round at door, and say berry low—O, like a woman's voice he say, "Omenee Pangeuk," dat is, Paul is dead—nebber see him since.

RATTS. That red-skin killed him.

SUNNYSIDE. So we believe; and so mad are the folks around, if they catch the red-skin they'll lynch him sure.

RATTS. Lynch him! Darn his copper carcass, I've got a set of Irish deckhands aboard that just loved that child; and after I tell them this, let them get a sight of the red-skin, I believe they would eat him, tomahawk and all. Poor little Paul!

THIBODEAUX. What was he worth?

RATTS. Well, near on five hundred dollars.

PETE. (*Scandalized.*) What, sar! You p'tend to be sorry for Paul, and prize him like dat! Five hundred dollars! (*To* THIBODEAUX.) Tousand dollars, Massa Thibodeau.

(*Enter* SCUDDER.)

SCUDDER. Gentlemen, the sale takes place at three. Good morning, Colonel. It's near that now, and there's still the sugar-houses to be inspected. Good day, Mr. Thibodeaux— shall we drive down that way? Mr. Lafouche, why, how do you do, sir? You're looking well.

LAFOUCHE. Sorry I can't return the compliment.

RATTS. Salem's looking a kinder hollowed out.

SCUDDER. What, Mr. Ratts, are you going to invest in swamps?

RATTS. No; I want a nigger.

SCUDDER. Hush.

PETE. Eh! wass dat?

SCUDDER. Mr. Sunnyside, I can't do this job of showin' round the folks; my stomach goes agin it. I want Pete here a minute.

SUNNYSIDE. I'll accompany them certainly.

SCUDDER. (*Eagerly.*) Will ye? Thank ye; thank ye.

SUNNYSIDE. We must excuse Scudder, friends. I'll see you round the estate.

(*Enter* GEORGE *and* MRS. PEYTON.)

LAFOUCHE. Good morning, Mrs. Peyton.

(*All salute.*)

SUNNYSIDE. This way, gentlemen.

RATTS. (*Aside to Sunnyside.*) I say, I'd like to say summit soft to the old woman; perhaps it wouldn't go well, would it?

THIBODEAUX. No; leave it alone.

RATTS. Darn it, when I see a woman in trouble, I feel like selling the skin off my back.

(*Exit* THIBODEAUX, SUNNYSIDE, RATTS, POINTDEXTER, GRACE, JACKSON, LAFOUCHE, CAILLOU, SOLON.)

SCUDDER. (*Aside to Pete.*) Go outside there; listen to what you hear, then go down to the quarters and tell the boys, for I can't do it. O, get out.

PETE. He said "I want a nigger." Laws, mussey! What am goin' to cum ob us! (*Exit slowly, as if trying to conceal himself.*)

GEORGE. My dear aunt, why do you not move from this painful scene? Go with Dora to Sunnyside.

MRS. PEYTON. No, George; your uncle said to me with his dying breath, "Nellie, never leave Terrebonne," and I never *will* leave it, till the law compels me.

SCUDDER. Mr. George, I'm going to say somethin' that has been chokin' me for some time. I know you'll excuse it. Thar's Miss Dora—that girl's in love with you; yes, sir, her eyes are startin' out of her head with it: now her fortune would redeem a good part of this estate.

MRS. PEYTON. Why, George, I never suspected this!

GEORGE. I did, aunt, I confess, but—

MRS. PEYTON. And you hesitated from motives of delicacy?

SCUDDER. No, ma'am; here's the plan of it. Mr. George is in love with Zoe.

GEORGE. Scudder!

MRS. PEYTON. George!

SCUDDER. Hold on, now! Things have got so jammed in on top of us, we ain't got time to put kid gloves on to handle them. He loves Zoe, and has found out that she loves him. (*Sighing.*) Well, that's all right; but as he can't marry her, and as Miss Dora would jump at him—

MRS. PEYTON. Why didn't you mention this before?

SCUDDER. Why, because *I* love Zoe, too, and I couldn't take that young feller from her; and she's jist living on the sight of him, as I saw her do; and they so happy in spite of this yer misery around them, and they reproachin' themselves with not feeling as they ought. I've seen it, I tell you; and darn it, ma'am, can't you see that's what's been a hollowing me out so—I beg your pardon.

MRS. PEYTON. O, George,—my son, let me call you,—I do not speak for my own sake, nor for the loss of the estate, but for the poor people here: they will be sold, divided, and taken away—they have been born here. Heaven has denied me children; so all the strings of my heart have grown around and amongst them, like the fibres and roots of an old tree in its native earth. O, let all go, but save them! With them around us, if we have not wealth, we shall at least have the home that they alone can make—

GEORGE. My dear mother—Mr. Scudder—you teach me what I ought to do; if Miss Sunnyside will accept me as I am, Terrebonne shall be saved: I will sell myself, but the slaves shall be protected.

MRS. PEYTON. *Sell* yourself, George! Is not Dora worth any man's—

SCUDDER. Don't say that, ma'am; don't say that to a man that loves another gal. He's going to do an heroic act; don't spile it.

MRS. PEYTON. But Zoe is only an Octoroon.

SCUDDER. She's won this race agin the white, anyhow; it's too late now to start her pedigree.

(*As* DORA *enters.*)

Come, Mrs. Peyton, take my arm. Hush! Here's the other one: she's a little too thoroughbred—too much of the grey-hound; but the heart's there, I believe.

(*Exeunt* SCUDDER *and* MRS. PEYTON.)

DORA. Poor Mrs. Peyton.

GEORGE. Miss Sunnyside, permit me a word: a feeling of delicacy has suspended upon my lips an avowal, which—

DORA. (*Aside.*) O, dear, has he suddenly come to his senses?

(*Enter* ZOE, *stopping at back.*)

GEORGE. In a word, I have seen and admired you!

DORA. (*Aside.*) He has a strange way of showing it. European, I suppose.

GEORGE. If you would pardon the abruptness of the question, I would ask you, Do you think the sincere devotion of my life to make yours happy would succeed?

DORA. (*Aside.*) Well, he has the oddest way of making love.

GEORGE. You are silent?

DORA. Mr. Peyton, I presume you have hesitated to make this avowal because you feared, in the present condition of affairs here, your object might be misconstrued, and that your attention was rather to my fortune than myself. (*A pause.*) Why don't he speak?—I mean, you feared I might not give you credit for sincere and pure feelings. Well, you wrong me. I don't think you capable of anything else but—

GEORGE. No, I hesitated because an attachment I had formed before I had the pleasure of seeing you had not altogether died out.

DORA. (*Smiling.*) Some of those sirens of Paris, I presume. (*Pausing.*) I shall endeavor not to be jealous of the past; perhaps I have no right to be. (*Pausing.*) But now that vagrant love is—eh, faded—is it not? Why don't you speak, sir?

GEORGE. Because, Miss Sunnyside, I have not learned to lie.

DORA. Good gracious—who wants you to?

GEORGE. I do, but I can't do it. No, the love I speak of is not such as you suppose—it is a passion that has grown up here since I arrived; but it is a hopeless, mad, wild feeling, that must perish.

DORA. Here! Since you arrived! Impossible: you have seen no one; whom can you mean?

ZOE. (*Advancing.*) Me.

GEORGE. Zoe!

DORA. You!

ZOE. Forgive him, Dora; for he knew no better until I told him. Dora, you are right. He is incapable of any but sincere and pure feelings—so are you. He loves me—what of that? You know you can't be jealous of a poor creature like me. If he caught the fever, were stung by a snake, or possessed of any other poisonous or unclean thing, you could pity, tend, love him through it, and for your gentle care he would love you in return. Well, is he not thus afflicted now? I am his love—he loves an Octoroon.

GEORGE. O, Zoe, you break my heart!

DORA. At college they said I was a fool—I must be. At New Orleans, they said, "She's pretty, very pretty, but no brains." I'm afraid they must be right; I can't understand a word of all this.

ZOE. Dear Dora, try to understand it with your heart. You love George; you love him dearly; I know it; and you deserve to be loved by him. He will love you—he must. His love for me will pass away—it shall. You heard him say it was hopeless. O, forgive him and me!

DORA. (*Weeping.*) O, why did he speak to me at all then? You've made me cry, then, and I hate you both! (*Exit through room.*)

(*Enter* MRS. PEYTON *and* SCUDDER, M'CLOSKY *and* POINT-DEXTER.)

M'CLOSKY. I'm sorry to intrude, but the business I came upon will excuse me.

MRS. PEYTON. Here is my nephew, sir.

ZOE. Perhaps I had better go.

M'CLOSKY. Wal, as it consarns you, perhaps you better had.

SCUDDER. Consarns Zoe?

M'CLOSKY. I don't know; she may as well hear the hull of it. Go on, Colonel—Colonel Pointdexter, ma'am—the mortgagee, auctioneer, and general agent.

POINTDEXTER. Pardon me, madam, but do you know these papers. (*He hands the papers to* MRS. PEYTON.)

MRS. PEYTON. (*Taking them.*) Yes, sir; they were the free papers of the girl Zoe; but they were in my husband's secretary. How came they in your possession?

M'CLOSKY. I—I found them.

GEORGE. And you purloined them?

m'closky. Hold on, you'll see. Go on, Colonel.

pointdexter. The list of your slaves is incomplete—it wants one.

scudder. The boy Paul—we know it.

pointdexter. No, sir, you have omitted the Octoroon girl, Zoe.

mrs. peyton. ⎱ Zoe!
zoe.   ⎰ Me!

pointdexter. At the time the judge executed those free papers to his infant slave, a judgment stood recorded against him; while that was on record he had no right to make away with his property. That judgment still exists: under it and others this estate is sold to-day. Those free papers ain't worth the sand that's on 'em.

mrs. peyton. Zoe a slave! It is impossible!

pointdexter. It is certain, madam: the judge was negligent, and doubtless forgot this small formality.

scudder. But creditors will not claim the gal?

m'closky. Excuse me; one of the principal mortgagees has made the demand.

(*Exeunt* m'closky *and* pointdexter.)

scudder. Hold on yere, George Peyton; you sit down there. You're trembling so, you'll fall down directly. This blow has staggered me some.

mrs. peyton. O, Zoe, my child! Don't think too hard of your poor father.

zoe. I shall do so if you weep. See, I'm calm.

scudder. Calm as a tombstone, and with about as much life. I see it in your face.

george. It cannot be! It shall not be!

scudder. Hold your tongue—it must. Be calm—darn the things; the proceeds of this sale won't cover the debts of the estate. Consarn those Liverpool English fellers, why couldn't they send something by the last mail? Even a letter, promising something—such is the feeling round amongst the planters. Darn me, if I couldn't raise thirty thousand on the envelope alone, and ten thousand more on the postmark.

george. Zoe, they shall not take you from us while I live.

scudder. Don't be a fool; they'd kill you, and then take her, just as soon as—stop: old Sunnyside, he'll buy her; that'll save her.

ZOE. No, it won't; we have confessed to Dora that we love each other. How can she then ask her father to free me?

SCUDDER. What in thunder made you do that?

ZOE. Because it was the truth, and I had rather be a slave with a free soul than remain free with a slavish, deceitful heart. My father gave me freedom—at least he thought so. May Heaven bless him for the thought, bless him for the happiness he spread around my life. You say the proceeds of the sale will not cover his debts. Let me be sold then, that I may free his name. I give him back the liberty he bestowed upon me; for I can never repay him the love he bore his poor Octoroon child, on whose breast his last sigh was drawn, into whose eyes he looked with the last gaze of affection.

MRS. PEYTON. O, my husband! I thank Heaven you have not lived to see this day.

ZOE. George, leave me! I would be alone a little while.

GEORGE. Zoe! (*Turning away overpowered.*)

ZOE. Do not weep, George. Dear George, you now see what a miserable thing I am.

GEORGE. Zoe!

SCUDDER. I wish they could sell *me!* I brought half this ruin on this family, with my all-fired improvements. I deserve to be a nigger this day—I feel like one, inside. (*Exit* SCUDDER.)

ZOE. Go now, George—leave me—take her with you.
(*Exit* MRS. PEYTON *and* GEORGE.)
A slave! A slave! Is this a dream—for my brain reels with the blow? He said so. What! Then I shall be sold!—sold! And my master—O! (*Falls on her knees, with her face in her hands.*) No—no master but one. George—George—hush —they come! Save me! No, (*Looks off.*) 't is Pete and the servants—they come this way. (*Enters the inner room.*)

(*Enter* PETE, GRACE, MINNIE, SOLON, DIDO, *and all the Negroes.*)

PETE. Cum yer now—stand round, 'cause I've got to talk to you darkies—keep dem chil'n quiet—don't make no noise, de missus up dar har us.

SOLON. Go on, Pete.

PETE. Gen'l'men, my colored frens and ladies, dar's mighty

bad news gone round. Dis yer prop'ty to be sold—old Terrebonne—whar we all been raised, is gwine—dey's gwine to tak it away—can't stop here nohow.

OMNES. O-o!—O-o!

PETE. Hold quiet, you trash o' niggers! Tink anybody wants you to cry? Who's you to set up screeching?—Be quiet! But dis ain't all. Now, my cullud brethren, gird up your lines, and listen—hold on yer bref—it's a comin'. We tought dat de niggers would belong to de ole missus, and if she lost Terrebonne, we must live dere allers, and we would hire out, and bring our wages to ole Missus Peyton.

OMNES. Ya! Ya! Well—

PETE. Hush! I tell ye, 't ain't so—we can't do it—we've got to be sold—

OMNES. Sold!

PETE. Will you hush? She will har you. Yes! I listen dar jess now—dar was ole lady cryin'—Mas'r George—ah! You seen dem big tears in his eyes. O, Mas'r Scudder, he didn't cry zackly; both ob his eyes and cheek look like de bad Bayou in low season—so dry dat I cry for him. (*Raising his voice.*) Den say de missus, " 'Tain't for de land I keer, but for dem poor niggers—dey'll be sold—dat wot stagger me." "No," say Mas'r George, "I'd rather sell myself fuss; but dey shan't suffer, nohow,—I see 'em dam fuss."

OMNES. O, bless 'um! Bless Mas'r George.

PETE. Hole yer tongues. Yes, for you, for me, for dem little ones, dem folks cried. Now, den, if Grace dere wid her chil'n were all sold, she'll begin screechin' like a cat. She didn't mind how kind old judge was to her; and Solon, too, he'll holler, and break de ole lady's heart.

GRACE. No, Pete; no, I won't. I'll bear it.

PETE. I don't tink you will any more, but dis here will; 'cause de family spile Dido, dey has. She nebber was worth much a' dat nigger.

DIDO. How dar you say dat, you black nigger, you? I fetch as much as any odder cook in Louisiana.

PETE. What's the use of your takin' it kind, and comfortin' de missus' heart, if Minnie dere, and Louise, and Marie, and Julie is to spile it?

MINNIE. We won't, Pete; we won't.

PETE. (*To the men.*) Dar, do ye hear dat, ye mis'able darkies; dem gals is worth a boat load of kinder men dem is. Cum,

for de pride of de family, let every darky look his best for
the judge's sake—dat ole man so good to us and dat ole
woman—so dem strangers from New Orleans shall say,
Dem's happy darkies, dem's a fine set of niggers; every one
say when he's sold, "Lor' bless dis yer family I'm gwine
out of, and send me as good a home."

OMNES. We'll do it, Pete; we'll do it.

PETE. Hush! Hark! I tell ye dar's somebody in dar. Who is it?

GRACE. It's Missy Zoe. See! See!

PETE. Come along; she har what we say, and she's cryin' for
us. None o' ye ign'rant niggers could cry for yerselves like
dat. Come here quite: now quite.

(*Exeunt* PETE *and all the Negroes, slowly.*)

(*Enter* ZOE *who is supposed to have overheard the last
scene.*)

ZOE. O! Must I learn from these poor wretches how much I
owe, and how I ought to pay the debt? Have I slept upon
the benefits I received, and never saw, never felt, never
knew that I was forgetful and ungrateful? O, my father!
My dear, dear father! Forgive your poor child. You made
her life too happy, and now these tears will flow. Let me
hide them till I teach my heart. O, my—my heart! (*Exit,
with a low, wailing, suffocating cry.*)

(*Enter* M'CLOSKY, LAFOUCHE, JACKSON, SUNNYSIDE *and*
POINTDEXTER.)

POINTDEXTER. (*Looking at his watch.*) Come, the hour is past.
I think we may begin business. Where is Mr. Scudder?

JACKSON. I want to get to Ophelensis to-night.

(*Enter* DORA.)

DORA. Father, come here.

SUNNYSIDE. Why, Dora, what's the matter? Your eyes are red.

DORA. Are they? Thank you. I don't care, they were blue this
morning, but it don't signify now.

SUNNYSIDE. My darling! Who has been teasing you?

DORA. Never mind. I want you to buy Terrebonne.

SUNNYSIDE. Buy Terrebonne! What for?

DORA. No matter—buy it!

SUNNYSIDE. It will cost me all I'm worth. This is folly, Dora.

DORA. Is my plantation at Comptableau worth this?

SUNNYSIDE. Nearly—perhaps.

DORA. Sell it, then, and buy this.

SUNNYSIDE. Are you mad, my love?

DORA. Do you want *me* to stop here and *bid* for it?

SUNNYSIDE. Good gracious, no!

DORA. Then I'll do it if you don't.

SUNNYSIDE. I will! I will! But for Heaven's sake go—here comes the crowd.

(*Exit* DORA.)

What on earth does that child mean or want?

(*Enter* SCUDDER, GEORGE, RATTS, CAILLOU, THIBODEAUX, PETE, GRACE, MINNIE, *and all the Negroes. A large table is in the center of the background.* POINTDEXTER *mounts the table with his hammer, his clerk sitting at his feet. The Negro mounts the table from behind. The rest sit down.*)

POINTDEXTER. Now, gentlemen, we shall proceed to business. It ain't necessary for me to dilate, describe or enumerate; Terrebonne is known to you as one of the richest bits of sile in Louisiana, and its condition reflects credit on them as had to keep it. I'll trouble you for that piece of baccy, Judge—thank you—so, gentlemen, as life is short, we'll start right off. The first lot on here is the estate in block, with its sugar-houses, stock, machines, implements, good dwelling-houses and furniture. If there is no bid for the estate and stuff, we'll sell it in smaller lots. Come, Mr. Thibodeaux, a man has a chance once in his life—here's yours.

THIBODEAUX. Go on. What's the reserve bid?

POINTDEXTER. The first mortgagee bids forty thousand dollars.

THIBODEAUX. Forty-five thousand.

SUNNYSIDE. Fifty thousand.

POINTDEXTER. When you have done joking, gentlemen, you'll say one hundred and twenty thousand. It carried that easy on mortgage.

LAFOUCHE. Then why don't you buy it yourself, Colonel?

POINTDEXTER. I'm waiting on your fifty thousand bid.

CAILLOU. Eighty thousand.

POINTDEXTER. Don't be afraid: it ain't going for that, Judge.

SUNNYSIDE. Ninety thousand.

POINTDEXTER. We're getting on.

THIBODEAUX. One hundred—

POINTDEXTER. One hundred thousand bid for this mag—

CAILLOU. One hundred and ten thousand—

POINTDEXTER. Good again—one hundred and—

SUNNYSIDE. Twenty.

POINTDEXTER. And twenty thousand bid. Squire Sunnyside is going to sell this at fifty thousand advance to-morrow. (*Looking round.*) Where's that man from Mobile that wanted to give one hundred and eighty thousand?

THIBODEAUX. I guess he ain't left home yet, Colonel.

POINTDEXTER. I shall knock it down to the Squire—going—gone—for one hundred and twenty thousand dollars. (*Raising hammer.*) Judge, you can raise the hull on mortgage—going for half its value. (*Knocking on the table.*) Squire Sunnyside, you've got a pretty bit o' land, Squire. Hillo, darkey, hand me a smash dar.

SUNNYSIDE. I got more than I can work now.

POINTDEXTER. Then buy the hands along with the property. Now, gentlemen, I'm proud to submit to you the finest lot of field hands and house servants that was ever offered for competition: they speak for themselves, and do credit to their owners. (*Reading.*) "No. 1, Solon, a guest boy, and a good waiter."

PETE. That's my son—buy him, Mas'r Ratts; he's sure to sarve you well.

POINTDEXTER. Hold your tongue!

RATTS. Let the old darkey alone—eight hundred for that boy.

CALLIOU. Nine.

RATTS. A thousand.

SOLON. Thank you, Mas'r Ratts: I die for you, sar; hold up for me, sar.

RATTS. Look here, the boy knows and likes me, Judge; let him come my way?

CALLIOU. Go on—I'm dumb.

POINTDEXTER. One thousand bid. He's yours, Captain Ratts, Magnolia steamer.

(SOLON *goes and stands behind* RATTS.)

"No. 2, the yellow girl, Grace, with two children—Saul, aged four, and Victoria, five."

(*They get on table.*)

SCUDDER. That's Solon's wife and children, Judge.

GRACE. (*To* RATTS.) Buy me, Mas'r Ratts, do buy me, sar?

RATTS. What in thunder should I do with you and those devils on board my boat?

GRACE. Wash, sar—cook, sar—anyting.

RATTS. Eight hundred agin, then—I'll go it.

JACKSON. Nine.

RATTS. I'm broke, Solon—I can't stop the Judge.

THIBODEAUX. What's the matter, Ratts? I'll lend you all you want. Go it, if you're a mind to.

RATTS. Eleven.

JACKSON. Twelve.

SUNNYSIDE. O, O!

SCUDDER. (*To* JACKSON.) Judge, my friend. The Judge is a little deaf. Hello! (*Speaking in his ear-trumpet.*) This gal and them children belong to that boy Solon there. You're bidding to separate them, Judge.

JACKSON. The devil I am! (*Rising.*) I'll take back my bid, Colonel.

POINTDEXTER. All right, Judge; I thought there was a mistake. I must keep you, Captain, to the eleven hundred.

RATTS. Go it.

POINTDEXTER. Eleven hundred—going—going—sold! "No. 3, Pete, a house servant."

PETE. Dat's me—yer, I'm comin'—stand around dar. (*Tumbles upon the table.*)

POINTDEXTER. Aged seventy-two.

PETE. What's dat? A mistake, sar—forty-six.

POINTDEXTER. Lame.

PETE. But don't mount to nuffin—kin work cannel. Come, Judge, pick up. Now's your time, sar.

JACKSON. One hundred dollars.

PETE. What, sar? Me! For me—look ye here! (*Dances.*)

GEORGE. Five hundred.

PETE. Mas'r George—ah, no, sar—don't buy me—keep your money for some udder dat is to be sold. I ain't no 'count, sar.

POINTDEXTER. Five hundred bid—it's a good price. He's yours, Mr. George Peyton.

(PETE *goes down.*)

"No. 4, the Octoroon girl, Zoe."

(*Enter* zoe, *very pale, and stands on table.* m'closky *who hitherto has taken no interest in the sale, now turns his chair.*)

SUNNYSIDE. (*Rising.*) Gentlemen, we are all acquainted with the circumstances of this girl's position, and I feel sure that no one here will oppose the family who desires to redeem the child of our esteemed and noble friend, the late Judge Peyton.

OMNES. Hear! Bravo! Hear!

POINTDEXTER. While the proceeds of this sale promises to realize less than the debts upon it, it is my duty to prevent any collusion for the depreciation of the property.

RATTS. Darn ye! You're a man as well as an auctioneer, ain't ye?

POINTDEXTER. What is offered for this slave?

SUNNYSIDE. One thousand dollars.

M'CLOSKY. Two thousand.

SUNNYSIDE. Three thousand.

M'CLOSKY. Five thousand.

GEORGE. Demon!

SUNNYSIDE. I bid seven thousand, which is the last dollar this family possesses.

M'CLOSKY. Eight.

THIBODEAUX. Nine.

OMNES. Bravo!

M'CLOSKY. Ten. It's no use, Squire.

SCUDDER. Jacob M'Closky, you shan't have that girl. Now, take care what you do. Twelve thousand.

M'CLOSKY. Shan't I! Fifteen thousand. Beat that any of ye.

POINTDEXTER. Fifteen thousand bid for the Octoroon.

(*Enter* DORA.)

DORA. Twenty thousand.

OMNES. Bravo!

M'CLOSKY. Twenty-five thousand.

OMNES. (*Groan.*) O! O!

GEORGE. Yelping hound—take that.

(*Rushes* M'CLOSKY. M'CLOSKY *draws his knife.*)

SCUDDER. (*Darting between them.*) Hold on, George Peyton—

stand back. This is your own house; we are under your uncle's roof; recollect yourself. And, strangers, ain't we forgetting there's a lady present? (*The knives disappear.*) If we can't behave like Christians, let's try and act like gentlemen. Go on, Colonel.

LAFOUCHE. He didn't ought to bid against a lady.

M'CLOSKY. O, that's it, is it? Then I'd like to hire a lady to go to auction and buy my hands.

POINTDEXTER. Gentlemen, I believe none of us have two feelings about the conduct of that man; but he has the law on his side—we may regret, but we must respect it. Mr. M'Closky has bid twenty-five thousand dollars for the Octoroon. Is there any other bid? For the first time, twenty-five thousand—last time! (*Brings hammer down.*) To Jacob M'Closky, the Octoroon girl, Zoe, twenty-five thousand dollars. (*Tableau.*)

ACT IV

SCENE. *The Wharf. The Steamer "Magnolia," alongside; a bluff rock.* RATTS *discovered, superintending the loading of ship.*

Enter LAFOUCHE *and* JACKSON.

JACKSON. How long before we start, captain?

RATTS. Just as soon as we put this cotton on board.

(*Enter* PETE, *with a lantern, and* SCUDDER, *with note book.*)

SCUDDER. One hundred and forty-nine bales. Can you take any more?

RATTS. Not a bale. I've got engaged eight hundred bales at the next landing, and one hundred hogsheads of sugar at Patten's Slide—that'll take my guards under—hurry up thar.

VOICE. (*Outside.*) Wood's aboard.

RATTS. All aboard then.

(*Enter* M'CLOSKY.)

SCUDDER. Sign that receipt, captain, and save me going up to the clerk.

M'CLOSKY. See here—there's a small freight of turpentine in the fore hold there, and one of the barrels leaks; a spark from your engines might set the ship on fire, and you'll go with it.

RATTS. You be darned! Go and try it, if you've a mind to.

LAFOUCHE. Captain, you've loaded up here until the boat is sunk so deep in the mud she won't float.

RATTS. (*Calling off.*) Wood up thar, you Pollo—hang on to the safety valve—guess she'll crawl off on her paddles.
(*Shouts heard.*)

JACKSON. What's the matter?

(*Enter* SOLON.)

SOLON. We got him!

SCUDDER. Who?

SOLON. The Injiun!

SCUDDER. Wahnotee? Where is he? D'ye call running away from a fellow catching him?

RATTS. Here he comes.

OMNES. Where? Where?

(*Enter* WAHNOTEE. *They are all about to rush on him.*)

SCUDDER. Hold on! Stan' round thar! No violence—the critter don't know what we mean.

JACKSON. Let him answer for the boy then.

M'CLOSKY. Down with him—lynch him.

OMNES. Lynch him!
(*Exit* LAFOUCHE.)

SCUDDER. Stan' back, I say! I'll nip the first that lays a finger on him. Pete, speak to the red-skin.

PETE. Whar's Paul, Wahnotee? What's come ob de child?

WAHNOTEE. Paul wunce—Paul pangeuk.

PETE. Pangeuk—dead!

WAHNOTEE. Mort!

M'CLOSKY. And you killed him?
(*They approach him.*)

SCUDDER. Hold on!

PETE. Um, Paul reste?

WAHNOTEE. Hugh vieu. (*Goes.*) Paul reste ci!

SCUDDER. Here, stay! (*Examining the ground.*) The earth has been stirred here lately.

WAHNOTEE. Weenee Paul. (*Points down, and shows by pantomime how he buried* PAUL.)

SCUDDER. The Injun means that he buried him there! Stop! Here's a bit of leather. (*Drawing out the mail-bags.*) The mail-bags that were lost! (*Sees the tomahawk in* WAHNOTEE's *belt—draws it out and examines it.*) Look! Here are marks of blood—look thar, red-skin, what's that?

WAHNOTEE. Paul! (*Makes a sign that* PAUL *was killed by a blow on the head.*)

M'CLOSKY. He confesses it; the Indian got drunk, quarrelled with him, and killed him.

(*Re-enter* LAFOUCHE, *with smashed apparatus.*)

LAFOUCHE. Here are evidences of the crime; this rum-bottle half emptied—this photographic apparatus smashed—and there are marks of blood and footsteps around the shed.

M'CLOSKY. What more d'ye want—ain't that proof enough? Lynch him!

OMNES. Lynch him! Lynch him!

SCUDDER. Stan' back, boys! He's an Injiun—fair play.

JACKSON. Try him, then—try him on the spot of his crime.

OMNES. Try him! Try him!

LAFOUCHE. Don't let him escape!

RATTS. I'll see to that. (*Drawing revolver.*) If he stirs, I'll put a bullet through his skull, mighty quick.

M'CLOSKY. Come, form a court then, choose a jury—we'll fix this varmin.

(*Enter* THIBODEAUX *and* CAILLOU.)

THIBODEAUX. What's the matter?

LAFOUCHE. We've caught this murdering Injiun, and are going to try him.

(WAHNOTEE *sits, rolled in blanket.*)

PETE. Poor little Paul—poor little nigger!

SCUDDER. This business goes agin me, Ratts—'t ain't right.

LAFOUCHE. We're ready; the jury's impanelled—go ahead—
who'll be accuser?

RATTS. M'Closky.

M'CLOSKY. Me?

RATTS. Yes; you was the first to hail Judge Lynch.

M'CLOSKY. Well, what's the use of argument whar guilt sticks
out so plain; the boy and Injiun were alone when last seen.

SCUDDER. Who says that?

M'CLOSKY. Everybody—that is, I heard so.

SCUDDER. Say what you know—not what you heard.

M'CLOSKY. I know then that the boy was killed with that
tomahawk—the redskin owns it—the signs of violence are
all round the shed—this apparatus smashed—ain't it plain
that in a drunken fit he slew the boy, and when sober concealed the body yonder?

OMNES. That's it—that's it.

RATTS. Who defends the Injiun?

SCUDDER. I will; for it is agin my natur' to b'lieve him guilty;
and if he be, this ain't the place, nor you the authority to
try him. How are we sure the boy is dead at all? There
are no witnesses but a rum bottle and an old machine. Is it
on such evidence you'd hang a human being?

RATTS. His own confession.

SCUDDER. I appeal against your usurped authority. This lynch
law is a wild and lawless proceeding. Here's a pictur' for
a civilized community to afford; yonder, a poor, ignorant
savage, and round him a circle of hearts, white with revenge and hate, thirsting for his blood: you call yourselves
judges—you ain't—you're a jury of executioners. It is such
scenes as these that bring disgrace upon our Western life.

M'CLOSKY. Evidence! Evidence! Give us evidence. We've had
talk enough; now for proof.

OMNES. Yes, yes! Proof, proof!

SCUDDER. Where am I to get it? The proof is here, in my heart.

PETE. (*Who has been looking about the camera.*) 'Top, sar!
'Top a bit! O, laws-a-mussey, see dis! Here's a pictur' I
found stickin' in that yar telescope machine, sar! Look, sar!

SCUDDER. A photographic plate.
    (PETE *holds his lantern up.*) What's this, eh? Two forms!
The child—'t is he! Dead—and above him—Ah! ah! Jacob
M'Closky, 't was you murdered that boy!

M'CLOSKY. Me?

SCUDDER. You! You slew him with that tomahawk; and as you stood over his body with the letter in your hand, you thought that no witness saw the deed, that no eye was on you—but there was, Jacob M'Closky, there was. The eye of the Eternal was on you—the blessed sun in heaven, that, looking down, struck upon this plate the image of the deed. Here you are, in the very attitude of your crime!

M'CLOSKY. 'T is false!

SCUDDER. 'T is true! The apparatus can't lie. Look there, jurymen. (*Showing plate to jury.*) Look there. O, you wanted evidence—you called for proof—Heaven has answered and convicted you.

M'CLOSKY. What court of law would receive such evidence? (*Going.*)

RATTS. Stop! *This* would! You called it yourself; you wanted to make us murder that Injiun; and since we've got our hands in for justice, we'll try it on *you*. What say ye? Shall we have one law for the red-skin and another for the white?

OMNES. Try him! Try him!

RATTS. Who'll be accuser?

SCUDDER. I will! Fellow-citizens, you are convened and assembled here under a higher power than the law. What's the law? When the ship's abroad on the ocean, when the army is before the enemy, where in thunder's the law? It is in the hearts of brave men, who can tell right from wrong, and from whom justice can't be bought. So it is here, in the wilds of the West, where our hatred of crime is measured by the speed of our executions—where necessity is law! I say, then, air you honest men? Air you true? Put your hands on your naked breasts, and let every man as don't feel a real American heart there, bustin' up with freedom, truth, and right, let that man step out—that's the oath I put to ye—and then say, Darn ye, go it!

OMNES. Go on! Go on!

SCUDDER. No! I won't go on; that man's down. I won't strike him, even with words. Jacob, your accuser is that picture of the crime—let that speak—defend yourself.

M'CLOSKY. (*Drawing knife.*) I will, quicker than lightning.

RATTS. Seize him, then!

(*They rush on* M'CLOSKY, *and disarm him.*)

He can fight though he's a painter: claws all over.

SCUDDER. Stop! Search him, we may find more evidence.

M'CLOSKY. Would you rob me first, and murder me afterwards?

RATTS. (*Searching him.*) That's his program—here's a pocketbook.

SCUDDER. (*Opening it.*) What's here? Letters! Hello! To "Mrs. Peyton, Terrebonne, Louisiana, United States." Liverpool postmark. Ho! I've got hold of the tail of a rat—come out. (*Reading.*) What's this? A draft for eighty-five thousand dollars, and credit on Palisse and Co., of New Orleans, for the balance. Hi! The rat's out. You killed the boy to steal this letter from the mail-bags—you stole this letter, that the money should not arrive in time to save the Octoroon; had it done so, the lien on the estate would have ceased, and Zoe be free.

OMNES. Lynch him! Lynch him! Down with him!

SCUDDER. Silence in the court: stand back, let the gentlemen of the jury retire, consult, and return their verdict.

RATTS. I'm responsible for the crittur—go on.

PETE. (*To* WAHNOTEE.) See, Injiun; look dar (*Showing him the plate.*), see dat innocent; look, dar's de murderer of poor Paul.

WAHNOTEE. Ugh! (*Examining the plate.*)

PETE. Ya! As he? Closky tue Paul—kill de child with your tomahawk dar: 't wasn't you, no—ole Pete allus say so. Poor Injiun lub our little Paul.

(WAHNOTEE *rises and looks at* M'CLOSKY—*he is in his war paint and fully armed.*)

SCUDDER. What say ye, gentlemen? Is the prisoner guilty, or is he not guilty?

OMNES. Guilty!

SCUDDER. And what is to be his punishment?

OMNES. Death!

(*All advance.*)

WAHNOTEE. (*Crosses to* M'CLOSKY.) Ugh!

SCUDDER. No, Injiun; we deal out justice here, not revenge. 'T ain't you he has injured, 't is the white man, whose laws he has offended.

RATTS. Away with him—put him down the aft hatch, till we rig his funeral.

M'CLOSKY. Fifty against one! O! If I had you one by one alone in the swamp, I'd rip ye all. (*He is borne off in boat struggling.*)

SCUDDER. Now, then, to business.

PETE. (*Re-enters from boat.*) O, law, sir, dat debil Closky, he tore hisself from de gen'lam, knock me down, take my light, and trows it on de turpentine barrels, and de shed's all afire! (*Fire seen.*)

JACKSON. (*Re-entering.*) We are catching fire forward: quick, cut free from the shore.

RATTS. All hands aboard there—cut the starn ropes—give her headway!

ALL. Ay, ay!

(*Cry of "Fire" heard—Engine bells heard—steam whistle noise.*)

RATTS. Cut all away, for'ard—overboard with every bale afire. (*The Steamer moves off with the fire still blazing.*)

(M'CLOSKY *re-enters, swimming.*)

M'CLOSKY. Ha! Have I fixed ye? Burn! Burn! That's right. You thought you had cornered me, did ye? As I swam down, I thought I heard something in the water, as if pursuing me— one of them darned alligators, I suppose—they swarm hereabout—may they crunch every limb of ye. (*Exit.*)

(WAHNOTEE *is seen swimming. He finds trail and follows* M'CLOSKY. *The Steamer floats on at back, burning.*)

ACT V

Scene 1

Negroes' Quarters.

Enter ZOE.

ZOE. It wants an hour yet to daylight—here is Pete's hut— (*Knocks.*) He sleeps—no: I see a light.

DIDO. (*Enters from hut.*) Who dat?

ZOE. Hush, aunty! 'T is I—Zoe.

DIDO. Missey Zoe? Why you out in de swamp dis time ob night; you catch de fever sure—you is all wet.

ZOE. Where's Pete?

DIDO. He gone down to de landing last night wid Mas'r Scudder; not come back since—kint make it out.

ZOE. Aunty, there is sickness up at the house; I have been up all night beside one who suffers, and I remembered that when I had the fever you gave me a drink, a bitter drink, that made me sleep—do you remember it?

DIDO. Didn't I? Dem doctors ain't no 'count; dey don't know nuffin.

ZOE. No; but you, aunty, you are wise—you know every plant, don't you, and what it is good for?

DIDO. Dat you drink is fust rate for red fever. Is de folks' head bad?

ZOE. Very bad, aunty; and the heart aches worse, so they can get no rest.

DIDO. Hold on a bit, I get you de bottle. (*Exit.*)

ZOE. In a few hours that man, my master, will come for me: he has paid my price, and he only consented to let me remain here this one night, because Mrs. Peyton promised to give me up to him to-day.

DIDO. (*Re-enters with phial.*) Here 't is—now you give one timble-full—dat's nuff.

ZOE. All there is there would kill one, wouldn't it?

DIDO. Guess it kill a dozen—nebber try.

ZOE. It's not a painful death, aunty, is it? You told me it produced a long, long sleep.

DIDO. Why you tremble so? Why you speak so wild? What you's gwine to do, missey?

ZOE. Give me the drink.

DIDO. No. Who dat sick at de house?

ZOE. Give it to me.

DIDO. No. You want to hurt yourself. O, Miss Zoe, why you ask old Dido for dis pizen?

ZOE. Listen to me. I love one who is here, and he loves me—George. I sat outside his door all night—I heard his sighs—his agony—torn from him by my coming fate; and he said, "I'd rather see her dead than his!"

DIDO. Dead!

ZOE. He said so—then I rose up, and stole from the house, and ran down to the bayou: but its cold, black, silent stream terrified me—drowning must be so horrible a death. I could not do it. Then, as I knelt there, weeping for courage, a snake rattled beside me. I shrunk from it and fled. Death was there beside me, and I dared not take it. O! I'm afraid to die; yet I am more afraid to live.

DIDO. Die!

ZOE. So I came here to you; to you, my own dear nurse; to you, who so often hushed me to sleep when I was a child; who dried my eyes and put your little Zoe to rest. Ah! Give me the rest that no master but One can disturb—the sleep from which I shall awake free! You can protect me from that man—do let me die without pain.

DIDO. No, no—life is good for young ting like you.

ZOE. O! good, good nurse: you will, you will.

DIDO. No—g'way.

ZOE. Then I shall never leave Terrebonne—the drink, nurse; the drink; that I may never leave my home—my dear, dear home. You will not give me to that man? Your own Zoe, that loves you, aunty, so much, so much. (*Gets the phial.*) Ah! I have it.

DIDO. No, missey. O! No—don't.

ZOE. Hush! (*Runs off.*)

DIDO. Here, Solon, Minnie, Grace.

(*They enter.*)

ALL. Was de matter?

DIDO. Miss Zoe got de pizen. (*Exit.*)

ALL. O! O! (*Exeunt.*)

Scene 2

In a Cane-brake Bayou, on a bank, with a canoe near by, M'CLOSKY *is seen asleep.*

M'CLOSKY. Burn, burn! Blaze away! How the flames crack. I'm not guilty; would ye murder me? Cut, cut the rope— I choke—choke!—Ah! (*Waking.*) Hello! Where am I? Why, I was dreaming—curse it! I can never sleep now without dreaming. Hush! I thought I heard the sound of a paddle in the water. All night, as I fled through the cane-brake, I heard footsteps behind me. I lost them in the cedar swamp —again they haunted my path down the bayou, moving as

I moved, resting when I rested—hush! There again!—No; it was only the wind over the canes. The sun is rising. I must launch my dug-out, and put for the bay, and in a few hours I shall be safe from pursuit on board of one of the coasting schooners that run from Galveston to Matagorda. In a little time this darned business will blow over, and I can show again. Hark! There's that noise again! If it was the ghost of that murdered boy haunting me! Well—I didn't mean to kill him, did I? Well, then, what has my all-cowardly heart got to skeer me so for?

(*Gets in canoe and rows off.* WAHNOTEE *appears in another canoe. Gets out and finds trail and paddles off after* M'CLOSKY.)

Scene 3

A cedar Swamp.

Enter SCUDDER *and* PETE.

SCUDDER. Come on, Pete, we shan't reach the house before midday.

PETE. Nebber mind, sa, we bring good news—it won't spile for de keeping.

SCUDDER. Ten miles we've had to walk, because some blamed varmin onhitched our dug-out. I left it last night all safe.

PETE. P'r'aps it floated away itself.

SCUDDER. No; the hitching line was cut with a knife.

PETE. Say, Mas'r Scudder, s'pose we go in round by de quarters and raise de darkies, den dey cum long wid us, and we 'proach dat ole house like Gin'ral Jackson when he took London out dar.

SCUDDER. Hello, Pete, I never heard of that affair.

PETE. I tell you, sa—hush!

SCUDDER. What?

PETE. Was dat?—A cry out dar in the swamp—dar again!

SCUDDER. So it is. Something forcing its way through the undergrowth—it comes this way—it's either a bear or a runaway nigger.

(*Draws a pistol.* M'CLOSKY *rushes on, and falls at* SCUDDER'S *feet.*)

SCUDDER. Stand off—what are ye?

PETE. Mas'r Clusky.

M'CLOSKY. Save me—save me! I can go no farther. I heard voices.

SCUDDER. Who's after you?

M'CLOSKY. I don't know, but I feel it's death! In some form, human, or wild beast, or ghost, it has tracked me through the night. I fled; it followed. Hark! There it comes—it comes—don't you hear a footstep on the dry leaves!

SCUDDER. Your crime has driven you mad.

M'CLOSKY. D'ye hear it—nearer—nearer—ah!

(WAHNOTEE *rushes on, and attacks* M'CLOSKY.)

SCUDDER. The Injiun! By thunder.

PETE. You'se a dead man, Mas'r Clusky—you got to b'lieve dat.

M'CLOSKY. No—no. If I must die, give me up to the law; but save me from the tomahawk. You are a white man; you'll not leave one of your own blood to be butchered by the red-skin?

SCUDDER. Hold on now, Jacob; we've got to figure on that— let us look straight at the thing. Here we are on the selvage of civilization. It ain't our side, I believe, rightly; but Nature has said that where the white man sets his foot, the red man and the black man shall up sticks and stand around. But what do we pay for that possession? In cash? No—in kind—that is, in protection, forbearance, gentleness, in all them goods that show the critters the difference between the Christian and the savage. Now, what have you done to show them the distinction? For, darn me, if I can find out.

M'CLOSKY. For what I have done, let me be tried.

SCUDDER. You have been tried—honestly tried and convicted. Providence has chosen your executioner. I shan't interfere.

PETE. O, no; Mas'r Scudder, don't leave Mas'r Closky like dat—don't, sa—'t ain't what good Christian should do.

SCUDDER. D'ye hear that, Jacob? This old nigger, the grand-father of the boy you murdered, speaks for you—don't that go through you? D'ye feel it? Go on, Pete, you've waked up the Christian here, and the old hoss responds. (*Throws bowie-knife to* M'CLOSKY.) Take that, and defend yourself. (*Exeunt* SCUDDER *and* PETE. WAHNOTEE *faces him. They fight.* M'CLOSKY *runs off,* WAHNOTEE *follows him.—Screams outside.*)

Scene 4

Parlor at Terrebonne.

Enter ZOE.

ZOE. My home, my home! I must see you no more. Those little
flowers can live, but I cannot. To-morrow they'll bloom
the same—all will be here as now, and I shall be cold. O!
My life, my happy life; why has it been so bright?

(*Enter* MRS. PEYTON *and* DORA.)

DORA. Zoe, where have you been?
MRS. PEYTON. We felt quite uneasy about you.
ZOE. I've been to the Negro quarters. I suppose I shall go
before long, and I wished to visit all the places, once again,
to see the poor people.
MRS. PEYTON. Zoe, dear, I'm glad to see you more calm this
morning.
DORA. But how pale she looks, and she trembles so.
ZOE. Do I?

(*Enter* GEORGE.)

Ah! He is here.
DORA. George, here she is.
ZOE. I have come to say good-by, sir; two hard words—so
hard, they might break many a heart; mightn't they?
GEORGE. O, Zoe! Can you smile at this moment?
ZOE. You see how easily I have become reconciled to my
fate—so it will be with you. You will not forget poor Zoe!
But her image will pass away like a little cloud that ob-
scured your happiness a while—you will love each other;
you are both too good not to join your hearts. Brightness
will return amongst you. Dora, I once made you weep;
those were the only tears I caused anybody. Will you
forgive me?
DORA. Forgive you—(*Kisses her.*)

ZOE. I feel you do, George.

GEORGE. Zoe, you are pale. Zoe!—She faints!

ZOE. No; a weakness, that's all—a little water.

(DORA *gets some water.*)

I have a restorative here—will you pour it in the glass?
(DORA *attempts to take it.*)

No; not you—George. (GEORGE *pours the contents of the phial into glass.*) Now, give it to me. George, dear George, do you love me?

GEORGE. Do you doubt it, Zoe?

ZOE. No! (*Drinks.*)

DORA. Zoe, if all I possess would buy your freedom, I would gladly give it.

ZOE. I am free! I had but one Master on earth, and he has given me my freedom!

DORA. Alas! But the deed that freed you was not lawful.

ZOE. Not lawful—no—but I am going to where there is no law—where there is only justice.

GEORGE. Zoe, you are suffering—your lips are white—your cheeks are flushed.

ZOE. I must be going—it is late. Farewell, Dora. (*Retiring.*)

PETE. (*Outside.*) Whar's Missus—whar's Mas'r George?

GEORGE. They come.

(*Enter* SCUDDER.)

SCUDDER. Stand around and let me pass—room thar! I feel so big with joy, creation ain't wide enough to hold me! Mrs. Peyton, George Peyton, Terrebonne is yours. It was that rascal M'Closky—but he got rats, I swow—he killed the boy, Paul, to rob this letter from the mail-bags—the letter from Liverpool you know—he sot fire to the shed—that was how the steamboat got burned up.

MRS. PEYTON. What d'ye mean?

SCUDDER. Read—read that. (*Gives letter to them.*)

GEORGE. Explain yourself.

(*Enter* SUNNYSIDE.)

SUNNYSIDE. Is it true?

SCUDDER. Every word of it, Squire. Here, you tell it, since you know it. If I was to try, I'd bust.

MRS. PEYTON. Read, George. Terrebonne is yours.

(*Enter* PETE, DIDO, SOLON, MINNIE, *and* GRACE.)

PETE. Whar is she—whar is Miss Zoe?

SCUDDER. What's the matter?

PETE. Don't ax me. Whar's de gal? I say.

SCUDDER. Here she is—Zoe!—Water—she faints.

PETE. No—no. 'T ain't no faint—she's a dying, sa: she got pizon from old Dido here, this mornin'.

GEORGE. Zoe!

SCUDDER. Zoe! Is this true?—No, it ain't—darn it, say it ain't. Look here, you're free, you know; nary a master to hurt you now: you will stop here as long as you're a mind to, only don't look so.

DORA. Her eyes have changed color.

PETE. Dat's what her soul's gwine to do. It's going up dar, whar dere's no line atween folks.

GEORGE. She revives.

ZOE. (*On the sofa.*) George—where—where—

GEORGE. O, Zoe! What have you done?

ZOE. Last night I overheard you weeping in your room, and you said, "I'd rather see her dead than so!"

GEORGE. Have I then prompted you to this?

ZOE. No; but I loved you so, I could not bear my fate; and then I stood between your heart and hers. When I am dead she will not be jealous of your love for me, no laws will stand between us. Lift me; so—(GEORGE *raises her head.*)—let me look at you, that your face may be the last I see of this world. O! George, you may, without a blush, confess your love for the Octoroon.

(*Dies.* GEORGE *lowers her head gently and kneels beside her.*)

SCUDDER. Poor child; she is free. (*Tableau.*)

RIP VAN WINKLE

Preface to RIP VAN WINKLE

Despite the appeal of *Rip Van Winkle* to many nineteenth-century actors and playwrights, its name is most closely associated with that of Joseph Jefferson (1829–1905). Jefferson achieved and maintained success in other roles; but popular demand as well as personal inclination consistently made him return to Rip, the fabulous Dutch-American comic hero. For years he devoted his career almost exclusively to this play, performing it in England and in practically every part of the United States, much as James O'Neill (the father of Eugene O'Neill) did so successfully with *The Count of Monte Cristo*.

He first played his Rip Van Winkle in 1865. Both his father and his grandfather had acted in the play, perhaps in John Kerr's dramatization of the Washington Irving story, which was first published in 1819 and is still among the best-known tales in the English language. It was Kerr, an Anglo-American actor, who had invented Rip's toast—"Here's your good health and your family's good health and may you all live long and prosper"—which was retained by subsequent adaptors of the play, including Jefferson. In 1850 Jefferson himself had played the part of Seth Slough, the innkeeper, to his half-brother Charles Burke's Rip, in the latter's own dramatization of the play. That version of the increasingly popular and frequently redramatized story eventually supplanted Kerr's, even in some of James Hackett's later performances, and contained Rip's oft-quoted line, "Are we so soon forgot when we are gone?" (Act IV, Scene 3). The next dramatization of interest was the first one that Jefferson himself made—a three-act play that was for the most part a collation of other versions. Produced in Washington in 1859, it was neither successful nor was Jefferson satisfied with it.

But his interest in the play continued. When he visited England in June 1865, after his four-year tour of Australia and South America, he asked Dion Boucicault to rework it for him. The resultant play, a three-act adaptation, was produced at the Adelphi Theatre in London on September 4, and it was an immediate and enormous success. Jefferson played in it for 170 nights in London and then repeated his triumph, first briefly in Manchester, then in New York and in other parts of America. Through the years he constantly kept altering and developing his role. He succeeded in producing a play that is a curious and appealing mixture of comedy, fantasy, and pathos—a "tall tale," Constance Rourke notes in her *American Humor* (1931), that "lived again in a transmuted mythology of death and dream and thunder." The text of the play that follows—first printed in 1895, thirty years after that of Boucicault—is Jefferson's acting script, and he continued to play it substantially in this form until the end of his career.

Joseph Jefferson was the most illustrious member of an illustrious theatre family. Its progenitor, an Englishman who acted with David Garrick at the Drury Lane, was Thomas Jefferson (1732?–1807). His son, the first Joseph Jefferson (1774–1832), sailed to America when he was twenty-one, and achieved fame on the New York stage. Among his seven children, all of whom became actors, was the second Joseph Jefferson (1804–1842). He did not inherit his father's considerable thespian talents (and he certainly lacked those of his son), although he had artistic talents and often did the scene painting in his theatre. He married an actress who was also an accomplished singer, Cornelia Frances Thomás (Charles Burke's mother by her first marriage), and they had four children; two of them survived infancy, the older being the third—and most famous—Joseph Jefferson.

In his *Autobiography* Jefferson tells about his early stage appearances—the first as the infant in the melodramatic rescue scene of Sheridan and Kotzebue's *Pizarro*, where, in a panic, he inadvertently scalped the Indian hero by pulling off the balding tragedian's wig; the second, at the age of four, when, carried onstage in a sack by T.D. Rice, he was emptied out at the end of the act to mimic the famous Jim Crow's dance and song:

> First on de heel tap, den on de toe,
> Ebery time I wheel about I jump Jim Crow.
> Wheel about and turn about and do jis so,
> And ebery time I wheel about I jump Jim Crow.

He first became successful in 1857 with 'his portrayals of Dr. Pangloss in George Colman's *The Heir at Law* and, the following year, Asa Trenchard in Tom Taylor's *Our American Cousin,* the play Lincoln was watching when he was assassinated. Later famous characterizations by Jefferson included Bob Acres in Richard Brinsley Sheridan's *The Rivals,* Caleb Plummer in Charles Dickens's *The Cricket on the Hearth,* and Salem Scudder in Boucicault's *The Octoroon.* He also lectured widely and with much acclaim on acting, drama, and the theatre. Performing for a total of more than seventy years, he reached the pinnacle of his profession when he succeeded Edwin Booth as President of the Players' Club in 1893. He retired in 1904, a year before his death on April 23, 1905.

The Autobiography of Joseph Jefferson (1890) was republished in 1949 as *Rip Van Winkle.* Biographies include William Winter's *Life and Art of Joseph Jefferson* (1894) and Montrose J. Moses's *Famous Actor-Families in America* (1906).

M.M.

RIP VAN WINKLE
as played by
Joseph Jefferson

Characters

RIP VAN WINKLE
DERRICK VON BEEKMAN, Village capitalist
NICHOLAS ("NICK") VEDDER, Innkeeper
HENDRICK, his son
COCKLES, Derrick's nephew
JACOB STEIN, Rip's drinking companion
SETH SLOUGH, Innkeeper

GRETCHEN, Rip's wife, later Derrick's wife
MEENIE, Rip's daughter
KÄTCHEN, Seth's wife

DEMONS AND VILLAGERS

ACT I

The village of Falling Waters, set amid familiar and un-mistakable Hudson River scenery, with the shining river itself and the noble heights of the Catskills visible in the distance. In the foreground, to the left of the stage, is a country inn bearing the sign of George III. *In the wall of the inn, a window closed by a solid wooden shutter. To the right of the stage, an old cottage with a door opening into the interior; before the cottage stands a bench holding a wash-tub, with a washboard, soap and clothes in the tub. In the center of the stage, a table and chairs, and on the table a stone pitcher and two tin cups.*

As the curtain rises, GRETCHEN *is discovered washing, and little* MEENIE *sitting nearby on a low stool. The sound of a chorus and laughter comes from the inn.*

GRETCHEN. Shouting and drinking day and night.

(*Laughter is heard from the inn.*)

Hark how they crow over their cups while their wives are working at home, and their children are starving.

(*Enter* DERRICK *from the inn with a green bag, followed by* NICK VEDDER. DERRICK *places his green bag on the table.*)

DERRICK. Not a day, not an hour. If the last two quarters' rent be not paid by this time tomorrow, out you go!

NICK. Oh, come, Derrick, you won't do it. Let us have a glass, and talk the matter over; good liquor opens the heart. Here, Hendrick! Hendrick!

(*Enter* HENDRICK.)

HENDRICK. Yes, Father.

DERRICK. So that is your brat?

NICK. Yes, that is my boy.

DERRICK. Then the best I can wish him is that he won't take after his father, and become a vagabond and a penniless outcast.

NICK. Those are hard words to hear in the presence of my child.

HENDRICK. Then why don't you knock him down, Father?

GRETCHEN. I'll tell you why—

DERRICK. Gretchen!

GRETCHEN. (*Wiping her arms and coming to front of tub.*) It is because your father is in that man's power. And what's the use of getting a man down, if you don't trample on him?

NICK. Oh, that is the way of the world.

GRETCHEN. (*To* HENDRICK.) Go in, boy. I want to speak to your father, and my words may not be fit for you to hear. Yonder is my little girl; go and play with her.

(HENDRICK *and* MEENIE *exeunt into the cottage.*)

GRETCHEN. Now, Derrick, Vedder is right; you won't turn him out of his house yonder.

DERRICK. And why not? Don't he owe me a year's rent?

GRETCHEN. And what do you owe him? Shall I sum up your accounts for you? Ten years ago, this was a quiet village, and belonged mostly to my husband, Rip Van Winkle, a foolish, idle fellow. That house yonder has since been his ruin. Yes; bit by bit, he has parted with all he had, to fill the mouths of sots and boon companions, gathered around him in yonder house. And you, Derrick—you supplied him with the money to waste in riot and drink. Acre by acre, you've sucked in his land to swell your store. Yonder miserable cabin is the only shelter we have left; but that is mine. Had it been his, he would have sold it you, Derrick, long ago, and wasted its price in riot.

(NICK, *who has been enjoying* DERRICK's *discomfiture during this speech, is unable to control himself, and at the end of the speech bursts into a loud laugh.*)

Aye, and you too, Nick Vedder; you have ruined my husband between you.

NICK. Oh, come, Mrs. Van Winkle, you're too hard. I couldn't refuse Rip's money in the way of business; I had my rent to pay.

GRETCHEN. And shall I tell you why you can't pay it? It is because you have given Rip credit, and he has ended by drinking you out of house and home. Your window-shutter is not wide enough to hold the score against him; it is full of chalk. Deny it if you can.

NICK. I do deny it. There now!

GRETCHEN. Then why do you keep that shutter closed? I'll show you why. (*Goes to inn, opens shutter, holds it open, pointing at* RIP's *score.*) That's why! Nick Vedder, you're a good man in the main, if there is such a thing.

(DERRICK *laughs.*)

Aye, and I doubt it. (*Turning on him.*) But you are the pest of this village; and the hand of every woman in it ought to help pull down that drunkard's nest of yours, stone by stone.

NICK. Come, Dame Van Winkle, you're too hard entire; now a man must have his odd time, and he's none the worse for being a jolly dog.

GRETCHEN. No, none the worse. He sings a good song; he tells a good story—oh, he's a glorious fellow! Did you ever see the wife of a jolly dog? Well, she lives in a kennel. Did you ever see the children of a jolly dog? They are the street curs, and their home is the gutter. (*Goes up to the washtub, and takes revenge on the clothing she scrubs.*)

NICK. (*Getting up and approaching* GRETCHEN *timidly.*) I tell you what it is, Dame Van Winkle. I don't know what your home may be, but judging from the rows I hear over there, and the damaged appearance of Rip's face after having escaped your clutches—

(GRETCHEN *looks up angrily;* NICK *retreats a few paces hastily.*)

—I should say that a gutter was a luxurious abode compared with it, and a kennel a peaceful retreat.

(*Exit hurriedly, laughing, to the inn.* GRETCHEN *looks up angrily, and throws the cloth she has been wringing after him, then resumes washing.* DERRICK *laughs at* NICK's *exit, walks up to* GRETCHEN, *and puts one foot on the bench.*)

DERRICK. Is it true, Gretchen? Are you truly miserable with Rip?

GRETCHEN. Ain't you pleased to hear it? Come then and warm your heart at my sorrow. Ten years ago I might have had you, Derrick. But I despised you for your miserly ways, and threw myself away on a vagabond.

DERRICK. You and I shared him between us. I took his estate, and you took his person. Now, I've improved my half. What have you done with yours?

GRETCHEN. I can't say that I have prospered with it. I've tried every means to reclaim him, but he is as obstinate and perverse as a Dutch pig. But the worst in him—and what I can't stand—is his good-humor. It drives me frantic when, night after night, he comes home drunk and helplessly good-humored! Oh, I can't stand that!

DERRICK. Where is he now?

GRETCHEN. We had a tiff yesterday, and he started. He has been out all night. Only wait until he comes back! The longer he stops out, the worse it will be for him.

DERRICK. Gretchen, you've made a great mistake, but there is time enough to repair it. You are comely still, thrifty, and that hard sort of grain that I most admire in woman. (*Looks cautiously around. Leans on tub.*) Why not start Rip for ever, and share my fortune?

GRETCHEN. Oh, no, Derrick; you've got my husband in your clutches, but you can't get them around me. If Rip would only mend his ways, he would see how much I love him; but no woman could love you, Derrick; for woman is not a domestic animal, glad to serve and fawn upon a man for the food and shelter she can get; and that is all she would ever get from you, Derrick. (*Piling the clothes on the washboard, and shouldering it.*)

DERRICK. The time may come when you'll change your tune.

GRETCHEN. Not while Rip lives, bad as he is. (*Exit into cottage.*)

DERRICK. Then I'll wait until you've killed him. Her spirit is not broken yet. But patience, Derrick, patience; in another month I'll have my claws on all that remains of Rip's property—yonder cottage and grounds; then I'll try you again my lady.

(*Enter* COCKLES, *with papers in his hand, running towards the inn.*)

How now, you imp? What brings you here so full of a hurry? Some mischief's in your head, or your heels would not be so busy.

COCKLES. I've brought a letter for you from my employer. There it is.

DERRICK. (*Examining letter.*) Why, the seal is broken!

COCKLES. Yes, I read it as I came along.

DERRICK. Now I apprenticed this vagabond to my lawyer, and this is his gratitude.

COCKLES. Don't waste your breath, Nunky,[1] for you'll want it; for when you read that, if it don't take you short in the wind, I'll admire you.

DERRICK. (*Reads.*) "You must obtain from Rip van Winkle a proper conveyance of the lands he has sold to you. The papers he has signed are in fact nothing but mortgages on his estate. If you foreclose, you must sell the property, which has lately much advanced in value; and it would sell for enough to pay off your loan, and all your improvements would enure to the benefit of Rip Van Winkle."

COCKLES. There, now, see what you've been doing—wasting your money and my expectations on another chap's property! Do you want to leave me a beggar?

DERRICK. (*Reads.*) "I enclose a deed for him to sign that will make him safe."

COCKLES. Of course he'll sign it; he won't wait to be asked—he'll be in such a hurry.

DERRICK. All my savings—all my money—sunk in improving this village!

COCKLES. Yes, instead of physicking[2] Rip, as you thought, you've been coddling him all the while.

DERRICK. All these houses I've built are on another man's land. What shall I do?

COCKLES. Pull them down again; pull them down.

DERRICK. Ass!—Dolt that I have been!

COCKLES. Calling yourself names won't mend it, Nunky.

DERRICK. The imp is right. Rip must be made to sign this paper. But how—how?

COCKLES. How? How? How's a big word sometimes, ain't it, Nunky?

DERRICK. Rip would not do it if he knew what he was about. But he can't read—nor write, for the matter of that. But he can make his cross, and I can cajole him.

COCKLES. Look sharp, Nunky. The man that's looking round for a fool and picks up Rip Van Winkle, will let him drop again very quick.

---

[1] Uncle.

[2] "Bleeding"; relieving someone of his money.

DERRICK. He is poor; I'll show him a handful of money. He's a drunkard; I'll give him a stomachful of liquor. Go in, boy, and leave me to work this; and let this be a lesson to you hereafter: beware of the fatal effects of poverty and drink.

COCKLES. Yes—and parting with my money on bad security. (*Exit. Laughter outside.*)

DERRICK. Here he comes now, surrounded by all the dogs and children in the district. They cling around him like flies around a lump of sugar.

(RIP *enters, running and skipping, carrying one small child pickaback, and surrounded by a swarm of others hanging on the skirts of his coat. He is laughing like a child himself, and his merry blue eyes twinkle with delight. He is dressed in an old deerskin coat, a pair of breeches which had once been red, now tattered, patched, and frayed, leather gaiters and shoes equally dilapidated, a shapeless felt hat with a bit of the brim hanging loose—the whole stained and weather-worn to an almost uniform clay-color, except for the bright blue of his jean shirt and the scarlet of his long wisp of a necktie. One of the boys carries his gun.*)

RIP. (*Taking his gun from the boy.*) There, run along mit you; run along.

DERRICK. (*The children scamper off.*) The vagabond looks like the father of the village.

RIP. (*Who has stood laughing and watching the children, suddenly calls after them.*) Hey! You let my dog Schneider alone there; you hear that, Sock der Jacob der bist eine for donner spits poo—yah—

DERRICK. Why, what's the matter, Rip?

RIP. (*Coming down and shaking hands with* DERRICK.) Oh, how you was, Derrick? How you was?

DERRICK. You seem in trouble.

RIP. Oh, yah; you know them fellers. Vell, I tole you such a funny thing. (*Laughing.*) Just now, as me and Schneider was comin' along through the willage—Schneider's my dawg; I don't know whether you know him? (RIP *always speaks of Schneider as if he were a person, and one in whom his hearer took as profound an interest as he does*

himself.) Well, them fellers went and tied a tin kettle mit
Scneider's tail, and how he did run then, mit the kettle
banging about. Well, I didn't hi him comin'. He run
betwixt me and my legs, an' spilt me an' all them children
in the mud;—yah, that's a fact.

(RIP *leans his gun against the cottage.*)

DERRICK. (*Aside.*) Now's my time. (*Aloud.*) Vedder! Vedder!
(NICK *appears at the door of the inn.*)
Bring us a bottle of liquor. Bring us your best, and be
quick.

NICK. What's in the wind now? The devil's to pay when
Derrick stands treat!
(*Exit. Re-enters, with bottle and cups in left hand. Hands
bottle to* DERRICK. RIP *lounges forward, and perches on the
corner of the table.*)

DERRICK. (*Rising and approaching* RIP.) Come, Rip, what
do you say to a glass?

RIP. (*Takes a cup and holds it to be filled.*) Oh, yah; now
what do I generally say to a glass? I say it's a fine thing—
when there's plenty in it. (Ve gates! Ve gates!) (*Shakes
hands with* NICK.) And then I says more to what's in it
than I do to the glass. Now you wouldn't believe it—that's
the first one I've had today.

DERRICK. How so?

RIP. (*Dryly.*) Because I couldn't get it before, I suppose.

DERRICK. Then let me fill him up for you.

RIP. No, that is enough for the first one.

NICK. Come, Rip, a bumper for the first one.

RIP. That is enough for the first one.

DERRICK. Come, Rip, let me fill him up for you.

RIP. (*With ludicrous decision and dignity.*) I believe I know
how much to drink. When I says a thing, I mean it.

DERRICK. Oh, well—(*Turns aside, and starts to fill his own
cup.*)

RIP. All right; come along. (*Holding out his glass, and laughing at his own inconsistency.*) Here's your good health and
your family's, and may they live long and prosper!
(*They all drink. At the end,* NICK *smacks his lips and
exclaims "Ah!"* DERRICK *repeats the same and* RIP *repeats
after* DERRICK.)
(*To* NICK, *sadly.*) Ah, you may well go "Ah!" and smack
your chops over that. You don't give me such schnapps

when I come. Derrick, my score is too big now. (*Jerking his head towards the shutter, he notices for the first time that it is open.*) What you go and open that window for? —That's fine schnapps, Nick. Where you got that?

NICK. That's high Dutch, Rip—high Dutch, and ten years in bottle. Why, I had that in the very day of your wedding. We broached the keg under yonder shed. Don't you recollect?

RIP. Is that the same?

NICK. Yes.

RIP. I thought I knowed that licker. You had it ten years ago? (*Laughing suddenly.*) I would not have kept it so long. But stop, mein freund; that's more than ten years ago.

NICK. No, it ain't.

RIP. It's the same day I got married?

NICK. Yes.

RIP. Well, I know by that. You think I forgot the day I got married? Oh, no, my friend; I remember that day long as I live. (*Serious for a moment. Takes off his hat, and puts it on the table.*)

DERRICK. Ah! Rip, I remember Gretchen then, ten years ago.—Zounds, how I envied you!

RIP. (*Looking up, surprised.*) Did you? (*Winks at* NICK. *Then, suddenly remembering.*) So did I. You didn't know what was comin', Derrick.

DERRICK. She was a beauty.

RIP. What, Gretchen?—Yes, she was. She was a pretty girl. My! My! Yah, we was a fine couple altogether. Well, come along.
(*Holding out his cup to* DERRICK, *who fills it from the bottle.*)

NICK. Yes, come along.
(*Takes water pitcher from the table, and starts to fill up* RIP's *cup.* RIP *stops him.*)

RIP. (*Who has been lounging against the table, sits on it, and puts his feet on the chair.*) Stop! I come along mitout that, Nick Vedder. (*Sententiously.*) Good licker and water is like man and wife.

DERRICK *and* NICK. How's that, Rip?

RIP. (*Laughing.*) They don't agree together. I always like my licker single. Well, here's your good health, and your family's, and may they live long and prosper!
(*They all drink.*)

NICK. That's right, Rip; drink away, and drown your sorrow.

RIP. (*Drolly.*) Yes; but she won't drown. My wife is my sorrow, and you cannick drown her. She tried it once, but couldn't do it.

DERRICK *and* NICK. Why, how so?

RIP. (*Puts down his cup and clasps his knee, still perched on the corner of the table.*) Didn't you know that Gretchen like to got drown?

DERRICK *and* NICK. No.

RIP. (*Puts hat on.*) That's the funniest thing of the whole of it. It's the same day I got married; she was comin' across the river there in the ferry-boat to get married mit me—

DERRICK *and* NICK. Yes.

RIP. Well, the boat she was comin' in got upsetted.

DERRICK *and* NICK. Ah!

RIP. Well, but she wasn't in it.

DERRICK *and* NICK. Oh!

RIP. (*Explaining quite seriously.*) No, that's what I say; if she had been in the boat what got upsetted, maybe she might have got drowned. (*More and more reflective.*) I don't know how it was she got left somehow or other. Women is always behind that way—always.

DERRICK. But surely, Rip, you would have risked your life to save such a glorious creature as she was.

RIP. (*Incredulously.*) You mean I would yump in and pull Gretchen out?

DERRICK. Yes.

RIP. Oh, would I? (*Suddenly remembering.*) Oh, you mean then—yes, I believe I would then. (*With simple conviction.*) But it would be more my duty now than it was then.

DERRICK. How so?

RIP. (*Quite seriously.*) Why, you see when a feller gets married a good many years mit his wife, he gets very much attached to her.

NICK. (*Pompously*). Ah, he does indeed.

RIP. (*Winks at* DERRICK, *and points at* NICK *with his thumb.*) But if Mrs. Van Winkle was a-drowning in the water now, an' she says to me, "Rip, come an' save your wife!" I would say, "Mrs. Van Winkle, I will yust go home and think about it." Oh, no, Derrick, if ever Gretchen tumbles in the water, she's got to swim now, you mind that.

DERRICK. She was here just now, anxiously expecting you home.

RIP. I know she's keeping it hot for me.

NICK. What, your dinner, Rip?

RIP. No, the broomstick.

(*Exit* NICK *into house, laughing.*)

(*Confidentially.*) Derrick, whenever I come back from the mountains, I always stick the game-bag in the window and creep in behind.

DERRICK. (*Seating himself on the table by the side of* RIP.) Have you anything now?

RIP. (*Dropping into the chair* DERRICK *has just left. Leaning back, and putting hands behind his head.*) What, for game? No, not a tail, I believe, not a feather. (*With humorous indifference.*)

DERRICK. (*Touching* RIP *on the shoulder and shaking a bag of money.*) Rip, suppose you were to hang this bagful of money inside, don't you think it would soothe her down, eh?

RIP. (*Sitting up.*) For me, is that?

DERRICK. Yes.

RIP. (*With a shrewd glance.*) Ain't you yokin' mit me?

DERRICK. No, Rip, I've prospered with the lands you've sold me, and I'll let you have a loan on easy terms. I'll take no interest.

RIP. (*Getting up and walking forward, with decision.*) No, I'm afraid I might pay you again some day, Derrick.

DERRICK. And so you shall, Rip, pay me when you please. (*Puts the bag in* RIP's *hands, and forces his fingers over it, turns, and goes to the table, speaking as he goes.*) Say in twenty years—twenty years from this day. Ah, where shall we be then?

RIP. (*Quizzically, and half to himself.*) I don't know about myself; but I think I can guess where you'll be about that time. (*Takes chair and sits down.*)

DERRICK. Well, Rip, I'll just step into the inn and draw out a little acknowledgement.

RIP. (*Who has been sitting, leaning forward with his elbows on his knees, softly chinking the bag of money in his hand, looks up suddenly.*) 'Knowledgment—for what is that?

DERRICK. Yes, for you to put your cross to.

RIP. (*Indifferently.*) All right; bring it along.

DERRICK. No fear of Gretchen now, eh, Rip?

RIP. (*Plunged in thought.*) Oh, no.

DERRICK. You feel quite comfortable now, don't you, Rip?
(*Exit to inn.*)

RIP. Oh, yah! (*Suddenly becoming serious and much mystified at* DERRICK's *conduct.*) Well, I don't know about that
Derrick! Derrick! (*Holding up the bag and chinking it.*)
It don't chink like good money neither. (*Grimly.*) It rattles
like a snake in a hole.

GRETCHEN. (*Inside the cottage.*) Out with that lazy, idle cur!
I won't have him here. Out, I say!

RIP. I'm glad I'm not in there now. I believe that's Schneider
what she's lickin'; he won't have any backbone left in him.
(*Sadly.*) I would rather she would lick me than the dog;
I'm more used to it than he is. (*Gets up, and looks in at
the window.*) There she is at the washtub. (*Admiring her
energy, almost envying it.*) What a hard-workin' woman
that is! Well, somebody must do it, I suppose. (*With the
air of a profound moral reflection.*) She's comin' here now;
she's got some broomstick mit her, too. (RIP *snatches up
his gun and slinks off around the corner of the house.*)

(*Enter* GRETCHEN *with broomstick, followed by* HENDRICK
and MEENIE, *carrying clothes-basket.*)

GRETCHEN. Come along, children. Now, you take the washing down to Dame Van Sloe's, then call at the butcher's
and tell him that my husband has not got back yet, so I
will have to go down myself to the marsh, and drive up
the bull we have sold to him. Tell him the beast shall be
in his stable in half an hour; so let him have the money
ready to pay me for it.

(*During this,* RIP *has crept in and sat on the bench by
the side of the tub behind* GRETCHEN.)

Ah, it is the last head of cattle we have left. Houses, lands,
beasts, everything gone—everything except a drunken
beast who nobody would buy or accept as a gift. Rip! Rip!
wait until I get you home!

(*Threatening an imaginary* RIP *with broomstick. With a
comical grimace,* RIP *tiptoes back behind the house.*)

Come, children, to work, to work! (*Exit.*)

(*Re-enter* RIP, *cautiously.*)

RIP. (*Laughing to himself.*) She gone to look after the bull.
She better not try the broomstick on him; he won't stand
it. (*Drops into the chair, with his back to the audience.*)

HENDRICK. Oh, Meenie, there's your father.

RIP. (*Holds out his arms, and* MEENIE *runs into them. Taking
her in his arms, and embracing her with great tenderness.*)
Ah, little gorl, was you glad to see your father come home?

MEENIE. Oh, yes!

RIP. (*Holding her close.*) I don't believe it, was you? Come
here. (*Getting up and leading her to the chair by the side
of the table.*) Let me look at you; I don't see you for such
a long time; come here. I don't deserve to have a thing
like that belong to me. (*Takes his hat off as if in rever-
ence.*) You're too good for a drunken, lazy feller like me,
that's a fact. (*Bites his underlip, looks up, and brushes
away a tear.*)

MEENIE. (*Kneeling by him.*) Oh, no, you are a good papa!

RIP. (*Makes this confession with a childlike simplicity. The
tears come, and he brushes them away once or twice.
When he asks for the cup, at the end, it seems but the
natural conclusion of his speech.*) No, I wasn't: no good
father would go and rob his child; that's what I've done.
Why, don't you know, Meenie, all the houses and lands in
the village was mine—they would all have been yours
when you grew up? Where they gone now? I gone drunk
'em up, that's where they gone. Hendrick, you just take
warnin' by that; that's what licker do; see that? (*Holds
up the skirt of coat.*) Bring a man to hunger and rags. Is
there any more in that cup over there? Give it to me.
(*Drinks.*)

HENDRICK. (*Hands him cup.*) Don't cry, Rip; Meenie does
not want your money, for when I'm a big man I shall work
for her, and she shall have all I get.

MEENIE. Yes, and I'll have Hendrick too.

RIP. (*Greatly amused.*) You'll have Hendrick, too. (*With
mock gravity.*) Well, is this all settled?

HENDRICK. Yes, Meenie and me have made it all up.

RIP. I didn't know, I only thought you might speak to me
about it, but if it's all settled, Meenie, then git married

mit him. (*Laughing silently, and suddenly.*) You goin' to marry my daughter? Well, now, that's very kind of you. Marry one another? (*The children nod.* RIP, *with immense seriousness.*) Well, here's your good health, and your family, may they live long and prosper. (*To* HENDRICK.) What you goin' to do when you get married, and grow up and so? (*Leans forward.*)

HENDRICK. I'm not going to stop here with Father; oh, no, that won't do. I'm going with Uncle Hans in his big ship to the North Pole, to catch whales.

RIP. Goin' to cotch wahales mit the North Pole? That's a long while away from here.

HENDRICK. Yes, but Uncle will give me ten shillings a month, and I will tell him to pay it all to Meenie.

RIP. There! He's goin' to pay it all to you; that's a good boy, that's a good boy.

MEENIE. Yes, and I'll give it all to you to keep for us.

RIP. (*With one of his little explosive laughs.*) I wouldn't do that, my darlin'; maybe if you give it to me, you don't get it back again. Hendrick! (*Suddenly earnest.*) You shall marry Meenie when you grow up, but you mustn't drink.

HENDRICK. (*Slapping* RIP *on the knee.*) I'll never touch a drop.

RIP. (*Quite seriously.*) You won't, nor me either; shake hands upon it. Now we swore off together. (*With a change of tone.*) I said so so many times, and never kept my word once, never. (*Drinks.*)

HENDRICK. I've said so once, and I'll keep mine.

DERRICK. (*Outside.*) Well, bring it along with you.

RIP. Here comes Derrick; he don't like some children; run along mit you.

(*Exit children with basket.*)

(*Enter* DERRICK *from inn with document.*)

DERRICK. There, Rip, is the little acknowledgement. (*Handing it to him.*)

RIP. 'Knowledgment. (*Putting on hat.*) For what is that?

DERRICK. That is to say I loaned you the money.

RIP. (*Lounging back in his chair.*) I don't want that; I would lose it if I had it. (*Fills his cup from the bottle. Blandly.*) I don't want it.

DERRICK. Don't you? But I do.

RIP. (*With simple surprise.*) For what?

DERRICK. Why, for you to put your cross to. Why, bless me, I've forgotten my pen and ink.

(*Enter* COCKLES.)

But luckily here comes my nephew with it. (*Aside.*) And in time to witness the signature.

RIP. Say, Derrick, have you been writing all that paper full in the little time you been in the house there? (*Turns the paper about curiously. Pours out more schnapps.*)

DERRICK. Yes, every word of it.

RIP. Have you? Well, just read it out loud to me. (*With an air of great simplicity.*)

DERRICK. (*Aside.*) Does he suspect? (*Aloud.*) Why, Rip, this is the first time you ever wanted anything more than the money.

RIP. (*Clasping his hands behind his head with an air of lordly indifference.*) Yes, I know; but I got nothing to do now. I'm a little curious about that, somehow.

COCKLES. (*Aside to* DERRICK.) The fish has taken the ground bait, but he's curious about the hook.

DERRICK. (*Aside.*) I dare not read a word of it.

COCKLES. (*Aside.*) Nunkey's stuck.

DERRICK. Well, Rip, I suppose you don't want to hear the formalities.

RIP. The what?

DERRICK. The preliminaries.

RIP. (*Indolently.*) I'll take it all—Bill, Claws, and Feathers. (*Leans forward and rests his head on his hand, and looks at the ground.*)

DERRICK. "Know all men by these presents, that I, Rip Van Winkle, in consideration of the sum of sixteen pounds received by me from Derrick Von Beekman"—(*Looks around at* COCKLES; *they wink knowingly at each other. Continues as if reading. Watching* RIP.)—"Do promise and undertake to pay the same in twenty years from date." (RIP *looks up; as he does so,* DERRICK *drops his eyes on document, then looks as if he had just finished reading.*) There, now are you satisfied?

RIP. (*Takes the document. In childlike surprise.*) Well, well, and does it take all that pen and ink to say such a little thing like that?

DERRICK. Why, of course it does.

COCKLES. (*Aside to* DERRICK.) Oh, the fool! he swallows it whole, hook and all.

RIP. (*Spreading the paper on the table.*) Where goes my cross, Derrick?

DERRICK. (*Pointing.*) There, you see I've left a nice little white corner for you.

RIP. (*Folds up paper in a leisurely manner and puts it in gamebag.*) W-e-l-l, I'll yust think about it. (*Looks up at* DERRICK *innocently.*)

DERRICK. Think about it? Why, what's the matter, Rip, isn't the money correct?

RIP. Oh, yes, I got the money all right. (*Chuckling.*) Oh! you mean about signing it. (*Rising. At a loss for a moment.*) Stop, yesterday was Friday, wasn't it?

DERRICK. So it was.

RIP. (*With an air of conviction.*) Well, I never do nothing like that the day after Friday, Derrick. (*Walks away towards his cottage.*)

DERRICK. (*Aside.*) The idiot! what can that signify? But I must not arouse his suspicions by pressing him. (*Aloud.*) You are right, Rip; sign it when you please; but I say, Rip, now that you're in funds, won't you help your old friend Nick Vedder, who owes me a year's rent?

RIP. (*Coming back to the table.*) Oh, yah, I will wipe off my schore, and stand treat to the whole willage.

DERRICK. Run, boy, and tell all the neighbors that Rip stands treat.

RIP. (*Leans on back of chair.*) An', Cockles, tell them we'll have a dance.

COCKLES. A dance! (*Runs off.*)

DERRICK. And I'll order the good cheer for you. (*Exit.*)

RIP. So do! So do! (*Cogitating dubiously.*) I don't understand it.

(*Re-enter* HENDRICK *with the basket over his head, followed by* MEENIE.)

Oh, you've come back?

HENDRICK. Yes, we've left the clothes.

RIP. Meenie, you take in the basket.

(*Exit* MEENIE *with the basket into the cottage.* HENDRICK *is following.*)

Hendrick, come here.

(HENDRICK *kneels between* RIP's *knees.*) So you are going to marry my daughter?

(HENDRICK *nods.*)

So, so. That's very kind of yer. (*Abruptly.*) Why you don't been to school today? You go to school some times, don't you?

HENDRICK. Yes, when father can spare me.

RIP. What do you learn mit that school,—pretty much something? (*Laughing at his mistake.*) I mean, everything?

HENDRICK. Yes; reading, writing and arithmetic.

RIP. Reading, and what?

HENDRICK. And writing, and arithmetic.

RIP. (*Puzzled.*) Writing and what?

HENDRICK. Arithmetic.

RIP. (*More puzzled.*) What meticks is that?

HENDRICK. Arithmetic.

RIP. (*With profound astonishment and patting* HENDRICK's *head.*) I don't see how the little mind can stand it all. Can you read?

HENDRICK. Oh, yes!

RIP. (*With a serious affectation of incredulity.*) I don't believe it; now, I'm just goin' to see if you can read. If you can't read, I won't let you marry my daughter. No, sir. (*Very drolly.*) I won't have nobody in my family what can't read. (*Taking out the paper that* DERRICK *has given him.*) Can you read ritmatics like that?

HENDRICK. Yes, that's writing.

RIP. (*Nonplussed.*) Oh! I thought it was reading.

HENDRICK. It's reading and writing, too.

RIP. What, both together. (*Suspiciously looking at the paper.*) Oh, yes; I didn't see that before; go long with it.

HENDRICK. (*Reads.*) "Know all men by these presents"—

RIP. (*Pleased, leaning back in his chair.*) Yah! that's right, what a wonderful thing der readin' is; why you can read it pretty nigh as good as Derrick, yes you do; go long.

HENDRICK. "That I, Rip Van Winkle"—

RIP. (*Taking off his hat, and holding it with his hands behind his head.*) Yah, that's right; you read it yust as well as Derrick; go long.

HENDRICK. "In consideration of the sum of sixteen pounds received do hereby sell and convey to Derrick Von Beekman all my estate, houses, lands whatsoever"—
(*Hat drops.*)

RIP. (*Almost fiercely.*) What are you readin', some ritmatics what ain't down there: where you got that? (*Looking sharply at* HENDRICK.)

HENDRICK. (*Pointing.*) There. "Houses, lands, whatsoever."

RIP. (*Looking not at the paper but at* HENDRICK *very earnestly, as if turning over in his mind whether the boy has read it correctly. Then satisfied of the deception* DERRICK *has practiced upon him and struck by the humor of the way in which he has discovered it, he laughs exultantly and looks towards the inn-door through which* DERRICK *disappeared a short time before.*) Yes, so it is. Go long mit the rest. (*He leans forward, and puts his ear close to* HENDRICK, *so as not to miss a word.*)

HENDRICK. "Whereof he now holds possession by mortgaged deeds, from time to time executed by me."

RIP. (*Takes paper, and looks towards the inn fiercely exultant.*) You read it better than Derrick, my boy, much better. (*After a moment's pause, recollects himself. Kindly to* HENDRICK.) That will do, run along mit you.
(*Exit* HENDRICK.)

RIP. Aha, my friend, Derrick! I guess you got some snakes in the grass. Now keep sober, Rip; I don't touch another drop so long what I live; I swore off now, that's a fixed fact.

(*Enter* DERRICK, NICK, STEIN, *and villagers.*)

DERRICK. Come, Rip, we'll have a rouse.

RIP. (*Seriously; half fiercely still.*) Here, Nick Vedder, here is the gelt; wipe off my score, and drink away. I don't join you; I swore off.

NICK. Why, Rip, you're king of the feast.

RIP. (*Absently, still intent on* DERRICK.) Am I dat?

OMNES. Swore off? What for?

RIP. I don't touch another drop.

JACOB STEIN. (*Coming down towards* RIP *with cup.*) Come, Rip, take a glass.

RIP. (*Turning on him, almost angry.*) Jacob Stein, you hear what I said?

STEIN. Yes.

RIP. (*Firmly.*) Well, when I said a thing, I mean it. (*Leans back in his chair with his hands behind his head.*)

STEIN. Oh, very well.

(*Turns away;* NICK *comes down and holds cup under* RIP's *nose.* RIP *looks to see if they are watching him. He can resist no longer, and takes the cup.*)

RIP. (*Laughing.*) Well, I won't count this one. Here's your good health and your family's, may they all live long and prosper.

DERRICK. Here come the fiddlers and the girls.

(*Enter girls.* RIP *walks over and closes the shutter which has held his score, then returns and seats himself on a low stool, and keeps time to the music as the villagers dance. Finally, the rhythm fires his blood. He jumps to his feet, snatches one of the girls away from her partner, and whirls into the dance. After a round or two, he lets go of her, and pirouettes two or three times by himself. Once more he catches her in his arms, and is in the act of embracing her, when he perceives* GRETCHEN *over her shoulder. He drops the girl, who falls on her knees at* GRETCHEN's *feet. There is a general laugh at his discomfiture, in which he joins half-heartedly. As the curtain descends,* RIP *is seen pointing at the girl as if seeking, like a modern Adam, to put the blame on her.*)

ACT II

The dimly lighted kitchen of RIP's *cottage. The door and window are at the back. It is night, and through the window a furious storm can be seen raging, with thunder, lightning, and rain. A fire smoulders on the hearth, to the right, and a candle gutters on the table in the center; a couple of chairs, a low stool, and a little cupboard, meagerly provided with cups and plates, complete the furniture of the room. Between the door and the window a clothes-horse, with a few garments hanging on it, forms a screen. To the left is a small door leading to the other rooms of the cottage.*

As the curtain rises, MEENIE *is seen sitting by the window, and* GRETCHEN *enters, takes off cloak, and throws a broomstick on the table.*

GRETCHEN. Meenie! Has your father come yet?

MEENIE. No, Mother.

GRETCHEN. So much the better for him. Never let him show his face in these doors again—never!

MEENIE. Oh, Mother, don't be so hard on him.

GRETCHEN. I'm not hard; how dare you say so?

(MEENIE *approaches her.*)

There, child, that father of yours is enough to spoil the temper of an angel. I went down to the marsh to drive up the bull. I don't know what Rip has been doing to the beast; he was howling and tearing about. I barely escaped with my life.

(*A crash outside.*)

What noise is that?

MEENIE. That's only Schneider, father's dog.

GRETCHEN. (*Picking up broomstick.*) Then I'll Schneider him. I won't have him here. (*Exit through the door leading to the rest of the cottage.*) Out, you idle, vagabond cur; out, I say!

MEENIE. (*Following her to the door, and crying.*) Oh, don't, don't hurt the poor thing!

(*Re-enter* GRETCHEN.)

GRETCHEN. He jumped out of the window before I could catch him. He's just like his master. Now, what are you crying for?

MEENIE. Because my poor father is out in all this rain.

(*A peal of thunder is heard.*)

Hark, how it thunders!

GRETCHEN. Serve him right—do him good. Is the supper ready?

MEENIE. Yes, Mother; it is there by the fireside. (*Pointing to the soup-bowl by the fire.*) Shall I lay the table?

GRETCHEN. Yes.

(*Again it thunders.*)

It's a dreadful night; I wonder where Rip is?

MEENIE. (*Bringing the cups and platters from the sideboard, together with a loaf of bread.*) Shall I lay the table for two, Mother, or for three?

GRETCHEN. For two, girl; he gets no supper here tonight.

(*Another peal of thunder.*)

Mercy, how the storm rages! the fool, to stop out in such a downpour. I hope he's found shelter. I must take out the old suit I washed and mended for him last week, and put them by the fire to air. The idiot, to stop out in such a downpour! I'll have him sick on my hands next; that's all I want to complete my misery. (*She fetches clothes from the horse and hangs them on the back of the chair in front of the fire.*) He knows what I am suffering now, and that's what keeps him out. (*Lightning.*) Mercy, what a flash that was! The wretch will be starved with the cold! Meenie!

MEENIE. Yes, mother.

GRETCHEN. You may lay the table for three.

(*There is a knock at the outer door.*)

There he is now!

(*Enter* HENDRICK, *who shakes rain from his hat.*)

Where's Rip? Is he not at your father's?

HENDRICK. No; I thought he was here.

GRETCHEN. He's gone back to the mountain. He's done it on purpose to spite me.

HENDRICK. (*Going to the fire.*) Shall I run after him, and bring him home? I know the road. We've often climbed it together.

GRETCHEN. No; I drove Rip from his house, and it's for me to bring him back again.

MEENIE. (*Still arranging the supper table.*) But, Mother— (*She pauses, with embarrassment.*) If he hears your voice behind him, he will only run away the faster.

GRETCHEN. Well, I can't help it; I can't rest under cover, while he is out in the storm. I shall feel better when I'm outside sharing the storm with him. Sit down, and take your suppers. I'll take my cloak along with me.

(*Exit.* MEENIE *has seated herself by the window.* HENDRICK *carries stool to the center of the stage, in front of the table.*)

HENDRICK. Meenie! Meenie!

MEENIE. Eh?

(HENDRICK *beckons to her. She runs to him. He stops her*
suddenly, then puts the stool down with great deliberation,
and sits on it, while MEENIE *kneels beside him.*)

HENDRICK. (*In a very solemn tone.*) I hope your father ain't
gone to the mountains tonight, Meenie!

MEENIE. (*In distress.*) Oh, dear! He will die of the cold there.

HENDRICK. (*Suddenly.*) Sh! (MEENIE *starts.*) It ain't for that.
(*Mysteriously.*) I've just heard old Clausen, over at
father's, saying, that on this very night, every twenty years,
the ghosts—

MEENIE. (*Catching his wrist.*) The what?

HENDRICK. (*In an awed tone.*) The ghosts of Hendrick Hudson, and his pirate crew, visit the Catskills above here.

(*The two children look around, frightened.*)

MEENIE. Oh, dear! Did he say so?

HENDRICK. Sh! (*Again they look around, frightened.*) Yes;
and the spirits have been seen there smoking, drinking,
and playing at tenpins.

MEENIE. Oh, how dreadful!

HENDRICK. Sh!

(*He goes cautiously to the chimney, and looks up, while*
MEENIE *looks under the table; then he returns to the stool,*
speaking as he comes.)

Yes; and every time that Hendrick Hudson lights his pipe
there's a flash of lightning.

(*Lightning and* MEENIE *gives a gasp of fear.*)

And when he rolls the balls along, there is a peal of
thunder.

(*Loud rumbles of thunder.* MEENIE *screams and throws*
herself into HENDRICK's *arms.*)

Don't be frightened, Meenie; I'm here. (*In a frightened*
tone, but with a manly effort to be courageous.)

(*Re-enter* GRETCHEN *with her cloak.*)

GRETCHEN. Here, stop that!

(*The children separate quickly.* HENDRICK *looks up at the*
ceiling and whistles, with an attempt at unconsciousness,
and MEENIE *assumes an innocent and unconcerned expres-*
sion.)

Now, don't you be filling that child's head with nonsense, but remain quietly here until I return. Hush, what noise is that? There is someone outside the window.

(*She steps behind the clothes-horse.* RIP *appears at the window, which he opens, and leans against the frame.*)

RIP. Meenie!

MEENIE *and* HENDRICK. (*Trying to make him perceive* GRETCHEN, *by a gesture in her direction.*) Sh!

(RIP *turns, and looks around outside to see what they mean, then, discovering nothing, drops his hat in at the window, and calls again, cautiously.*)

RIP. Meenie!

MEENIE *and* HENDRICK. (*With the same warning gesture.*) Sh!

(GRETCHEN *shakes her fist at the children, who assume an air of innocence.*)

RIP. What's the matter? Meenie, has the wildcat come home? (RIP *reaches in after his hat.* GRETCHEN *catches him by his hair, and holds his head down.*) Och, my darlin', don't do that, eh!

HENDRICK *and* MEENIE. (*Who run towards* GRETCHEN.) Don't, Mother! Don't, Mother! Don't!

RIP. (*Imitating their tone.*) Don't, Mother, don't! Don't you hear the children? (*Getting angry.*) Let go my head, won't you?

GRETCHEN. No; not a hair.

RIP. (*Bantering.*) Hold on to it then, what do I care?

HENDRICK *and* MEENIE. (*Catching* GRETCHEN's *dress.*) Don't, Mother! Don't, Mother! Don't!

(GRETCHEN *lets go of* RIP, *and turns upon them. They escape, and disappear through the door to the left.*)

RIP. (*Getting in through the window, and coming forward, apparently drunk, but jolly; and his resentment for the treatment he has just received is half humorous.*) For what you do dat, hey? You must want a bald-headed husband, I reckon!

(GRETCHEN *picks up chair, and bangs it down;* RIP *imitates her with the stool. She sits down angrily, and slaps the table.* RIP *throws down his felt hat with a great show of violence, and it makes no noise; then seats himself on the stool.*)

GRETCHEN. Now, then!

RIP. Now, den; I don't like it den, neider_ (*When* RIP *is drunk, his dialect grows more pronounced.*)

GRETCHEN. Who did you call a wildcat?

RIP. (*With a sudden little tipsy laugh, and confused.*) A wildcat—dat's when I come in at the window?

GRETCHEN. Yes; that's when you came in the window.

RIP. (*Rising, and with a tone of finality.*) Yes; that's the time I said it.

GRETCHEN. Yes; and that's the time I heard it.

RIP. (*With drunken assurance.*) That's all right; I was afraid you wouldn't hear it.

GRETCHEN. Now who did you mean by that wildcat?

RIP. (*Confused.*) Who did I mean? Now, let me see.

GRETCHEN. Yes; who did you mean?

RIP. How do I know who-oo I mean? (*With a sudden inspiration.*) Maybe it's the dog Schneider, I call that.

GRETCHEN. (*Incredulously.*) The dog Schneider; that's not likely.

RIP. (*Argumentatively.*) Of course it is likely; he's my dog. I'll call him a wildcat much as I please. (*Conclusively. He sits down in the chair on which his clothes are warming, in front of the fire.*)

GRETCHEN. And then, there's your disgraceful conduct this morning. What have you got to say to that?

RIP. How do I know what I got to say to that, when I don't know what I do-a, do-a? (*Hiccoughs.*)

GRETCHEN. Don't know what you do-a-oo! Hugging and kissing the girls before my face; you thought I wouldn't see you.

RIP. (*Boldly.*) I knowed you would—I knowed you would; because, because—(*Losing the thread of his discourse.*) Oh-h, don' you bodder me. (*He turns and leans his head against the back of the chair.*)

GRETCHEN. You knew I was there?

RIP. (*Laughing.*) I thought I saw you.

GRETCHEN. I saw you myself, dancing with the girl.

RIP. You saw the girl dancin' mit me.

(GRETCHEN *remembers* RIP's *clothes, and goes over to see if he is wet, and pushes him towards the center of the stage.* RIP *mistakes her intention.*)

You want to pull some more hair out of my head?

GRETCHEN. Why, the monster! He isn't wet a bit! He's as dry as if he'd been aired!

RIP. Of course I'm dry. (*Laughing.*) I'm always dry—always dry.

GRETCHEN. (*Examines game-bag, and pulls out a flask, which she holds under* RIP's *nose.*) Why, what's here? Why, it's a bottle—a bottle!

RIP. (*Leaning against the table.*) Yes; it's a bottle. (*Laughs.*) You think I don't know a bottle when I see it?

GRETCHEN. That's pretty game for your game-bag, ain't it?

RIP. (*Assuming an innocent air.*) Somebody must have put it there.

GRETCHEN. (*Putting the flask in her pocket.*) Then, you don't get it again.

RIP. (*With a show of anger.*) Now mind, If I don't get it again—well—all there is about it—(*Breaking down.*) I don't want it. I have had enough. (*With a droll air of conviction.*)

GRETCHEN. I'm glad you know when you've had enough.

RIP. (*Still leaning against the table.*) That's the way mit me. I'm glad I know when I got enough—(*Laughs.*) An' I'm glad when I've got enough, too. Give me the bottle; I want to put it in the game-bag.

GRETCHEN. For what?

RIP. (*Lounging off the table, and coming forward and leaning his arms on* GRETCHEN's *shoulders.*) So that I can't drink it. Here's the whole business—(*He slides his hand down to* GRETCHEN's *pocket and tries to find the bottle while he talks to her.*) Here's the whole business about it. What is the use of anybody—well—wash the use of anybody, any-how—well—oh(*Missing the pocket.*) What you talkin' 'bout. (*Suddenly his hand slips in her pocket, and he begins to pull the bottle out, with great satisfaction.*) Now, now I can tell you all 'bout it.

GRETCHEN. (*Discovering his tactics, and pushing him away.*) Pshaw!

RIP. If you don't give me the bottle, I just break up every-thing in the house.

GRETCHEN. If you dare!

RIP. If I dare! Haven't I done it two or three times before? I just throw everything right out of the window.

(RIP *throws the plates and cups on the floor and overturns a chair, and seats himself on the table.* GRETCHEN *picks them up again.*)

GRETCHEN. Don't Rip; don't do that! Now stop, Rip, stop! (GRETCHEN *bangs down a chair by the table and seats herself.*) Now, then, perhaps you will be kind enough to tell where you've been for the last two days. Where have you been? Do you hear?

RIP. Where I've been? Well, it's not my bottle, anyhow. I borrowed that bottle from another feller. You want to know where I been?

GRETCHEN. Yes; and I will know.

RIP. (*Good-humoredly.*) Let's see. Last night I stopped out all night.

GRETCHEN. But why?

RIP. Why? You mean the reason of it?

GRETCHEN. Yes, the reason.

RIP. (*Inconsequently.*) The reason is why. Don't bother me.

GRETCHEN. (*Emphasizing each word with a bang on the table.*) Why—did—you—stop—out—all—night?

RIP. (*Imitating her tone.*) Because—I—want—to—get—up—early—in—the—morning. (*Hiccough.*) Come don't get so mad mit a feller. Why, I've been fillin' my game-bag mit game.

(*Rip gets down off the table, and* GRETCHEN *comes towards him and feels his game-bag.*)

GRETCHEN. Your game-bag is full of game, isn't it?

RIP. (*Taking her hand and holding it away from her pocket.*) That? Why, that wouldn't hold it. (*Finding his way into* GRETCHEN's *pocket.*) Now I can tell you all about it. You know last night I stopped out all night—

GRETCHEN. Yes; and let me catch you again.

(*He is pulling the bottle out, when* GRETCHEN *catches him, and slaps his hand.*)

You paltry thief!

RIP. Oh, you ain't got no confidence in me. Now what do you think was the first thing I saw in the morning? (*Dragging a chair to the front of the stage.*)

GRETCHEN. I don't know. What?

RIP. (*Seating himself.*) A rabbit.

GRETCHEN. (*Pleased.*) I like a rabbit. I like it in a stew.

RIP. (*Looking at her, amused.*) I guess you like everything in a stew—everything what's a rabbit I mean. Well, there was a rabbit a-feedin' mit the grass; you know they always come out early in der mornin' and feed mit the grass?

GRETCHEN. Never mind the grass. Go on.

RIP. Don't get so patient; you wait till you get the rabbit. (*Humorously.*) Well, I crawl up—

GRETCHEN. Yes, yes!

RIP. (*Becoming interested in his own powers of invention.*) An' his little tail was a-stickin' up so—(*With a gesture of his forefinger.*)

GRETCHEN. (*Impatiently.*) Never mind his tail. Go on.

RIP. (*Remonstrating at her interruption.*) The more fatter the rabbit, the more whiter is his tail—

GRETCHEN. Well, well, go on.

RIP. (*Taking aim.*) Well, I haul up—

GRETCHEN. Yes, yes!

RIP. And his ears was a-stickin' up so—(*Making the two ears with his two forefingers.*)

GRETCHEN. Never mind his ears. Go on.

RIP. I pull the trigger.

GRETCHEN. (*Eagerly.*) Bang went the gun, and—

RIP. (*Seriously.*) And the rabbit run away.

GRETCHEN. (*Angrily.*) And so you shot nothing?

RIP. How will I shot him when he run away? (*He laughs at her disappointment.*) There, don't get so mad mit a feller. Now I'm going to tell you what I did shot; that's what I didn't shot. You know that old forty-acre field of ours?

GRETCHEN. (*Scornfully.*) Ours! Ours, did you say?

RIP. (*Shamefacedly.*) You know the one I mean well enough. It used to be ours.

GRETCHEN. (*Regretfully.*) Yes; it used, indeed!

RIP. It ain't ours now, is it?

GRETCHEN. (*Sighing.*) No, indeed, it is not.

RIP. No? Den I won't bodder about it. Better let somebody bodder about that field what belongs to it. Well, in that field there's a pond; and what do you think I see in that pond?

GRETCHEN. I don't know. Ducks?

RIP. Ducks! More an' a thousand.

GRETCHEN. (*Walking to where broomstick is.*) More than a thousand ducks?

RIP. I haul up again—

GRETCHEN. (*Picking up broomstick.*) Yes, and so will I. And if you miss fire this time—(*She holds it threateningly over* RIP's *shoulder.*)

RIP. (*Looking at it askance out of the corner of his eye, then putting up his hand and pushing it aside.*) You will scare the ducks mit that. Well, I take better aim this time as I did before. I pull the trigger, and—bang!

GRETCHEN. How many down?

RIP. (*Indifferently.*) One.

GRETCHEN. (*Indignantly.*) What! only one duck out of a thousand?

RIP. Who said one duck?

GRETCHEN. You did!

RIP. (*Getting up and leaning on the back of the chair.*) I didn't say anything of the kind.

GRETCHEN. You said "one."

RIP. Ah! *One*. But I shot more as one duck.

GRETCHEN. Did you?

RIP. (*Crosses over, and sits on the low stool, laughing silently.*) I shot our old bull.

(GRETCHEN *flings down the broomstick, and throws herself into the chair at the right of the table, in dumb rage.*)

I didn't kill him. I just sting him, you know. Well, then the bull come right after me; and I come right away from him. O, Gretchen, how you would laugh if you could see that— (*With a vain appeal to her sense of humor.*) the bull was a-comin', and I was a-goin'. Well, he chased me across the field. I tried to climb over the fence so fast what I could,—(*Doubles up with his silent laugh.*) an' the bull come up an' save me the trouble of that. Well, then, I rolled over on the other side.

GRETCHEN. (*With disgust.*) And then you went fast asleep for the rest of the day.

RIP. That's a fact. That's a fact.

GRETCHEN. (*Bursting into tears, and burying her head in her arms on the table.*) O, Rip, you'll break my heart! You will.

RIP. Now she's gone crying mit herself! Don't cry, Gretchen, don't cry. My d-a-r-l-i-n', don't cry.

GRETCHEN. (*Angrily.*) I will cry.

RIP. Cry 'way as much as you like. What do I care? All the better soon as a woman gets cryin'; den all the danger's over. (RIP *goes to* GRETCHEN, *leans over, and puts his arm around her.*) Gretchen, don't cry; my angel, don't. (*He succeeds in getting his hand into her pocket, and steals the bottle.*) Don't cry, my daarlin'. (*Humorously.*)

Gretchen won't you give me a little drop out of that bottle what you took away from me? (*He sits on the table, just behind her, and takes a drink from the bottle.*)

GRETCHEN. Here's a man drunk, and asking for more.

RIP. I wasn't. I swore off. (*Coaxingly.*) You give me a little drop an' I won't count it.

GRETCHEN. (*Sharply.*) No!

RIP. (*Drinking again.*) Well, den, here's your good health, an' your family's, and may they live long and prosper! (*Puts bottle in his bag.*)

GRETCHEN. You unfeeling brute. Your wife's starving. And, Rip, your child's in rags.

RIP. (*Holding up his coat, and heaving a sigh of resignation.*) Well, I'm the same way; you know dat.

GRETCHEN. (*Sitting up, and looking appealingly at* RIP.) Oh, Rip, if you would only treat me kindly!

RIP. (*Putting his arms around her.*) Well, den, I will. I'm going to treat you kind. I'll treat you kind.

GRETCHEN. Why, it would add ten years to my life.

RIP. (*Over her shoulder, and after a pause.*) That's a great inducement; it is, my darlin'. I know I treat you too bad, an' you deserve to be a widow.

GRETCHEN. (*Getting up, and putting her arms on* RIP's *shoulder.*) Oh, Rip, if you would only reform!

RIP. Well, den, I will. I won't touch another drop so long as I live.

GRETCHEN. Can I trust you?

RIP. You mustn't suspect me.

GRETCHEN. (*Embracing him.*) There, then, I will trust you. (*She takes the candle and goes to fetch the children.*) Here, Hendrick, Meenie? Children, where are you? (*Exit through the door on the left.*)

RIP. (*Seats himself in the chair to the right of the table, and takes out flask.*) Well, it's too bad; but it's all a woman's fault anyway. When a man gets drinkin' and that, they ought to let him alone. So soon as they scold him, he goes off like a sky-rocket.

(*Re-enter* GRETCHEN *and the children.*)

GRETCHEN. (*Seeing the flask in* RIP's *hand.*) I thought as much.

RIP. (*Unconscious of her presence.*) How I did smooth her
down! I must drink her good health. Gretchen, here's your
good health. (*About to drink.*)

GRETCHEN. (*Snatching the bottle, and using it to gesticulate
with.*) Oh, you paltry thief!

RIP. (*Concerned for the schnapps.*) What you doin'? You'll
spill the licker out of the bottle. (*He puts in the cork.*)

GRETCHEN. (*Examining the flask.*) Why, the monster, he's
emptied the bottle!

RIP. That's a fac'. That's a fac'.

GRETCHEN. (*Throwing down the flask.*) Then that is the last
drop you drink under my roof!

RIP. What! What!

(MEENIE *approaches her father on tiptoe, and kneels beside him.*)

GRETCHEN. Out, you drunkard! Out, you sot! You disgrace
to your wife and to your child! This house is mine.

RIP. (*Dazed, and a little sobered.*) Yours! Yours!

GRETCHEN. (*Raising her voice above the storm, which seems
to rage more fiercely outside.*) Yes, mine, mine! Had it
been yours to sell, it would have gone along with the rest
of your land. Out then, I say— (*Pushing open the door.*)
for you have no longer any share in me or mine.
(*A peal of thunder.*)

MEENIE. (*Running over, and kneeling by* GRETCHEN.) Oh,
mother, hark at the storm!

GRETCHEN. (*Pushing her aside.*) Begone, man, can't you
speak? Are you struck dumb? You sleep no more under my
roof.

RIP. (*Who has not moved, even his arm remaining out-
stretched, as it was when* MEENIE *slipped from his side,
murmurs in a bewildered, incredulous way.*) Why,
Gretchen, are you goin' to turn me out like a dog?
(GRETCHEN *points to the door.* RIP *rises and leans against
the table with a groan. His conscience speaks.*) Well,
maybe you are right. (*His voice breaks, and with a despair-
ing gesture.*) I have got no home. I will go. But mind,
Gretchen, after what you say to me tonight, I can never
darken your door again—never— (*Going towards the door.*)
I will go.

HENDRICK. (*Running up to* RIP.) Not into the storm, Rip.
Hark, how it thunders!

RIP. (*Putting his arm around him.*) Yah, my boy; but not as bad to me as the storm in my home. I will go. (*At the door by this time.*)

MEENIE. (*Catching* RIP's *coat.*) No, Father, don't go!

RIP. (*Bending over her tenderly, and holding her close to him.*) My child! Bless you, my child, bless you!

(MEENIE *faints.* RIP *gives a sobbing sigh.*)

GRETCHEN. (*Relenting.*) No, Rip—I—

RIP. (*Waving her off.*) No, you have drive me from your house. You have opened the door for me to go. You may never open it for me to come back. (*Leaning against the doorpost, overcome by his emotion. His eyes rest on* MEENIE, *who lies at his feet.*) You say I have no share in this house. (*Points to* MEENIE *in profound despair.*) Well, see, then, I wipe the disgrace from your door. (*He staggers out into the storm.*)

GRETCHEN. No, Rip! Husband, come back! (GRETCHEN *faints, and the curtain falls.*)

ACT III

A steep and rocky clove in the Catskill Mountains, down which rushes a torrent, swollen by the storm. Overhead, the hemlocks stretch their melancholy boughs. It is night.

RIP *enters, almost at a run, with his head down, and his coat-collar turned up, beating his way against the storm. With the hunter's instinct, he protects the priming of his gun with the skirt of his jacket. Having reached a comparatively level spot, he pauses for breath, and turns to see what has become of his dog.*

RIP. (*Whistling to the dog.*) Schneider! Schneider! What's the matter with Schneider? Something must have scared that dog. There he goes head over heels down the hill. Well, here I am again—another night in the mountains! Heigho! these old trees begin to know me, I reckon. (*Taking off his hat.*) How are you, old fellows? Well, I like the trees; they keep me from the wind and the rain, and they never blow me up; and when I lay me down on the broad of my back, they seem to bow their heads to me, an' say: "Go to sleep, Rip, go to sleep." (*Lightning.*) My, what a flash that was! Old Hendrick Hudson's lighting his pipe in the mountains tonight; now, we'll hear him roll the big balls along. (*Thunder.* RIP *looks back over the path he has come and whistles again for his dog.*) Well, I—no—Schneider! No; whatever it is, it's on two legs. Why, what a funny thing is that a comin' up the hill? I thought nobody but me ever come nigh this place.

(*Enter a strange dwarfish figure, clad all in gray like a Dutch seaman of the seventeenth century, in short-skirted doublet, hose and high-crowned hat drawn over his eyes. From beneath the latter his long gray beard streams down till it almost touches the ground. He carries a keg on his shoulder. He advances slowly towards* RIP, *and, by his gesture, begs* RIP *to set the keg down for him.* RIP *does so, and the dwarf seats himself upon it.*)

(*With good-humored sarcasm.*) Sit down, and make yourself comfortable. (*A long pause and silence.*) What? What's the matter? Ain't ye goin' to speak to a feller? I don't want to speak to you, then. Who you think you was, that I want to speak to you, any more than you want to speak to me; you hear what I say?
(RIP *pokes the dwarf in the ribs, who turns, and looks up.* RIP *retreats hastily.*)
Donner an' Blitzen! What for a man is das? I have been walking over these mountains ever since I was a boy, an' I never saw a queer looking codger like that before. He must be an old sea-snake, I reckon.
(*The dwarf approaches* RIP, *and motions* RIP *to help him up the mountain with the keg.*)
Well, why don't you say so, den? You mean you would like me to help you up with that keg?
(*The dwarf nods in the affirmative.*)
Well, sir, I don't do it.
(*The dwarf holds up his hands in supplication.*)
No, there's no good you speakin' like that. I never seed you before, did I?
(*The dwarf shakes his head,* RIP, *with great decision, walking away, and leaning against a tree.*)

I don't want to see you again, needer. What have you got
in that keg, schnapps?

(*The dwarf nods.*)

I don't believe you.

(*The dwarf nods more affirmatively.*)

Is it good schnapps?

(*The dwarf again insists.*)

Well, I'll help you. Go 'long; pick up my gun, there, and
I follow you mit that keg on my shoulder. I'll follow you,
old broadchops.

(*As* RIP *shoulders the keg, a furious blast whirls up the
valley, and seems to carry him and his demon companion
before it. The rain that follows blots out the landscape.
For a few moments, all is darkness. Gradually, the topmost
peak of the Catskill Mountains becomes visible, far above
the storm. Stretching below, the country lies spread out
like a map. A feeble and watery moonlight shows us a
weird group, gathered upon the peak—Hendrick Hudson,
and his ghostly crew. In the foreground, one of them poises
a ball, about to bowl it, while the others lean forward in
attitudes of watchful expectancy. Silently he pitches it;
and, after a momentary pause, a long and rumbling peal
of thunder reverberates among the valleys below. At this
moment, the demon, carrying* RIP's *gun, appears over the
crest of the peak in the background, and* RIP *toils after
with the keg on his shoulder. Arrived at the summit, he
drops the keg on his knee, and gasps for breath.*)

(*Glancing out over the landscape.*) I say, old gentleman,
I never was so high up in the mountains before. Look
down into the valley there; it seems more as a mile. I—
(*Turning to speak to his companion, and perceiving another of the crew.*) You're another feller!

(*The second demon nods assent.*)

You're that other chap's brother?

(*The demon again assents.* RIP *carries the keg a little
further, and comes face to face with a third.*)

You're another brother?

(*The third demon nods assent.* RIP *takes another step, and
perceives* HENDRICK HUDSON *in the center, surrounded by
many demons.*)

You're his old gran'father?

(HUDSON *nods.* RIP *puts down the keg in perplexity, not
untinged with alarm.*)

Donner and Blitzen! here's the whole family; I'm a dead man to a certainty.

(*The demons extend their arms to* HUDSON, *as if inquiring what they should do. He points to* RIP, *they do the same.*) My, my, I suppose they're speakin' about me! (*Looking at his gun, which the first demon has deposited on the ground, and which lies within his reach.*) No good shootin' at 'em; family's to big for one gun.

(HENDRICK HUDSON *advances, and seats himself on the keg facing* RIP. *The demons slowly surround the two.*)

(*Looking about him with growing apprehension.*) My, my, I don't like that kind of people at all! No, sir! I don't like any sech kind. I like that old gran'father worse than any of them. (*With a sheepish attempt to be genial, and appear at his ease.*) How you was, old gentleman? I didn't mean to intrude on you, did I?

(HUDSON *shakes his head.*) What? (*No reply.*) I'll tell you how it was; I met one of your gran'children, I don't know which is the one— (*Glancing around.*) They're all so much alike. Well— (*Embarrassed and looking at one demon.*) That's the same kind of a one. Anyway, this one, he axed me to help him up the mountain mit dat keg. Well, he was an old feller, an' I thought I would help him. (*Pauses, troubled by their silence.*) Was I right to help him? (HUDSON *nods.*) I say, was I right to help him?

(HUDSON *nods again.*)

If he was here, he would yust tell you the same thing any way, because— (*Suddenly perceiving the demon he had met below.*) Why, dat's the one, ain't it?

(*The demon nods.*)

Yes; dat is the one, dat's the same kind of a one dat I met. Was I right to come? (HUDSON *nods approval.*) I didn't want to come here, anyhow; no, sir, I didn't want to come to any such kind of a place. (*After a pause, seeing that no one has anything to say.*) I guess I better go away from it.

(RIP *picks up his gun, and is about to return by the way he came; but the demons raise their hands threateningly, and stop him. He puts his gun down again.*)

I didn't want to come here, anyhow— (*Grumbling to himself, then pulling himself together with an effort, and facing* HUDSON.) Well, old gentleman, if you mean to do me any harm, just speak it right out— (*Then with a little laugh.*) Oh! I will die game—(*Glancing around for a means of escape, and half to himself.*) If I can't run away.

(HUDSON *extends a cup to* RIP, *as if inviting him to drink.*)

(*Doubtfully.*) You want me to drink mit you?

(HUDSON *nods.* RIP *approaches him cautiously, unable to resist the temptation of a drink.*)

Well, I swore off drinkin'; but as this is the first time I see you, I won't count this one—

(*He takes the cup.* HUDSON *holds up another cup.* RIP *is reassured, and his old geniality returns.*)

You drink mit me? We drink mit one another?

(HUDSON *nods affirmatively.* RIP *feels at home under these familiar circumstances, and becomes familiar and colloquial again.*)

What's the matter mit you, old gentleman, anyhow? You go and make so (*Imitating the demon.*) mit your head every time; was you deaf?

(HUDSON *shakes his head.*)

Oh, nein. (*Laughing at his error.*) If you was deaf, you wouldn't hear what I was sayin'. Was you dumb?

(HUDSON *nods yes.*)

So? You was dumb?

(HUDSON *nods again.*)

Has all of your family the same complaint?

(HUDSON *nods.*)

All the boys dumb, hey? All the boys dumb.

(*All the demons nod. Then, suddenly, as if struck with an idea.*)

Have you got any girls?

(HUDSON *shakes his head.*)

Don't you? Such a big family, and all boys?

(HUDSON *nods.*)

(*With profound regret.*) That's a pity; my, that's a pity. Oh, my, if you had some dumb girls, what wives they would make— (*Brightening up.*) Well, old gentleman, here's your good health, and all your family—(*Turning, and waving to them.*)—may they live long and prosper.

(RIP *drinks. As he does so, all the demons lean forward, watching the effect of the liquor.* RIP *puts his hand to his head. The empty cup falls to the ground.*)

(*In an awed and ecstatic voice.*) What for licker is that!

(*As he turns, half reeling, he sees* HUDSON *holding out to him another cup. He snatches it with almost frantic eager-*

ness.) Give me another one! (*He empties it at a draught. A long pause follows during which the effect of the liquor upon* RIP *becomes apparent; the light in his eyes fades, his exhilaration dies out, and he loses his grasp on the reality of his surroundings. Finally, he clasps his head with both hands, and cries in a muffled, terrified voice.*) Oh, my, my head was so light, and now, it's heavy as lead!
(*He reels, and falls heavily to the ground. A long pause. The demons begin to disappear.* RIP *becomes dimly conscious of this, and raises himself on his elbow.*)
Are you goin' to leave me, boys? Are you goin' to leave me all alone? Don't leave me; don't go away. (*With a last effort.*) I will drink your good health, and your family's—
(*He falls back heavily, asleep*)

CURTAIN

ACT IV

Scene 1

As the curtain rises, the same high peaks of the Catskills, and the far-stretching valley below, are disclosed in the gray light of dawn.

RIP *is still lying on the ground, as in the last act, but he is no longer the* RIP *we knew. His hair and beard are long and white, bleached by the storms that have rolled over his head during the twenty years he has been asleep.*

As he stirs and slowly rises to a half-sitting posture, we see that his former picturesque rags have become so dilapidated that it is a matter of marvel how they hold together. They have lost all traces of color, and have assumed the neutral tints of the moss and lichens that cover the rocks. His voice, when he first speaks, betrays even more distinctly than his appearance the lapse of time. Instead of the full round tones of manhood, he speaks in the high treble of feeble old age. His very hands have grown old and weather-beaten.

RIP. (*Staring vacantly around.*) I wonder where I was. On top of the Catskill Mountains as sure as a gun! Won't my wife give it to me for stopping out all night? I must get

up and get home with myself. (*Trying to rise.*) Oh, I feel
very bad! Vat is the matter with my elbow? (*In trying to
rub it, the other one gives him such a twinge that he cries
out.*) Oh! the other elbow is more badder than the other
one. I must have cotched the rheumatix a-sleepin' mit the
wet grass. (*He rises with great difficulty.*) Och! I never
had such rheumatix like that. (*He feels himself all over,
and then stands for a moment pondering, and bewildered
by a strange memory.*) I wasn't sleeping all the time,
needer. I know I met a queer kind of a man, and we got
drinkin' and I guess I got pretty drunk. Well, I must pick
up my gun, and get home mit myself. (*After several painful attempts, he succeeds in picking up his gun, which
drops all to pieces as he lifts it.* RIP *looks at it in amazement.*) My gun must have cotched the rheumatix too.
Now, that's too bad. Them fellows have gone and stole my
good gun, and leave me this rusty old barrel. (RIP *begins
slowly to climb over the peak towards the path by which
he had ascended, his memory seeming to act automatically.
When he reaches the highest point, where he can look out
over the valley, he stops in surprise.*) Why, is that the
village of Falling Waters that I see? Why, the place is
more than twice the size it was last night. I—(*He sinks
down.*) I don't know whether I am dreaming, or sleeping,
or waking. (*Then pulling himself together with a great
effort, and calling up the image of his wife to act as whip
and spur to his waning powers, with humorous conviction,
as he gets up painfully again.*) I go home to my wife.
She'll let me know whether I'm asleep or awake or not.
(*Almost unable to proceed.*) I don't know if I will ever
get home, my k-nees are so stiff. My backbone, it's broke
already. (*As the curtain falls,* RIP *stands leaning on the
barrel of his gun as on a staff, with one hand raised, looking out over the valley.*)

Scene 2

A comfortable-looking room in DERRICK'S *house. As the
curtain rises,* MEENIE *and* GRETCHEN *enter.* MEENIE *is a tall
young woman of twenty-six, and* GRETCHEN *is a matronly
figure with white hair. They are well dressed, and have every
appearance of physical and material prosperity.*

GRETCHEN. I am sent to you by your father, Meenie.

MEENIE. Oh, don't call him so; he is not my father! He is your husband, Mother; but I owe him no love. And his cruel treatment of you—

GRETCHEN. Hush, child! Oh, if he heard you, he would make me pay for every disrespectful word you utter.

MEENIE. Yes; he would beat you, starve and degrade you. You are not his wife, Mother, but his menial.

GRETCHEN. My spirit is broken, Meenie. I cannot resent it. Nay, I deserve it; for as Derrick now treats me, so I treated your poor father when he was alive.

MEENIE. You, Mother? You, so gentle? You, who are weakness and patience itself?

GRETCHEN. Yes; because for fifteen years I have been Derrick's wife. But it was my temper, my cruelty, that drove your father from our home twenty years ago. You were too young then to remember him.

MEENIE. No, Mother, I recollect dear Father taking me on his knee, and saying to Hendrick that I should be his wife; and I promised I would.

GRETCHEN. Poor Rip! Poor, good-natured, kind creature that he was! How gently he bore with me; and I drove him like a dog from his home. I hunted him into the mountains, where he perished of hunger or cold, or a prey to some wild beast.

MEENIE. Don't cry, Mother!

(*Enter* DERRICK, *now grown old and bent over his cane, and infinitely more disagreeable than before. He, too, has thriven, and is dressed in a handsome full suit of black silk.*)

DERRICK. Snivelling again, eh? Teaching that girl of yours to be an obstinate hypocrite?

MEENIE. Oh, sir, she—

DERRICK. Hold your tongue, Miss. Speak when you're spoken to. I'll have you both to understand that there's but one master here. Well, mistress, have you told her my wishes, and is she prepared to obey them?

GRETCHEN. Indeed, sir, I was trying to—

DERRICK. Beating about the bush, prevaricating, and sneaking, as you usually do.

MEENIE. If you have made her your slave, you must expect her to cringe.

DERRICK. (*Approaching her threateningly.*) What's that?

GRETCHEN. Meenie! Meenie! For Heaven's sake, do not anger him!

DERRICK. (*Raising his cane.*) She had better not.

MEENIE. (*Defiantly.*) Take care how you raise your hand to me, for I'll keep a strict account of it. And when Hendrick comes back from sea, he'll make you smart for it, I promise you.

DERRICK. Is the girl mad?

MEENIE. He thrashed your nephew once for being insolent to me. Go and ask him how Hendrick pays my debts; and then when you speak to me you'll mind your stops.

DERRICK. (*To* GRETCHEN.) Oh, you shall pay for this!

GRETCHEN. No, Derrick, indeed, indeed I have not urged her to this! O, Meenie, do not speak so to him; for my sake forbear!

MEENIE. For your sake, yes, dear Mother. I forgot that he could revenge himself on you.

DERRICK. As for your sailor lover, Hendrick Vedder, I've got news of him at last. His ship, the *Mayflower*, was lost three years ago, off Cape Horn.

MEENIE. No, no. Not lost?

DERRICK. If you doubt it, there's the *Shipping Gazette*, in on my office table. You can satisfy yourself that your sailor bully has gone to the bottom.

GRETCHEN. Oh, sir, do not convey the news to her so cruelly.

DERRICK. That's it. Because I don't sneak and trick and lie about it, I'm cruel. The man's dead, has been dead and gone these two years or more. The time of mourning is over. Am I going to be nice about it this time of day?

MEENIE. Then all my hope is gone, gone forever!

DERRICK. So much the better for you. Hendrick's whole fortune was invested in that ship. So there's an end of him and your expectations. Now you are free, and a beggar. My nephew has a fancy for you. He will have a share of my business now, and my money when—when I die.

GRETCHEN. Do not ask her to decide now!

DERRICK. Why not? If she expects to make a better bargain by holding off, she's mistaken.

GRETCHEN. How can you expect her to think of a husband at this moment?

DERRICK. Don't I tell you the other one is dead these two years?

GRETCHEN. (*Leading* MEENIE *away.*) Come, my child. Leave her to me, sir; I will try and persuade her.

DERRICK. Take care that you do; for if she don't consent to accept my offer, she shall pack bag and baggage out of this house. Aye, this very day! Not a penny, not a stitch of clothes but what she has on her back, shall she have! Oh, I've had to deal with obstinate women before now, and I've taken them down before I've done with them. You know who I mean? Do you know who I mean? Stop. *Answer me! Do you know who I mean?*

GRETCHEN. (*Submissively.*) Yes, sir.

DERRICK. Then why didn't you say so before? Sulky, I suppose. There, you may be off.

(*Exeunt.*)

Scene 3

The village of Falling Waters, which has grown to be a smart and flourishing town, but whose chief features remain unchanged.

To the left, as of yore, is the inn, bearing scarcely any mark of the lapse of time, save that the sign of George III *has been replaced by a portrait of George Washington. To the right, where* RIP's *cottage used to stand, nothing remains, however, but the blackened and crumbling ruins of a chimney. A table and chairs stand in front of the inn porch.*

Into this familiar scene RIP *makes his entrance, but not as before, in glee, with children clinging about him. Faint, weak, and weary, he stumbles along, followed by a jeering, hooting mob of villagers; while the children hide from him in fear, behind their elders. His eyes look dazed and uncomprehending, and he catches at the back of a chair as if in need of physical as well as mental support.*

KÄTCHEN. (*As* RIP *enters.*) Why, what queer looking creature is this, that all the boys are playing—

SETH. Why, he looks as though he's been dead for fifty years, and dug up again!

RIP. My friends, *Kannst du Deutsch sprechen?*[1]

FIRST VILLAGER. I say, old fellow, you ain't seen anything of an old butter-tub with no kiver[2] on, no place about here, have you?

RIP. (*Bewildered, but with simplicity.*) What is that? I don't know who that is.

SECOND VILLAGER. I say, old man, who's your barber?

(*The crowd laughs, and goes off repeating, "Who's your barber?" Some of the children remain to stare at* RIP; *but when he holds out his hand to them, they, too, run off frightened.*)

RIP. Who's my barber; what dey mean by dat? (*Noticing his beard.*) Why is that on me? I didn't see that before. My beard and hair is so long and white. Gretchen won't know me with that, when she gets me home. (*Looking towards the cottage.*) Why, the home's gone away! (RIP *becomes more and more puzzled, like a man in a dream who sees unfamiliar things amid familiar surroundings, and cannot make out what has happened; and as in a dream a man preserves his individuality, so* RIP *stumbles along through his bewilderment, exhibiting flashes of his old humor, wit, and native shrewdness. But with all this he never laughs.*)

SETH. I say, old man, hadn't you better go home and get shaved?

RIP. (*Looking about for the voice.*) What?

SETH. Here, this way. Hadn't you better go home and get shaved?

RIP. My wife will shave me when she gets me home. Is this the village of "Falling Waters" where we was?

SETH. Yes.

RIP. (*Still more puzzled, not knowing his face.*) Do you live here?

SETH. Well, rather. I was born here.

RIP. (*Reflectively.*) Then you live here?

SETH. Well, rather; of course I do.

RIP. (*Feeling that he has hold of something certain.*) Do you know where I live?

SETH. No; but I should say you belong to Noah's Ark.

RIP. (*Putting his hand to his ear.*) That I belong mit vas?

SETH. Noah's Ark.

[1] "Do you speak German?"
[2] Cover.

RIP. (*Very much hurt.*) Why will you say such thing like that? (*Then, with a flash of humor, and drawing his beard slowly through his fingers.*) Well, look like it, don't I? (*Beginning all over again to feel for his clue.*) My friend, did you never hear of a man in this place whose name was Rip Van Winkle?

SETH. Rip Van Winkle, the laziest, drunken vagabond in the country?

RIP. (*Somewhat taken aback by this description, but obliged to concur in it.*) Yah, that is the one; there is no mistaking him, eh?

SETH. I know all about him.

RIP. (*Hopefully.*) Do you?

SETH. Yes.

RIP. (*Quite eagerly.*) Well, if you know all about him; well, what has become of him?

SETH. What has become of him? Why, bless your soul, he's been dead these twenty years!

RIP. (*Looking at* SETH.) Then I am dead, I suppose. So Rip Van Winkle was dead, eh?

SETH. Yes; and buried.

RIP. (*Humorously.*) I'm sorry for that; for he was a good fellow, so he was.

SETH. (*Aside.*) There appears to be something queer about this old chap; I wonder who he is. (*Rising and taking chair over to* RIP.) There, old gentleman, be seated.

RIP. (*Seating himself with great difficulty, assisted by* SETH.) Oh, thank you; every time I move a new way, I get another pain. My friend, where is the house what you live in?

SETH. (*Pointing at inn.*) There.

RIP. Did you live there yesterday?

SETH. Well, rather.

RIP. No, it is Nick Vedder what live in that house. Where is Nick Vedder?

SETH. Does he? Then I wish he'd pay the rent for it. Why, Nick Vedder has been dead these fifteen years.

RIP. Did you know Jacob Stein, what was with him?

SETH. No; but I've heard of him. He was one of the same sort as Rip and Nick.

RIP. Yes, them fellows was all pretty much alike.

SETH. Well, he went off the hooks a short time after Rip.

RIP. Where has he gone?

SETH. Off the hooks.

RIP. What is that, when they go off the hooks?

SETH. Why, he died.

RIP. (*With an air of hopelessness.*) Is there anybody alive
here at all? (*Then, with a sudden revulsion of feeling, convinced of the impossibility of what he hears.*) That man is
drunk what talks to me.

SETH. Ah, they were a jolly set, I reckon.

RIP. Oh, they was. I knowed them all.

SETH. Did you?

RIP. Yes, I know Jacob Stein, and Nick Vedder, and Rip Van
Winkle, and the whole of them. (*A new idea strikes him,
and he beckons to* SETH, *whom he asks, very earnestly.*)
Oh, my friend, come and see here. Did you know
Schneider?

SETH. Schneider! Schneider! No, I never heard of him.

RIP. (*Simply.*) He was a dog. I thought you might know him.
Well, if dat is so, what has become of my child Meenie,
and my wife Gretchen? Are they gone, too? (*Turning to
look at the ruins of the house.*) Yah, even the house is
dead.

SETH. Poor, old chap! He seems quite cast down at the loss
of his friends. I'll step in and get a drop of something to
cheer him up. (*Exit.*)

RIP. (*Puzzling it out with himself.*) I can't make it out how
it all was; because if this here is me, what is here now, and
Rip Van Winkle is dead, then who am I? That is what I
would like to know. Yesterday, everybody was here; and
now they was all gone. (*Very forlorn.*)

(*Re-enter* SETH, *followed by the villagers.*)

SETH. (*Offering* RIP *the cup.*) There, old gent, there's a drop
of something to cheer you up.

RIP. (*Shaking hands with* SETH *and* KÄTCHEN.) Oh, thank
you. I—I—I swore off; but this is the first time what I see
you. I won't count this one. (*His voice breaks.*) My friend,
you have been very kind to me. Here is your good health,
and your family's, and may they all live long and prosper!

SETH. I say, wife, ain't he a curiosity fit for a show?

RIP. (*Aside.*) That gives me courage to ask these people
anodder question. (*He begins with difficulty.*) My friend, I
don't know whether you knowed it or not, but there was
a child of Rip—Meenie her name was.

SETH. Oh, yes; that's all right.

RIP. (*With great emotion, leaning forward.*) She is not gone? She is not dead? No, no!

SETH. No; she is alive.

RIP. (*Sinking back with relief.*) Meenie is alive. It's all right now—all right now.

SETH. She's the prettiest girl in the village.

RIP. I know dat.

SETH. But if she wastes her time waiting on Hendrick Vedder, she'll be a middle-aged woman before long.

RIP. (*Incredulously.*) She's a little child, only six years old.

SETH. Six-and-twenty, you mean.

RIP. (*Thinking they are making fun of him.*) She's a little child no bigger than that. Don't bodder me; I don't like that.

SETH. Why she's as big as her mother.

RIP. (*Very much surprised that* SETH *knows* GRETCHEN.) What, Gretchen?

SETH. Yes, Gretchen.

RIP. Isn't Gretchen dead?

SETH. No. She's alive.

RIP. (*With mixed emotions.*) Gretchen is alive, eh! Gretchen's alive!

SETH. Yes; and married again.

RIP. (*Fiercely.*) How would she do such a thing like that?

SETH. Why, easy enough. After Rip died, she was a widow, wasn't she?

RIP. Oh, yes. I forgot about Rip's being dead. Well, and then?

SETH. Well, then Derrick made love to her.

RIP. (*Surprised, and almost amused.*) What for Derrick? Not Derrick Von Beekman?

SETH. Yes, Derrick Von Beekman.

RIP. (*Still more interested.*) Well, and then?

SETH. Well, then her affairs went bad; and at last she married him.

RIP. (*Turning it over in his mind.*) Has Derrick married Gretchen?

SETH. Yes.

RIP. (*With a flash of his old humor, but still with no laughter.*) Well, I didn't think he would come to any good; I never did. So she cotched Derrick, eh? Poor Derrick!

SETH. Yes.

RIP. Well, here's their good health, and their family's, and may they all live long and prosper! (*Drinks.*)

SETH. Now, old gent, hadn't you better be going home, wherever that is?

RIP. (*With conviction.*) Where my home was? Here's where it is.

SETH. What, here in this village? Now do you think we're going to keep all the half-witted strays that choose to come along here? No; be off with you. Why, it's a shame that those you belong to should allow such an old tramp as you to float around here.

VILLAGERS. (*Roughly, and trying to push him along.*) Yes; away with him!

RIP. (*Frightened, and pleading with them.*) Are you going to drive me away into the hills again?

FIRST VILLAGER. Yes; away with him! He's an old tramp.

(*Enter* HENDRICK, *with stick and bundle, followed by some of the women of the village.*)

VILLAGERS. Away with him!

HENDRICK. (*Throwing down bundle.*) Avast there, mates. Where are you towing that old hulk to? What, you won't? (*Pushing crowd aside, and going forward.*) Where are you towing that old hulk to?

SETH. Who are you?

HENDRICK. I'm a man, every inch of me; and if you doubt it, I'll undertake to remove the suspicions from any two of you in five minutes. Ain't you ashamed of yourselves? Don't you see the poor old creature has but half his wits?

SETH. Well, this is no asylum for worn out idiots.

VILLAGERS. (*Coming forward.*) No, it ain't!

HENDRICK. Ain't it?

OMNES. No, it ain't.

HENDRICK. Then I'll make it a hospital for broken heads if you stand there much longer. Clear the decks, you lubberly swabs! (*Drives them aside. Turns to* RIP, *who stands bewildered.*) What is the cause of all this?

RIP. (*Helplessly.*) I don't know, do you?

HENDRICK. (*To villagers.*) Do any of you know him?

FIRST VILLAGER. No; he appears to be a stranger.

HENDRICK. (*To* RIP.) You seem bewildered. Can I help you?

RIP. (*Feebly.*) Just tell me where I live.

HENDRICK. And don't you know?

RIP. No; I don't.

HENDRICK. Why, what's your name?

RIP. (*Almost childishly.*) I don't know; but I believe I know vat it used to be. My name, it used to be Rip Van Winkle.

VILLAGERS. (*In astonishment.*) Rip Van Winkle?

HENDRICK. Rip Van Winkle? Impossible!

RIP. (*Pathetically feeble, and old.*) Well, I wouldn't swear to it myself. I tell you how it was: Last night, I don't know about the time, I went away up into the mountains, and while I was there I met a queer kind o' man, and we got drinkin'; and I guess I got pretty drunk. And then I went to sleep; and when I woke up this morning, I was dead. (*All laugh.*)

HENDRICK. Poor old fellow; he's crazy. Rip Van Winkle has been dead these twenty years. I knew him when I was a child.

RIP. (*Clutching at a faint hope.*) You don't know me?

HENDRICK. No; nor anybody else here, it seems.

(*The villagers, finding that there is to be no amusement for them straggle off to their occupations.*)

SETH. (*As he goes into the inn.*) Why, wife, he's as cracked as our old teapot.

RIP. (*With simple pathos.*) Are we so soon forgot when we are gone? No one remembers Rip Van Winkle.

HENDRICK. Come, cheer up, my old hearty, and you shall share my breakfast. (*Assists* RIP *to sit at the table.* RIP *has fallen into a dream again. To* KÄTCHEN.) Bring us enough for three, and of your best.

KÄTCHEN. That I will. (*Exit into inn.*)

HENDRICK. So here I am, home again. And yonder's the very spot where, five years ago, I parted from Meenie.

RIP. (*Roused by the name.*) What, Meenie Van Winkle?

HENDRICK. And she promised to remain true to Hendrick Vedder.

RIP. Oh, yah; that was Nick Vedder's son.

HENDRICK. (*Turning to* RIP.) That's me.

RIP. (*Resentfully.*) That was you! You think I'm a fool? He's a little child, no bigger than that, the one I mean.

HENDRICK. How mad he is!

(*Enter* KÄTCHEN *from inn with tray, on which is laid a breakfast. She puts it on table, and exits into inn.*)

There, that's right. Stow your old locker full while I take a cruise around yonder house where, five years ago, I left the dearest bit of human nature that was ever put together. I'll be back directly. Who comes here? It's surely Derrick and his wife. Egad, I'm in luck; for now the old birds are out, Meenie will surely be alone. I'll take advantage of the coast being clear, and steer into harbor alongside. (*Exit.*)

(*Enter* DERRICK, *followed by* GRETCHEN.)

DERRICK. So you have come to that conclusion, have you?

GRETCHEN. I cannot accept this sacrifice.

RIP. (*Starting from his reverie, and turning to look at her.*) Why, that is Gretchen's voice. (*As he recognizes her, and sees how aged she is.*) My, my! Is that my wife?

DERRICK. Oh, you can't accept! Won't you kindly allow me a word on the subject?

RIP. (*Aside, humorously.*) No, indeed, she will not. Now, my friend, you are going to cotch it.

GRETCHEN. There is a limit even to my patience. Don't drive me to it.

RIP. (*Aside, drolly.*) Take care, my friend; take care.

DERRICK. Look you, woman; Meenie has consented to marry my nephew. She has pledged her word to do so on condition that I settle an annuity on you.

GRETCHEN. I won't allow my child to break her heart.

DERRICK. You won't allow? Dare to raise your voice, dare but to speak except as I command you, you shall repent it to the last hour of your life.

RIP. (*Expectantly.*) Now she'll knock him down, flat as a flounder.

DERRICK. (*Sneeringly.*) You won't allow? This is something new. Who are you; do you think you are dealing with your first husband?

GRETCHEN. Alas, no; I wish I was.

RIP. (*Lost in wonderment.*) My, my, if Rip was alive, he never would have believed it!

DERRICK. So you thought to get the upper hand of me, when you married me; didn't you?

GRETCHEN. I thought to get a home for my little girl—shelter, and food; want drove me to your door, and I married you for a meal's victuals for my sick child.

DERRICK. So you came to me as if I was a poorhouse, eh? Then you can't complain of the treatment you received. You sacrificed yourself for Meenie, and the least she can do now is to do the same for you. In an hour the deeds will be ready. Now, just you take care that no insolent interference of yours spoils my plans; do you hear?

GRETCHEN. Yes, sir.

DERRICK. Why can't you be kind and affectionate to her, as I am to you. There, go and blubber over her; that's your way. You are always pretending to be miserable.

GRETCHEN. Alas, no sir! I am always pretending to be happy.

DERRICK. Don't cry. I won't have it; come now, none of that. If you come home today with red eyes, and streaky cheeks, I'll give you something to cry for; now you know what's for supper. (*Exit.*)

RIP. (*Still amazed.*) Well, if I hadn't seen it, I never would have believed it!

GRETCHEN. (*Absorbed in her grief.*) Oh, wretch that I am, I must consent, or that man will surely thrust her out of doors to starve, to beg, and to become—(*Seeing* RIP.) Yes, to become a thing of rags and misery, like that poor soul.

RIP. She always drived the beggars away; I suppose I must go. (*Getting up, and starting to go.*)

GRETCHEN. (*Taking penny from her pocket.*) Here, my poor man, take this. It is only a penny; but take it, and may God bless you, poor wanderer, so old, so helpless. Why do you come to this strange place, so far from home?

RIP. (*Keeping his face turned away from her.*) She don't know me; she don't know me!

GRETCHEN. Are you alone in the world?

RIP. (*Trying to bring himself to look directly at* GRETCHEN.) My wife asks me if I'm alone.

GRETCHEN. Come with me. How feeble he is; there, lean on me. Come to yonder house, and there you shall rest your limbs by the fire.

(GRETCHEN *takes his arm, and puts it in her own. As they move towards her house,* RIP *stops, and, with an effort, turns and looks her full in the face, with a penetrating gaze, as if imploring recognition, but there is none; and,*

*sadly shaking his head, he shrinks into himself, and allows
her to lead him tottering off.*)

Scene 4

The same room in DERRICK'S *home as in Scene 2.*

Enter DERRICK.

DERRICK. I don't know what women were invented for, except
to make a man's life miserable. I can get a useful, hard-
working woman to keep my house clean, and order my
dinner for me, for half that weak, snivelling creature costs
me.

(*Enter* COCKLES.)

COCKLES. Well, uncle, what news; will she have me?

DERRICK. Leave it to me; she must, she shall.

COCKLES. If she holds out, what are we to do? It was all very
well, you marrying Rip's widow, that choked off all inquiry
into his affairs; but here's Meenie, Rip's heiress, who
rightly owns all this property; if we don't secure her, we're
not safe.

DERRICK. You've got rid of Hendrick Vedder; that's one obstacle removed.

COCKLES. I'm not so sure about that. His ship was wrecked
on a lonely coast; but some of the crew may have, unfor-
tunately, been saved.

DERRICK. If he turns up after you're married, what need you
care?

COCKLES. I'd like nothing better; I'd like to see his face when
he saw my arm around his sweetheart—my wife. But if he
turns up before our marriage—

DERRICK. I must put the screw on somewhere.

COCKLES. I'll tell you, Meenie will do anything for her
mother's sake. Now you are always threatening to turn
her out, as she turned out Rip. That's the tender place.
Meenie fears more for her mother than she cares for herself.

DERRICK. Well, what am I to do?

COCKLES. Make Gretchen independent of you; settle the little fortune on her, that you are always talking about doing, but never keeping your word. The girl will sell herself to secure her mother's happiness.

DERRICK. And it would be a cheap riddance for me. I was just talking about it to Gretchen this morning. You shall have the girl; but I hope you are not going to marry her out of any weak feeling of love. You're not going to let her make a fool of you by and by?

COCKLES. I never cared for her until she was impudent to me, and got that sailor lover of hers to thrash me; and then I began to feel a hunger for her I never felt before.

DERRICK. That's just the way I felt for Gretchen.

COCKLES. 'T ain't revenge that I feel; it's enterprise. I want to overcome a difficulty.

DERRICK. (*Chuckling.*) And so you shall. Come, we'll put your scheme in train at once; and let this be a warning to you hereafter: never marry another man's widow.

COCKLES. No, uncle; I'll take a leaf out of your book, and let it be a warning to her.

(*Exeunt.*)

Scene 5

A plain sitting-room in DERRICK's *house. A table stands in the center with several chairs around it. There are cups, a jug, and a workbasket on the table. As the curtain rises,* MEENIE *is discovered seated by the table.*

MEENIE. Why should I repine? Did my mother hesitate to sacrifice her life to make a home for me? No; these tears are ungrateful, selfish.

(*The door at the back opens.*)

(GRETCHEN *enters, leading* RIP, *who seems very feeble and a little wild.*)

GRETCHEN. Come in and rest a while.

RIP. This your house, your home?

GRETCHEN. Yes. Meenie, Meenie, bring him a chair.

RIP. (*Turning aside so as to shield his face from* MEENIE.) Is that your daughter?

GRETCHEN. That is my daughter.

RIP. (*Looking timidly at* MEENIE, *as* GRETCHEN *helps him into a chair.*) I thought you was a child.

GRETCHEN. (*Crossing to go into another room, and speaking to* MEENIE, *who starts to follow her.*) Stay with him until I get some food to fill his wallet. Don't be frightened, child, he is only a simple, half-witted creature whose misery has touched my heart.

(*Exit.* MEENIE *takes her workbasket and starts to follow.*)

RIP. (*Holding out his hand to detain her, and speaking with hardly suppressed excitement.*) One moment, my dear. Come here, and let me look at you. (*Pathetically.*) Are you afraid? I won't hurt you. I only want to look at you; that is all. Won't you come? (MEENIE *puts down her workbasket, and* RIP *is relieved of his great fear that she might leave him. His excitement increases as he goes on in his struggle to make her recognize him.*) Yes, I thought you would. Oh, yah, that is Meenie! But you are grown!

(MEENIE *smiles.*)

But see the smile and the eyes! That is just the same Meenie. You are a woman, Meenie. Do you remember something of your father? (*He looks at her eagerly and anxiously, as if on her answer hung his reason and his life.*)

MEENIE. I do. I do. Oh, I wish he was here now!

RIP. (*Half rising in his chair, in his excitement.*) Yah? But he isn't? No? No?

MEENIE. No; he's dead. I remember him so well. No one ever loved him as I did.

RIP. No; nobody ever loved me like my child.

MEENIE. Never shall I forget his dear, good face. Tell me—

RIP. (*Eagerly and expectantly.*) Yah?—

MEENIE. Did you know him?

RIP. (*Confused by her question, and afraid to answer.*) Well —I thought I did. But I— When I say that here, in the village, the people all laugh at me.

MEENIE. He is wandering. (*She starts to go.*)

RIP. (*Making a great effort of will, and resolved to put the question of his identity to the test.*) Don't go away from me. I want you to look at me now, and tell me if you have ever seen me before.

MEENIE. (*Surprised.*) No.

RIP. (*Holding out his arms to her.*) Try, my darlin', won't you?

MEENIE. (*Frightened.*) What do you mean? Why do you gaze so earnestly and fondly on me?

RIP. (*Rising from his chair, in trembling excitement, and approaching her.*) I am afraid to tell you, my dear, because if you say it is not true, it may be it would break my heart. But, Meenie, either I dream, or I am mad; but I am your father.

MEENIE. My father!

RIP. Yes; but hear me, my dear, and then you will know. (*Trying to be logical and calm, but laboring under great excitement.*) This village here is the village of Falling Waters. Well, that was my home. I had here in this place my wife, Gretchen, and my child Meenie—little Meenie— (*A long pause, during which he strives to reassemble his ideas and memories more accurately.*) and my dog Schneider. That's all the family what I've got. Try and remember me. Dear, won't you? (*Pleadingly.*) I don't know when it was.— This night there was a storm; and my wife drove me from my house; and I went away—I don't remember any more till I come back here now. And see, I get back now, and my wife is gone, and my home is gone. My home is gone, and my child—my child looks in my face, and don't know who I am!

MEENIE. (*Rushing into his arms.*) I do! Father!

RIP. (*Sobbing.*) Ah, my child! Somebody knows me now! Somebody knows me now!

MEENIE. But can it be possible?

RIP. Oh, yah; it is so, Meenie! (*With a pathetic return of his uncertainty.*) Don't say it is not, or you will kill me if you do.

MEENIE. No. One by one your features come back to my memory. Your voice recalls that of my dear father, too. I cannot doubt; yet it is so strange.

RIP. Yah, but it is me, Meenie; it is me.

MEENIE. I am bewildered. Surely mother will know you.

RIP. (*Smiling.*) No, I don't believe she'll know me.

MEENIE. She can best prove your identity. I will call her.

RIP. No. You call the dog Schneider. He'll know me better than my wife.

(*They retire to a sofa in the background, where* RIP *sits with his arm around* MEENIE.)

(*Enter* DERRICK, *with documents.*)

DERRICK. What old vagabond is this?

(MEENIE *starts to resent insult.*)

DERRICK. Here, give him a cold potato, and let him go.

(*To* GRETCHEN, *who has entered, followed by* COCKLES. GRETCHEN *seats herself in the chair at the right of the table.*)

Come you here, mistress. Here are the papers for the young couple to sign.

COCKLES. (*Aside.*) And the sooner, the better. Hush, Uncle, Hendrick is here.

DERRICK. Young Vedder? Then we must look sharp. (*To* GRETCHEN.) Come, fetch that girl of yours to sign this deed.

GRETCHEN. Never shall she put her name to that paper with my consent. Never.

DERRICK. Dare you oppose me in my own house? Dare you preach disobedience under my roof?

GRETCHEN. I dare do anything when my child's life's at stake. No, a thousand times, no! You shall not make of her what you have of me. Starvation and death are better than such a life as I lead.

DERRICK. (*Raising cane.*) Don't provoke me.

GRETCHEN. (*Kneeling.*) Beat me, starve me. You can only kill me. After all, I deserve it. (*Rising.*) But Meenie has given her promise to Hendrick Vedder, and she shall not break her word.

COCKLES. (*Seated at right of table.*) But Hendrick Vedder is dead.

(*The door is flung open, and* HENDRICK *enters.*)

HENDRICK. That's a lie! He's alive!

GRETCHEN *and* MEENIE. (*Rushing to him.*) Alive!

HENDRICK. (*To* MEENIE). I've heard all about it. They made you believe that I was dead. (*To* DERRICK.) Only wait till I get through here. (*Embracing* MEENIE.) What a pleasure I've got to come! (*To* DERRICK.) And what a thrashing I've brought back for you two swabs.

DERRICK. (*Angrily.*) Am I to be bullied under my own roof by a beggarly sailor? Quit my house all of you. (*Seizes* GRETCHEN, *and drags her away from the crowd.*) As for you, woman, this is your work, and I'll make you pay for it.

GRETCHEN. Hendrick, save me from him. He will kill me.

HENDRICK. Stand off!

DERRICK. (*Raising cane.*) No; she is my wife, mine.

GRETCHEN. Heaven help me, I am!

(RIP *has risen from the sofa, and comes forward, and leans against the center of the table, with one hand in his game-bag. He is fully awake now, and has recovered all his old shrewdness.*)

RIP. Stop. I am not so sure about that. If that is so, then what has become of Rip Van Winkle?

COCKLES. He's dead.

RIP. That's another lie. He's no more dead than Hendrick Vedder. Derrick Von Beekman, you say this house and land was yours?

DERRICK. Yes.

RIP. Where and what is the paper what you wanted Rip Van Winkle to sign when he was drunk, but sober enough not to do it? (*Taking an old paper out of game-bag, and turning to* HENDRICK.) Have you forgot how to read?

HENDRICK. No.

RIP. Then you read that.

(HENDRICK *takes the document from* RIP, *and looks it over.*)

DERRICK. What does this mad old vagabond mean to say?

RIP. I mean, that is my wife, Gretchen Van Winkle.

GRETCHEN. (*Rushing to* RIP.) Rip! Rip!

COCKLES. I say, Uncle, are you going to stand that? That old impostor is going it under your nose in fine style.

DERRICK. I'm dumb with rage. (*To the villagers, who have come crowding in.*) Out of my house, all of you! Begone, you old tramp!

HENDRICK. Stay where you are. (*To* DERRICK.) This house don't belong to you. Not an acre of land, not a brick in the town is yours. They have never ceased to belong to Rip Van Winkle; and this document proves it.

DERRICK. 'Tis false. That paper is a forgery.

HENDRICK. Oh, no, it is not; for I read it to Rip twenty years ago.

RIP. Clever boy! Clever boy! Dat's the reason I didn't sign it then, Derrick.

DERRICK. (*Approaching* HENDRICK.) And do you think I'm fool enough to give up my property in this way?

HENDRICK. No. You're fool enough to hang on to it, until we make you refund to Rip every shilling over and above the paltry sum you loaned him upon it. Now, if you are wise, you'll take a hint. There's the door. Go! And never let us see your face again.

RIP. Yah; give him a cold potato, and let him go.

(*Exit* DERRICK *in a great rage. All the villagers laugh at him.* HENDRICK *follows him to the door.*)

COCKLES. (*Kneeling to* MEENIE.) O, Meenie! Meenie!

HENDRICK. (*Coming down, and taking him by the ear.*) I'll Meenie you!

(*Takes him and pushes him out. All the villagers laugh.* MEENIE *gives* RIP *a chair.*)

GRETCHEN. (*Kneeling by the side of* RIP.) O, Rip! I drove you from your home; but do not desert me again. I'll never speak an unkind word to you, and you shall never see a frown on my face. And Rip—

RIP. Yah.

GRETCHEN. You may stay out all night, if you like.

RIP. (*Leaning back in his chair.*) No, thank you. I had enough of that.

GRETCHEN. And, Rip, you can get tight as often as you please.

RIP. (*Taking bottle, and filling the cup from it.*) No; I don't touch another drop.

MEENIE. (*Kneeling by the other side of* RIP.) Oh, yes, you will, Father. For see, here are all the neighbors come to welcome you home.

(GRETCHEN *offers* RIP *the cup.*)

RIP. (*With all his old kindliness and hospitality.*) Well, bring in all the children, and the neighbors, and the dogs, and— (*Seeing the cup which* GRETCHEN *is offering to him.*) I swore off, you know. Well, I won't count this one; for this will go down with a prayer. I will take my cup and pipe and tell my strange story to all my friends. Here is my child Meenie, and my wife Gretchen, and my boy Hendrick. I'll drink all your good health, and I'll drink your good health, and your families', and may they all live long and prosper!

CURTAIN

MARGARET FLEMING

Preface to MARGARET FLEMING

Margaret Fleming was a *succès d'estime*, warmly encouraged and supported by important literary figures of the day. After a trial run in Lynn, Massachusetts, in July, 1890, however, managers in Boston and New York would not lease their theatres for the production of a play they considered too daring in theme and treatment, particularly at the third-act curtain. Its author finally rented a small Boston auditorium, where *Margaret Fleming* had its first production—a three-week run beginning on May 4, 1891, and then another three-week run in October. According to William Dean Howells, "It became the talk of the whole city wherever cultivated people met." He further wrote, in *Harper's Magazine* (August 1891): "The power of this story as presented in Mr. Herne's every-day phrase, and in the naked simplicity of Mrs. Herne's acting of the wife's part, was terrific. It clutched at the heart. It was common; it was pitilessly plain; it was ugly; but it was true, and it was irresistible." But such realism, which had naturally found champions in Howells, Hamlin Garland, and others, was precisely that which repelled mass audiences.

Both in theme and in dramaturgy the play was considerably ahead of its time. Contemporaneous with the plays of Henrik Ibsen, *Margaret Fleming* shows the influence of the great Norwegian, who was, in fact, one of Herne's idols. The "problem" in the play is less neatly solved than it would have been by Ibsen. But it is there, in the form of the rising ghost of Philip's adultery and its effects on himself and Margaret. *Margaret Fleming* is thus America's first modern drama of ideas, a play that frankly discusses problems heretofore shunned, and does so without the traditional melodrama. Also strongly reminiscent of Ibsen is the dramaturgy, which constitutes an equally significant turning point in American theatre history. What distinguishes *Margaret Fleming* from the other plays in this volume—and indeed from the other plays produced before it—are the absence of heroes, villains, soliloquies, and asides; dramatic climaxes that are devoid of violent action or words; frequent anticlimactic curtains; lifelike details in action and setting; and other devices of the "realistic" drama that have remained dominant (or have become clichés) in our age.

After the trial run, where he had played Philip, Herne played the part of Joe Fletcher—and "deliciously," according to Howells. *Margaret Fleming* was given a special matinée performance at Palmer's Theatre in New York on December 9, 1891, but was coldly received by New York audiences and critics alike. The play never achieved popularity, even after Herne rewrote the last act. Its earlier version is not extant, but Hamlin Garland, in an article in *The Arena* (October 1891), incidentally furnishes the following interesting account of what happened in that version, after Margaret's blindness and the daring third-act curtain:

> . . . It all ends in the flight of Fleming, and the destruction of their home. Several years later a chain of events brings wife and husband together in the office of the Boston Inspector of Police. Joe Fletcher, a street peddler, and husband of Maria, the sister of Lena Schmidt, was the means of bringing them together again. Fleming runs across Joe on the Common, and Joe takes him to see Maria. Margaret has found Maria and her child, which Maria had taken. Philip's altercation with Maria brings them into the police office. After explanations, the inspector turns to the husband and wife, and voicing conventional morality, advises them to patch it up. "When you want me, ring that bell," he says, and leaves them alone. There is a hush of suspense, and then Fleming, seeing the work he had wrought in the blind face before him, speaks.
>
> PHILIP. Margaret!
>
> MARGARET. Well!
>
> PHILIP. This is terrible.
>
> MARGARET. You heard the inspector. He calls it a "common case."
>
> PHILIP. Yes, I was wondering whether he meant that or only said it.
>
> MARGARET. I guess he meant it, Philip. We'll be crowded out of his thoughts before he goes to bed to-night.

❈   ❈   ❈

MARGARET. Ah, well, it's done now, and—

PHILIP. Yes, it's done. For four years I've been like an escaped prisoner that wanted to give himself up and dreaded the punishment. I'm captured at last, and without hope or fear,—I *was* going to say without shame,—I ask you, my judge, to pronounce my sentence.

MARGARET. That's a terrible thing to ask me to do, Philip. . . . (*She hesitates.*)

PHILIP. Of course you'll get a divorce?

MARGARET. Don't let us have any more ceremonies, Philip. . . . I gave myself to you when you asked me to. We were married in my mother's little home. Do you remember what a bright, beautiful morning it was?

PHILIP. Yes.

MARGARET. That was seven years ago. To-day we're *here!* . . .

❈   ❈   ❈

MARGARET. I *am* calm. My eyes have simply been turned in upon myself for four years. I see clearer than I used to.

PHILIP. Suppose I could come to you some day and say, Margaret, I'm *now* an honest man. Would you live with me again?

MARGARET. The wife-heart has gone out of me, Philip.

PHILIP. I'll wait, Margaret. Perhaps it may come back again. Who knows?

❈   ❈   ❈

PHILIP. Is it degrading to forgive?

MARGARET. No; but it is to condone. Suppose *I* had broken faith with you?

PHILIP. Ah, Margaret!

MARGARET. I know! But suppose I had? Why should a wife bear the whole stigma of infidelity? Isn't it just as revolting in a husband? . . . Then can't you see that it is simply impossible for me to live with you again?

PHILIP. That's my sentence. . . . We'll be friends?

MARGARET. Yes, friends. We'll respect each other as
friends. We never could as man and wife.

As they clasp hands, something latent, organic rushes
over her. She masters it, puts his hand aside: "Ring
that bell!"

Herne rewrote this last act into the present version, with
its promise of an eventual reconciliation of the Flemings, for
the McVicker's Theatre production in Chicago in 1892, and
it has been thus performed in the few revivals and in the
amateur productions that it still receives occasionally. The
script of this later version, too, is lost, but Mrs. Herne, who
not only created the part of Margaret but was also closely
associated with the composition of the play, later recon-
structed it for publication in its present form.

Born in Cohoes, New York, in 1839, James A. Herne
(originally Ahern) was a prominent actor, playwright, and
stage manager. He became the leading man for Lucille
Western, to whose sister Helen he had been briefly married.
While managing Maguire's New Theatre in San Francisco
he began dramatizing some of the novels of Dickens, who
was a strong influence on Herne's work. There also began
his association with David Belasco, at the time (1874) a bit
player in Herne's *Rip Van Winkle*; they collaborated on a
number of plays, including the long popular *Hearts of Oak*
(1879). By then Herne had become stage manager and
leading actor at San Francisco's Baldwin Theatre, where he
met the Irish-born player Katharine Corcoran (1857–1943),
whom he married in 1878. An excellent actress, who was
Herne's leading lady in most of his plays, Mrs. Herne also
inspired—to the point of suggesting "scenes, lines, and stage
business," according to Hamlin Garland—his playwriting,
which in time became less and less melodramatic and more
realistic.

Herne had great faith in art, which he persistently attempted to elevate in his own profession. The Syndicate that
was formed in 1896 and almost totally dominated American
theatres for a decade was not, of course, given to artistic
experimentation. Herne therefore joined others who were
striving to establish something like André Antoine's Théâtre
Libre in Paris and Otto Brahm's Freie Bühne in Berlin. They

called for the "establishment of a distinctively American Theatre," where "the Drama shall be considered a Work of Art, and produced as such—independent of cheap popularity." *Margaret Fleming* was hailed by his associates in this unsuccessful project, and Herne himself invested—and lost— thousands of dollars in his attempts to make the play popular. He formulated his artistic creed, "Art for Truth's Sake," a manifesto published in *The Arena* (February 1897). But it was the maudlin and the melodramatic that was popular, and Herne's *Shore Acres* (1892)—in which he played the sentimental Yankee Uncle Nat—was more attuned to such tastes and made a fortune for him. Among his other plays in which he and Mrs. Herne starred are *The Reverend Griffith Davenport* (1899), a Civil War drama that had little commercial success, and his last play, *Sag Harbor* (1899), a very successful revamping of *Hearts of Oak*, in which Herne took the part of Captain Marble. It was during the run of this play that he died, in New York City, on June 2, 1901.

Margaret Fleming was first published in Arthur Hobson Quinn's *Representative American Plays* (1917). For Herne's biography and a study of his work and milieu, see Herbert J. Edwards and Julie A. Herne's *James A. Herne, The Rise of Realism in the American Drama* (University of Maine, 1964) and John Perry's *James A. Herne, the American Ibsen* (Chicago, 1978).

M.M.

MARGARET FLEMING
By James A. Herne

Characters

PHILIP FLEMING, a mill owner
MARGARET FLEMING, his wife
LUCY, their baby
BOBBY, office boy
MR. FOSTER, manager of the mill
WILLIAMS, foreman
JOE FLETCHER
DOCTOR LARKIN
MARIA BINDLEY, the nursemaid
JANE, the maid
HANNAH, the cook
MRS. BURTON
CHARLIE BURTON, her 10-year-old son
INFANT

Setting: Canton, Massachusetts;
May and June, 1890.

ACT I

SCENE 1

It is a morning in Spring in PHILIP FLEMING's *private office at the mill. Bright sunlight floods the room at first. Later it becomes cloudy until at the end of the act, rain is falling fitfully. The room is handsomely furnished. There is a table in the center at the back between two windows. Above the table and attached to the wall is a cabinet with a mirror in the door. In the right corner is an umbrella-stand and hat-rack beside a door leading to the street. There are two windows below the door. A little to the right of the center of the room is an armchair, and in the same position on the left is a flat-top office desk, with a chair on either side. Behind it on the left is a door leading to the mill. There is a bunch of flowers on the desk, and two silver frames holding pictures of* MARGARET *and* LUCY. *There are also pictures on the wall, including one of the mill and one of* PHILIP's *father as a young man.*

As the curtain rises, BOBBY *enters from the left with a desk-basket of mail, which he places on the desk. He re-arranges the chairs slightly. As he is about to go out a key is heard in the door on the right.* BOBBY *pauses expectantly.* PHILIP FLEMING, *carrying an umbrella and a rain-coat, enters from the street door on the right. He is a well dressed, prosperous, happy-looking man about thirty-five. He hangs up his hat and coat, and places his umbrella in the stand. Then he glances carelessly into the hat-rack mirror and runs his hand lightly over his hair.*

PHILIP. (*In a friendly manner.*) Good morning, Bobby.
BOBBY. (*Grinning appreciatively.*) Good morning, sir.
   (PHILIP *goes to his desk and, shifting one or two articles out of his way, begins the duties of the day.*)
PHILIP. Did you get wet this morning in that big shower?
BOBBY. Yes, sir, a little, but I'm all right now.

(PHILIP *glances rapidly through the letters and with an eager manner selects two large envelopes, opens one, glances through a document it contains and places it in his inside coat-pocket with a satisfied smile.*)

PHILIP. (*Chatting, as he continues his work.*) Still doing the four mile sprint?

BOBBY. Yes, sir. Oh, I like it, sir—when it don't rain.

(PHILIP *opens other letters rapidly, glancing with a quick, comprehensive eye through each before placing it in the growing heap on the desk.*)

PHILIP. How about the bicycle?

BOBBY. Well, sir, Mr. Foster says he thinks he'll be able to recommend me for a raise pretty soon, if I keep up my record.

PHILIP. (*Looking at him quizzically.*) A raise, Bobby?

BOBBY. Yes, Mr. Fleming, and my mother says I can save all I get and I guess I'll have a bicycle pretty soon then.

PHILIP. How long have you been here?

BOBBY. Six months the day after tomorrow.

PHILIP. (*Smiling kindly.*) I guess I'll have to talk to Foster, myself.

BOBBY. Oh, thank you, Mr. Fleming.

(PHILIP *opens a letter which appears to disturb him. He pauses over it with a worried frown.*)

PHILIP. Ask Mr. Foster to come here at once, please.

(*As* BOBBY *starts to go.*)

And tell Williams I want to see him.

BOBBY. Yes, sir.

(*He goes out the door on the left. There is a moment's pause, and then* FOSTER *enters from the same door. He is a bright, active young man about twenty-eight or thirty.*)

PHILIP. Good morning, Foster.

FOSTER. Good morning, Mr. Fleming.

PHILIP. Here's a letter from the receiver for Reed and Vorst. He wants to know if we'll accept an immediate settlement of forty percent.

FOSTER. (*Becoming serious.*) Gee, Mr. Fleming, I don't see how we can. I was depending on at least fifty percent to carry us through the summer. It's always a dull season, you know, and—

PHILIP. Why, we have more orders now than we had this time last year.

FOSTER. Yes, I know, sir. But, I was going to speak to you. The Cotton Exchange Bank doesn't want to renew those notes.

PHILIP. Doesn't, eh? Well, then, we'll have to accept Reed and Vorst's offer.

FOSTER. I think it would be a mistake just now, sir. If we hold out they've got big assets.

PHILIP. Can't be helped. I'm hard-pressed. We're short of ready money.

FOSTER. I don't understand it. We've had a better winter than we've had for years.

PHILIP. (*Smiling.*) That last little flier I took wasn't as successful as the former ones.

FOSTER. You've been too lenient with the retailers.

PHILIP. "Live and let live" 's my motto.

FOSTER. I'd hate to see anything happen to the mill.

PHILIP. Nothing's going to happen. Let me do the worrying. Our credit's good. I'll raise the money tomorrow.

FOSTER. I hope so, sir. Anything else?

PHILIP. (*Giving him the letters.*) Wire the answers to these right away. That's all.

FOSTER. All right, sir. (*He goes out.*)

(PHILIP *takes up a large sheet of paper which contains a report from one of the departments of the mill. He scans it closely and makes some calculations upon a sheet of paper.* WILLIAMS *enters.*)

PHILIP. (*Looking up.*) Good morning, Williams.

(WILLIAMS *is quite an old man, but has the attitude of one who knows his business and can do things. He stands with bent shoulders and arms hanging limp. He is chewing tobacco, and speaks with a quick, sharp, New England accent.*)

WILLIAMS. Good morning, Mr. Fleming.

PHILIP. (*Holding the report in his hand.*) Williams, a short time ago you told me that the main supply belt in the finishing room was only repaired a few times during the last six months. I find here from your report that it has broken down about twice a week since last January. How long does it take to make a repair?

WILLIAMS. Oh, sometimes about ten minutes—other times again, twenty minutes. We have done it in five minutes.

PHILIP. There are about one hundred and ten operators in that room?

WILLIAMS. One hundred and seven.

PHILIP. Why, you should have reported this condition the first week it arose. Poor economy, Williams. (*He makes a few, rapid calculations upon the back of a report.*) Twelve hundred dollars lost time. (*He shakes his head.*) We could have bought a new belt a year ago and saved money in the bargain.

WILLIAMS. I told Mr. Baker several times, sir, in the beginning and he didn't seem to think anything of it.

PHILIP. Well, report all such details to me in the future.

(*He writes a few lines rapidly and rings the bell.* BOBBY *enters briskly.*)

Tell Mr. Foster to get those firms over long distance, and whichever one can make the quickest delivery to place orders there—see?

BOBBY. Yes, sir. (*He has a soiled card in his hand, which he offers to* PHILIP *with a grin.*) A man outside told me to hand you his visiting card.

WILLIAMS. Is that all, sir?

PHILIP. Yes. (*He smiles as he reads the card.*) Joe Fletcher! Tell him to come in.

(*He resumes work at his desk.* WILLIAMS *goes out.*)

BOBBY. Yes, sir. (*He follows* WILLIAMS.)

(*After a moment* JOE FLETCHER *enters. He is a man of middle age, well made but heavy and slouching in manner. He has a keen, shrewd eye in a weak and dissipated face, which is made attractive, nevertheless, by a genial and ingratiating smile. He is wearing a shabby linen coat called a "duster," which hangs, crushed and limp, from his neck to his ankles. Strung from his left shoulder is a cord hung with sponges of various sizes. Several lengths of chamois are dangling with the sponges across his breast and back, draping his right hip and leg. In one hand he has a weather-beaten satchel. He carries by a leather thong a heavy stone hanging from a cracked plate. There are two holes in the rim of the plate through one of which runs the thong by which it is carried. The other, the big stone, is fastened to it with a piece of chain. He carries it unconscious of its weight. There is a pervading sense of intimacy between the man and his equipment, and from his*

*battered hat to his spreading shoes the stains of the road,
like a varnish, bind them together in a mellow fellowship.*)

PHILIP. Hello, Joe. (*He looks at him with humorous curiosity.*)

JOE. (*Light-heartedly.*) How d'do, Mr. Fleming. (*His voice
is broken and husky. He gives a little, dry cough now and
then in an ineffectual attempt to clear it. He crosses to the
corner of the table, and shows by his step that his feet are
sore and swollen.*)

PHILIP. What are you doing now, Joe?

JOE. (*Indicating his effects. While he talks he places the
stone against a corner of the table on the floor, and puts
the valise on the edge of the table.*) Traveling merchant;
agent for Brummell's Giant Cement; professional corn doctor—soft and hard corns—calluses—bunions removed instantly, ingrowing nails treated 'thout pain or loss of blood
—*or* money *re*funded. Didn't ye read m'card? (*He coughs.*)

PHILIP. (*Laughing.*) Well, not all of it, Joe.

JOE. (*Reminiscently.*) Inventor of Dr. Fletcher's famous
cough mixture, warranted to cure coughs—colds, hoarseness and loss o' voice. An infallible remedy fur all chronic
conditions of the *pul-mon*-ary organs. (*He coughs again.*)
When not too fur gone. (*He takes a labelled bottle, containing a brown mixture from his inside pocket, shakes it
and holds it up proudly before* PHILIP.) Kin I sell ye a
bottle? (*He smiles ingratiatingly.*)

PHILIP. (*Smiling but shaking his head.*) No, Joe, I guess not
today.

JOE. (*Opening the satchel insinuatingly.*) Mebbe a few
boxes o' corn salve? It's great. (PHILIP *shakes his head.*)
Would ye like to consider a box o' cement?

PHILIP. (*Still smiling.*) No, but I'll take one of those big
sponges.

JOE. I thought I could sell ye something.
(*He unhooks a large sponge and lays it upon the desk.*
PHILIP *hands him a bill. He takes it carelessly, looks at it,
shakes his head regretfully and puts it into his pocket.
Then he feels in his other pocket and taps his vest
pockets.*) Gosh, I'm sorry, but I ain't got a bit of change.

PHILIP. Oh, never mind the change, Joe. (*He laughs indulgently.*)

JOE. (*Regretfully.*) Well, I'd feel better if *I hed* the change.

(JOE *has been standing to the left of the desk.*) Kin I set down fur a minnit, Mr. Fleming? M'feet gets so tired.

PHILIP. Yes, Joe, sit down.

JOE. I got pretty wet a while ago in that shower. My, but it did come down.

PHILIP. (*Warmly.*) Perhaps you'd like a hot drink?
(*He indicates with a nod of the head, the cabinet back of* JOE, *as the latter is about to sit down.* JOE *shows a lively interest.*)

JOE. (*Glancing at* PHILIP *with a shy twinkle in his eye.*) Oh, kin I, Mr. Fleming? Thank ye. (*He shuffles over to the cabinet, opens the door and gloats over the vision of joy which greets him. He selects a bottle.*)

PHILIP. Hold on, Joe. Wait for some hot water.

JOE. (*Hastily.*) No, thank ye. I'm afraid I'd be like the Irishman in the dream.

PHILIP. What was that, Joe?

JOE. (*As he pours out a generous portion.*) Well, the Irishman was dreaming that he went to see the priest, and the priest asked him to have a drink. "I will, thank ye kindly," says Pat. "Is it hot or cold, ye'll have it?" says the priest? "Hot, if ye plaze, yer Riverence," says Pat, and while they were waiting fur the hot water, Pat wakes up. "Bad luck to me," says he, "why didn't I take it cold?" (*He drains the glass, smacks his lips and chuckles.*) My, but that's good stuff! Mr. Fleming, are ye as fond of it yourself as ye used to be?

PHILIP. (*Smiling and shaking his head.*) No, Joe. I've got through with all that foolishness. I've sowed my wild oats.

JOE. (*Chuckling as he sits in the chair.*) You must have got a pretty slick crop out o' yourn.

PHILIP. Every man gets a pretty full crop of those, Joe, before he gets through.

JOE. Ye've turned over a new leaf, eh?

PHILIP. Yes—married.

JOE. Married?

PHILIP. Yes, and got a baby.

JOE. Thet so! Did ye marry out'n the mill?

PHILIP. Oh, no. She was a Miss Thorp, of Niagara. (*He hands the picture of the child to* JOE.)

JOE. (*Showing interest immediately, and gazing at the picture, while gradually a gentle responsive smile plays over his features. He says, admiringly.*) By George! that's a great baby! (*He gives a chuckling laugh at it.*) Boy?

PHILIP. (*Proudly.*) No. Girl!

JOE. Thet so! Should a thought you'd a wanted a boy. (*With sly significance, and chuckling at his own joke.*) Ye've hed so many girls.

PHILIP. (*He laughs lightly.*) Tut, tut, Joe, no more of that for me. (*He hands him the frame containing* MARGARET'S *picture.*) My wife.

JOE. (*His expression becoming grave as the sweetness and dignity of the face touches him. He takes a long breath.*) My, but that's a fine face. Gee, if she's as good as that, you're a lucky man, Mr. Fleming.

PHILIP. Yes, Joe, I've got more than I deserve, I guess. (*He becomes serious for the first time and a shadow flits over his face. He sighs.*)

JOE. (*Sympathetically.*) Oh, I understand just how you feel. I'm married m'self. (*He sits down facing the audience, his hands clasped, his thumbs gently rolling over each other. A far-away tender look comes into his eyes.*)

PHILIP. (*Surprised.*) Married?

(JOE *nods his head.*)

Where's your wife?

JOE. Left me. (*He gives a sigh of self pity.*)

PHILIP. (*Touched.*) Left you! (*He shakes his head compassionately, then the thought comes to him.*) If my wife left me I'd kill myself.

JOE. (*Philosophically.*) Oh, no, no, ye wouldn't. You'd get over it, just as I did. (*He sighs.*)

PHILIP. How did it happen? What did you do?

JOE. (*Innocently.*) Not a durn thing! She was a nice, German woman, too. She kept a gent's furnishing store down in South Boston, and I married her.

PHILIP. (*Recovering himself and speaking gaily.*) Oh, Joe. (*He shakes his head in mock reproval.*) You married her for her money, eh? (*He laughs at him.*)

JOE. (*Ingenuously.*) No, I didn't, honest. I thought I might get a whack at the till once in a while, but I didn't.

PHILIP. (*Quizzing him.*) Why not, Joe?

JOE. She fixed me up a pack and sent me out on the road to sell goods, and when I got back, she was gone. There was a new sign on the store, "Isaac Litchenstein, Ladies and Gents' Drygoods." (*He draws a big sigh.*)

PHILIP. And you've never seen her since?

JOE. (*Shaking his head sadly.*) No, siree, never!

PHILIP. (*Serious again, impressed by* JOE.) That's pretty tough, Joe.

(BOBBY *enters.*)

BOBBY. Doctor Larkin would like to see you, sir.

JOE. (*Gathering himself and his merchandise together.*) Well, I guess I'll get out and drum up a few sales. Much obliged to you, Mr. Fleming.

PHILIP. Oh, stop at the house, Joe. Mrs. Fleming might want something. It's the old place on Linden Street.

JOE. Got a dog?

PHILIP. Yes.

JOE. That settles it.

PHILIP. Only a pug, Joe.

JOE. Oh, a snorer. I'll sell him a bottle of cough mixture.

(*As* DR. LARKIN *enters.*)

Hello, Doc! How are you? Raining?

(JOE *goes to the door on the right, crossing the* DOCTOR *who is walking toward* PHILIP *on the left.*)

DOCTOR. (*Looking at him, mystified.*) Good morning, sir. No, it's not raining.

(JOE *goes out.* DR. LARKIN *is a tall, gaunt man who looks older than he is, with quite a stoop in his shoulders. He has dark brown hair and a beard, streaked with grey, and soft, kind blue eyes. He carries the medicine satchel of a homeopathic physician. His manner is usually distant and cold but extremely quiet and gentle. In the opening of this scene he is perturbed and irritated, later he becomes stern and authoritative.*)

PHILIP. Good morning, Doctor Larkin.

DOCTOR. (*Turning to* PHILIP.) Who is that fellow? (*He looks after* JOE *as he goes out.*)

PHILIP. Don't you remember him? That's Joe Fletcher. (PHILIP *is standing to the right of the desk, and* DOCTOR LARKIN *at the left center of the stage.*)

DOCTOR. Is that Joe Fletcher? Why he used to be quite a decent sort of fellow. Wasn't he a foreman here in your father's time?

PHILIP. Yes, he was one of the best men in the mill.

DOCTOR. (*Shaking his head.*) He is a sad example of what

liquor and immorality will bring a man to. He has indulged his appetites until he has no real moral nature left.

PHILIP. (*Lightly.*) Oh, I don't think Joe ever had much "moral nature."

(*The sunlight leaves the room. It is growing cloudy outside.*)

DOCTOR. Every man has a moral nature. In this case it is love of drink that has destroyed it. There are some men who are moral lepers, even lacking the weakness of the tippler as an excuse.

PHILIP. Have you been to the house, doctor? About midnight Margaret thought little Lucy had a fever. She was going to call you up—but—

DOCTOR. (*Abruptly.*) She would not have found me in at midnight.

PHILIP. Ah, is that so? Someone very ill?

(*The telephone rings.*)

Excuse me, doctor. Hello. Oh, is that you, Margaret? How is Lucy now? Good! I knew she'd be all right. Yes, of course. Do—bring her. (*To the* DOCTOR.) She's bringing baby to the 'phone. Hello, Lucy. Many happy returns of the day. Good-bye. Yes, I'll be home at twelve sharp. Apple pie? Yes, of course, I like it. That is, *your* apple pie. (*He leaves the phone with a joyous air.*) This is baby's birthday, you know, doctor.

DOCTOR. I've just left a baby (*He speaks bitterly, looking at* PHILIP *significantly.*) that should never have had a birthday.

PHILIP. (*Without noticing the* DOCTOR's *manner, he goes to the cabinet and, taking a box of cigars, offers the box to the* DOCTOR.) Why, Doctor, you're morbid today. Take a cigar, it will quiet your nerves.

(*The rain begins to fall, beating heavily agains the windows.*)

DOCTOR. No, thank you. (*With a subtle shade of repugnance in his tone.*) I'll smoke one of my own.

(PHILIP *smiles indulgently, goes to the desk, sits in the chair to the left of it, lights a cigar, leans back luxuriously, with his hands in his pockets, and one leg over the other, and tips back the legs of the chair.*)

PHILIP. (*Carelessly.*) What's the matter, doctor? You used to respect my cigars.

DOCTOR. (*Hotly.*) I used to respect you.

PHILIP. (*Rather surprised but laughing good-naturedly.*) Well, doctor, and don't you now? (*He is bantering him.*)

DOCTOR. (*Quietly but sternly.*) No, I don't.

PHILIP. (*Smoking placidly.*) Good Lord—why?

DOCTOR. (*His satchel resting upon his knees, his hands clasping the metal top, he leans over a trifle and, looking impressively into* PHILIP's *face, says, in a low, calm voice.*) At two o'clock last night Lena Schmidt gave birth to a child.

PHILIP. (*Becoming livid with amazement and fear, and staring blankly before him, the cigar dropping from his parted lips.*) In God's name, how did they come to send for you?

DOCTOR. Doctor Taylor—he called me in consultation. He was frightened after the girl had been in labor thirty-six hours.

PHILIP. (*Murmuring to himself.*) Thirty-six hours! Good God! (*There is a pause, then he partly recovers himself.*) I suppose she told you?

DOCTOR. She told me nothing. It was a lucky thing for you that I was there. The girl was delirious.

PHILIP. Delirious! Well, I've done all I could for her, doctor.

DOCTOR. Have you? (*His tone is full of scorn.*)

PHILIP. She's had all the money she wanted.

DOCTOR. Has she? (*He speaks in the same tone.*)

PHILIP. I tried to get her away months ago, but she wouldn't do it. She was as stubborn as a mule.

DOCTOR. Strange she should want to remain near the father of her child, isn't it?

PHILIP. If she'd done as I told her to, this thing would never have happened.

DOCTOR. You'd have forced some poor devil to run the risk of state's prison. By God, you're worse than I thought you were.

PHILIP. Why, doctor, you must think I'm—

DOCTOR. I don't think anything about it. I know just what brutes such men as you are.

PHILIP. Well, I'm not wholly to blame. You don't know the whole story, doctor.

DOCTOR. I don't want to know it. The *girl's* not to blame. She's a product of her environment. Under present social conditions, she'd probably have gone wrong anyhow. But you! God Almighty! If we can't look for decency in men like you—representative men—where in God's name are we to look for it, I'd like to know?

PHILIP. If my wife hears of this, my home will be ruined.

DOCTOR. (*Scornfully.*) Your home! Your home! It is just such damn scoundrels as you that make and destroy homes.

PHILIP. Oh, come now, doctor, aren't you a little severe?

DOCTOR. Severe! Severe! Why, do you realize, if this thing should become known, it will stir up a stench that will offend the moral sense of every man, woman and child in this community?

PHILIP. Well, after all, I'm no worse than other men. Why, I haven't seen the girl for months.

DOCTOR. Haven't you? Well, then suppose you go and see her now.

PHILIP. (*He springs to his feet.*) I'll do nothing of the sort.

DOCTOR. Yes, you will. She shan't lie there and die like a dog.

PHILIP. (*He walks around the room greatly perturbed.*) I tell you I'll not go!

DOCTOR. Yes, you will.

PHILIP. (*He comes over to the* DOCTOR *and looks down upon him.*) What'll you do if I don't?

DOCTOR. I don't know, but you'd best go and see that girl.

PHILIP. (*He turns away.*) Well, what do you want me to say to her?

DOCTOR. Lie to her as you have before. Tell her you love her.

PHILIP. I never lied to her. I never told her I loved her.

DOCTOR. Faugh!

PHILIP. I tell you I never did!

DOCTOR. (*Rising from his chair.*) You'd better get Mrs. Fleming away from here until this thing blows over. When I think of a high-minded, splendid little woman like her married to a man like you—ugh! (*The* DOCTOR *goes out quickly.*)

(PHILIP, *left alone, walks about like an old man, seems dazed for a moment, then goes mechanically to the telephone.*)

PHILIP. Linden, 3721. Margaret. (*He speaks in a broken, hushed voice.*) Margaret! Yes, it's I, Philip. Yes! Well, I'm tired. No, I can't come home now. I will not be home to luncheon. I have a business engagement. No, I cannot break it off. It's too important. Eh? Why, with a man from

Boston. Yes, certainly, I will, just as soon as I can get
away. Yes, dear—I will—good-bye.

(*Just before he finishes,* FOSTER *enters.*)

Hello, Foster.

FOSTER. (*Consulting a memorandum.*) I couldn't get the
Harry Smith Company, New York, until noon, sir. They
say that the belting can be shipped by fast express at once.
The Boston people want ten cents a square foot more than
they ask, but we can save that in time and express rates.

PHILIP. When would the New York shipment get here?

FOSTER. At the earliest, tomorrow afternoon.

PHILIP. White and Cross can ship at once, you say?

FOSTER. Yes, sir.

PHILIP. Well, give them the order. Their stuff is better, anyhow. Have a covered wagon at the station for the four-ten
train. Keep enough men over time tonight to put it up.

FOSTER. Yes, sir, the sooner it's done, the better.

PHILIP. Yes, Williams is getting old. He's not the best man
for that finishing room. Put him where you can keep an
eye on him. He's all right. I have an appointment and will
not be in the office again today. Get the interest on those
notes off.

FOSTER. Yes, I've attended to that already. Anything else?

PHILIP. No.

FOSTER. All right, sir. Good morning.

(PHILIP *who has braced himself for this, relaxes again. The
rain continues. He goes about the room, lights a cigar,
puts on a raincoat, looks at his watch, buttons his coat,
all the while sunk in deep thought. He takes his umbrella
and hat and goes out quietly, shutting the door so that
the click of the latch is heard, as the curtain falls.*)

SCENE 2

The scene is the living room in MARGARET's *home. At the
back large glass doors open on to a spacious porch with a
garden beyond. There is a fireplace with logs burning, in the
corner on the left, and beside it a French window opening
on the garden. Below it is a door leading to another room.
There is another door on the right going to the main part of
the house. There is a table in the center, a baby grand piano*

*on the lower right, and a baby carriage close by the doors
at the back. The room is furnished in exquisite taste, showing
in its distinct character the grace and individuality of a well-
bred woman.*

MARGARET *is seated in a low rocking-chair near the fire
with the baby in her lap. A large bath towel is spread
across her knees. She is exquisitely dressed in an evening
gown.*

MARIA BINDLEY, *the nursemaid, is dressed in a black dress,
cap and apron. She is a middle-aged German woman,
dark in complexion, and of medium build and height. She
speaks with a not too pronounced German accent. She is
gathering up the baby's garments which are scattered about*
MARGARET'S *feet. She is furtively weeping and makes an
occasional effort to overcome her emotion.* MARGARET *is
putting the last touches to the baby's night toilet. She is
laughing and murmuring mother talk to her.*

*A shaded lamp is burning on the table to the right. The
effect of the light is subdued. The glare of the fire is the
high note, making a soft radiance about* MARGARET *and
the child.* MARIA *is in the shadow, except as she flits into
the light whenever she moves near* MARGARET. *The sound
of the rain beating against the windows is heard now and
then.*

MARGARET. (*In a low, laughing tone.*) No—no—*no!* You little
beggar. You've had your supper! (*She fastens the last two
or three buttons of her dress.*) No more! Time to go to
sleep now! No use staying awake any longer for naughty
father. Two—whole—hours—late! No, he doesn't care a bit
about you; not a bit! (*She shakes her head.*) No, nor me
either. Never mind, darling, we'll punish him well for this.
Yes, we will. Perhaps we'll leave *him* some day, and then
we'll see how he likes being left alone. Naughty, bad
father—isn't he? *Yes he is!* Staying away all day! Never
mind, ladybird—hush, go to sleep now—Mother loves her!
Go to sleep—close your eyes. (*This is all said in a cooing,
soothing voice. She begins to sing a lullaby.*) Go—to—
sleep—blossom—go to sl—

(MARIA *comes close to* MARGARET *and picks up two little
socks. As she rises, she sniffs in an effort to suppress her*

tears. This attracts MARGARET'S *attention, and immediately she is all commiseration.*)

MARGARET. Don't cry, Maria—please don't—it distresses me to see you cry.

MARIA. (*Smiling a little at* MARGARET'S *sympathy. As she talks, she smooths the socks and folds them.*) I cannot help it, Mrs. Fleming—I am an unhappy woman. I try not to cry, but I cannot keep back de tears. (*She puts the socks in the basket on the table.*) I have had an unhappy life—my fadder vas a brute. (*She picks up the dress and shakes it.*) My first husband, Ralph Bindley, vas a goot, honest man. (*She puts the dress in the basket.*) Und my second husband vas dot tramp vot vas here dis morning. Vat I have told you aboudt already. (*She gathers together the other garments.*) Und now my sister—my little Lena—is dying.

MARGARET. (*In dismay.*) Dying! Why, you didn't tell me *that*, Maria!

MARIA. Vell, she is not dying yust this very moment, but the doctor says she vill never leave dot bed alive. My sweet little Lena! My lovely little sister. I have nursed her, Mrs. Fleming, yust like you nurse your baby now.

MARGARET. (*Holding the child to her breast.*) What did you say her name was?

MARIA. (*Working mechanically and putting the things neatly away.*) Lena,—Lena Schmidt. She does not go by my name—she goes by my fadder's name.

MARGARET. And, you say, she ran away from you?

MARIA. Ya—I tried to find her every place. I hunted high und low, but she does not come, und von day I meet an olt friend on Vashington Street, Chris Anderson, und Chris, he tell me that two or three weeks before he see her by the public gartens. Und she vas valking by the arm of a fine, handsome gentleman—und she look smiling and happy, und Chris, he says dot he knows *dot* gentleman— *dot* he vas a rich man vot lives down in Canton where Chris vonce worked when he comes to dis country first.

MARGARET. And didn't you ask the man's name?

MARIA. Ach, I forget. Und Chris go back to de olt country, und I never find out. Und den I tink maybe she is married to dot man—und she is ashamed of me and dot miserable husband of mine. I say to myself, "I vill go and see—und

find oudt if she is happy." Den I vill go far away, where
she vill never see me again. Und I come here to Canton,
und at last I find her—und Ach Gott! She is going to be a
mutter—und she is no man's vife! (*She has been weeping
silently but has continued to work, only pausing at some
point in her story that moved her.*)

MARGARET. (*Deeply touched.*) Did she tell you the man's
name?

MARIA. Ach! No! You could not drag dot oudt of her mit
red-hot irons. She says she loves dis man, und she vill
make him no trouble. But, by Gott, I vill find dot man
oudt, und I vill choke it from his troat. (*She is beside herself with vindictive passion.*)

MARGARET. (*Terrified at her ferocity and crushing her child
to her breast.*) Oh, Maria—don't—please don't! You frighten
me!

MARIA. (*At once all humility.*) Excuse me, Mrs. Fleming. I
did not mean to do dot.

MARGARET. (*Kindly.*) You need not remain any longer. I can
manage baby myself. You had best go to your sister at
once. If I can be of any help to you, please tell me, won't
you?

MARIA. Ya, Mrs. Fleming, I tank you. Und if she is vorse
maybe I stay all night.

MARGARET. Yes, certainly. You need not come back tonight.

MARIA. (*Very softly and humbly.*) I am much obliged to you,
Mrs. Fleming.

MARGARET. (*As* MARIA *is going.*) Oh! You had best take my
raincoat.

MARIA. Ah, you are very goot, Mrs. Fleming. (*She has
finished her work and is going but hesitates a moment and
turns back.*) If you please, don't tell Mr. Fleming about me
und my poor sister!

MARGARET. (*Slightly annoyed.*) Decidedly not! Why should
I tell such things to him?

MARIA. Vell—men don't have sympathy mit peoples like us.
He is a fine gentleman, und if he knowed about *her*—he
might not like to have *me* by his vife und child. He might
tink *I* vas as badt as she was. Good night, Mrs. Fleming.

MARGARET. Good night, Maria. No need to hurry back in the
morning. (*There is a wistful sympathy in her face. As her
eyes rest upon the door through which* MARIA *has passed,*

she is lost in thought. Presently a door slams, then she is all alert with expectation. There is a moment's pause, she listens then quickly puts the child in the baby carriage and runs to the door.) Is that you, Philip?

JANE. (*Outside.*) No, ma'am, it is not Mr. Fleming. It was only the post man.

(MARGARET *turns away with a sigh of disappointment, goes to the French window and peers out at the rain. The* MAID *enters with several letters, leaves them on the table and goes out.* MARGARET *turns from the window, brushes the tears away impatiently, and drifts purposelessly across the room toward the right, her hands clasped behind her back. Finding herself at the piano she listlessly sits before it and plays a plaintive air, softly. Then suddenly she dashes into a prelude to a gay love song. As she sings half through a stanza, the song gradually loses spirit. Her hands grow heavy over the keys, her voice breaks, and the words come slow and faltering. She ends by breaking into tears, with her head lowered and her fingers resting idly upon the keys. The child attracts her and she goes quickly to her. She laughs through her tears into the wide-open eyes, and begins scolding her for not going to sleep. Soft endearing notes come and go in her voice. A tender joy takes possession of her spirit. She takes the child in her arms.*)

MARGARET. Well, my lady, wide awake! Come, come, no more nonsense, now! No. Go to sleep! Late hours—will—certainly spoil—your beauty. Yes! Close up your eyes—quick! Come! There, that's nice. She's a sweet, good child! (*She hums.*) Go—to—sleep! (*She sways slowly from right to left, then swinging with a rhythmic step with the lullaby, she lilts softly.*) Blow, blow, Blossom go—into the world below—I am the west wind wild and strong—blossoms must go when they hear my song. (*She puts out the lamp, leaving the room in the warm glare of the firelight.*) Go, little blossom, go—into the world below. Rain, rain, rain is here. Blossoms must learn to weep.

(*She reaches the French window. As she turns* PHILIP *is seen through the filmy curtains. He enters unnoticed.*)

I am the east wind, bleak and cold, poor little blossoms their petals must fold. Weep, little blossoms, weep, into your cradles creep.

(*She is unconscious of* PHILIP'S *presence. His raincoat and hat are dripping wet. He is pale and weary, his manner is listless and abstracted and he looks as though he had been wandering about in the rain for hours. He drifts into the room.* MARGARET *turns around and takes a step, her eyes upon the child, then her lullaby grows indistinct as she notices that the baby is asleep. Another step takes her into* PHILIP's *arms. She gives a cry of alarm.*)

MARGARET. . . Oh, Philip! You frightened me! Why did you do that?

PHILIP. Why are you in the dark, Margaret? (*He goes toward her as if to take her in his arms.*) Dearest!

MARGARET. (*Drawing back from him with a shade of petulance.*) You're all wet. Don't come near baby. She was wakeful. I've put her to sleep. Where have you been all day?

PHILIP. Didn't I tell you over the 'phone I had an engagement?

MARGARET. (*As she flits swiftly into the room on the left.*) Did it take you all day to keep it? (*She remains in the room long enough to put the child in the crib and then returns.*)

PHILIP. Yes. A lot of things came up—that I didn't expect. I've been detained. (*He is still standing where she left him.*)

MARGARET. (*Turning up the lamp.*) Why, dear, look! Your umbrella is dripping all over the floor.

PHILIP. (*Noticing the little puddle of water.*) Oh, how stupid of me! (*He hurries out the door on the right, removes his hat and raincoat, leaves the umbrella, and returns quickly.*) (MARGARET, *meanwhile has mopped up the water. Then she turns on the lamp on the table to the right.*)

MARGARET. (*Reproachfully.*) We've been awfully lonesome here all day, baby and I!

PHILIP. (*By the fire.*) Forgive me, sweetheart. I've had a very hard day.

MARGARET. Did you forget it was Lucy's birthday?

PHILIP. (*Smiling gravely.*) No, I didn't forget. You have both been in my mind the whole day.

MARGARET. (*Glowing with love and a welcome that she refused to give until now.*) Oh, Philip! (*She throws herself in his arms.*) It's good to get you back. So good!
(*After a moment she rings the bell. The* MAID *answers.*) Jane, I wish you would serve dinner in here.

JANE. Yes, Mrs. Fleming.

PHILIP. (*Drawing her close to him again.*) Dear little wife!
(*As though a long time had passed since he parted from
her.*)

JANE. (*Coming in with a tray containing food and silver, and
going to the center table.*) Shall I lay the table here, Mrs.
Fleming?

MARGARET. No—here—cosy—by the fire.
(JANE *dresses the table deftly and without bustle. She
goes away and returns with the dinner.*)
You need not return, Jane. I'll ring if we need you.

JANE. Very well, Mrs. Fleming. (*She goes off.*)

PHILIP. (*Sitting to the right of the table, and taking a large
envelope from his pocket, he withdraws a bank book and
hands it to* MARGARET, *who is about to sit down on the
left.*) Here, Margaret—I want you to look over that.

MARGARET. (*Taking the book and reading the cover.*) Margaret Fleming in account with Boston Providence Savings
Bank. (*She opens the book and reads.*) "By deposit, May
3, 1890, $5,000." Five thousand dollars! Oh, Philip!

PHILIP. (*Smiling complacently.*) There's something else.

MARGARET. Yes? (PHILIP *nods his head, and hands her a
large envelope which he has taken from his pocket. She
looks at it and reads.*) "Margaret Fleming, guardian for
Lucy Fleming." (*She takes a document from the envelope.*) A certificate for $20,000 worth of United States
bonds, maturing 1930. Why, Philip! How wonderful. But,
can you afford it?
(*He smiles and nods his head, and then begins to serve
the dinner.* MARGARET, *in childish joy, rushes to the door
of the room where the child is.*)
Oh, baby! Lucy! You are rich, rich! (*She stops and peeps
in.*) Oh, my, I must not wake her. *The little heiress!* (*She
sits at the table and begins to serve.*)

PHILIP. (*Handing her another envelope. Tenderly.*) For you,
Margaret!

MARGARET. (*Taking it and becoming breathless as she reads
it.*) It's a deed for this house and all the land! Ah, Philip,
how generous you are, and this is what has kept you away
all day! And I was cross with you. (*Tears come to her
eyes.*) Forgive me, dear, please do. (*She goes to him and
kneels by his side.*) But, why do you do all this? What
need? What necessity for me to have a deed of property
from you?

PHILIP. Well, things have not been going just our way at the mill. The new tariff laws may help some, but I doubt it. At all events, before anything serious—

MARGARET. (*A little awed.*) Serious?

PHILIP. Well, you never can be sure. At any rate, in times of stress a business man should protect his family.

MARGARET. Is there danger—of—trouble?

PHILIP. No! I hope not. I think I'll be able to tide it over.

MARGARET. But, dear—you—this property, is worth a lot of money. Why not sell it? Wouldn't that be a great help? A resource in case—

PHILIP. Sell the home?

MARGARET. No, sell the house. The home is where we are. (*She rises and stands partly back of his chair with her arms about his neck.*) Where *love is*—no matter *where,* just so long as we three are there together. A big house—a little house—of course, I do love this place, where you were born, and baby— (*Taking a long breath.*) It's very precious—but— (*She has moved back to the head of the table and now lays down the deed.*) I cannot take it, dear. It frightens me. It's too valuable—all this—land—no—let us guard it together and if bad times come, it will be—a fine thing to have—

PHILIP. (*Protesting.*) Now, my dear!

MARGARET. I don't want the responsibility. Suppose something happened to me. (*She sits at the table, on the left.*)

PHILIP. Ah—Margaret—

MARGARET. (*Laughing.*) Well—I just said "suppose."

PHILIP. (*Laughing.*) Well—*don't say it.* We'll think of nothing "suppose." *Nothing,* but bright—*beautiful* things.

MARGARET. Come dear, eat. I should think you were famished. You've touched nothing yet.

PHILIP. I don't feel hungry. I'm tired—awfully tired.

MARGARET. No wonder, after all you've been through today. I'll make you a cup of tea.

(*She rings the bell.* JANE *enters.*)

Boiling water, Jane, please, and bring the tea things. (*While she is busy over the tea things she stops and looks at him quizzically.*) Who was that tramp you sent here this morning?

PHILIP. (*Innocently.*) What tramp?

MARGARET. Why, the one with the plate and the big stone—

the cough medicine,—the sponges and *the voice.* (*She imitates* JOE.)

PHILIP. (*Laughing.*) Ah, he's not a tramp—that's Joe Fletcher.

MARGARET. Did you know that he was Maria's husband?

PHILIP. (*Amazed.*) What! Maria's husband? What did he say to her?

MARGARET. (*Smiling reminiscently.*) He didn't say much— *She* did all the talking.

PHILIP. What did *she* say?

MARGARET. I don't know. She spoke in German. I think, she was swearing at him. When I came she had him by the ears and was trying to pull his head off. Then she got him to the floor and threw him down the front steps. It was the funniest thing I ever saw. I couldn't help laughing, yet my heart ached for her.

PHILIP. Poor Joe! That's the second time she's thrown him out.

MARGARET. She never did that before?

PHILIP. He says she did.

MARGARET. Well, she didn't. He robbed her and left her.

PHILIP. What?

MARGARET. She went out on the road to sell goods and left him in charge of the shop. When she came back he was gone and he had sold out the place to a secondhand dealer.

PHILIP. (*In wonderment.*) What a liar that fellow is!

MARGARET. Well, if he told you any other story—he certainly is. (*She notices a change in his face.*) Why, Philip! You look awfully white! Are you ill? Are you keeping anything from me? Oh, please tell me—do. Let me share your trouble. (*She goes to him, and puts her arms about his shoulders, with her face against his as she finishes the last line.*)

PHILIP. No—no—dear heart—nothing! There's nothing more to tell. I'm very tired.

MARGARET. Oh, how selfish of me. You should have gone to bed the moment you came.

PHILIP. I'll be all right in the morning. I must have caught a chill. (*He shudders.*) My blood seems to be congealed.

MARGARET. (*Alarmed.*) Oh, my dear—my poor boy! It was a dreadful thing you did. (*He starts guiltily.*) Going about in the rain all day. (*She goes swiftly into the room on the left and returns with a handsome dressing gown and slip-*

pers. PHILIP *has gone over to the fire.*) I must give you some aconite. A hot drink—and a mustard foot bath. (*She fusses over him, helps him to get into his dressing gown, and warms his slippers by the fire.*)

PHILIP. I don't think I need anything, dear, but a hot drink, perhaps, and a night's rest. I'll be all right in the morning. I think I'll take a little brandy.

MARGARET. (*Quickly.*) I'll get it for you, dear. Keep by the fire. (*She rushes out the door on the right, and returns quickly with a silver tray holding a cut-glass decanter of brandy and a glass. She pours out some and holds up the glass.*) Is that enough?

PHILIP. Plenty—thank you! (*He drinks it, while* MARGARET *replaces the tray on the small table at the back.*)

MARGARET. Now, dear, I'll look after that mustard bath.

PHILIP. (*Protesting.*) Oh, Margaret, please don't bother. I really don't need it.

MARGARET. (*Laughing at him.*) Yes, you do. (*She shakes her finger threateningly at him.*) You might just as well make up your mind that you've got to have it.

PHILIP. (*Smiling resignedly.*) All right—"boss."

MARGARET. (*Laughing at him as she starts to go.*) You know, Philip, dear, you gave me the strangest feeling when you stood there—the rain dripping from you—you didn't look a bit like yourself. (*She gives an apologetic laugh.*) You gave me a dreadful fright. Just like a spirit! A lost spirit. (*She laughs again.*) Now, wasn't that silly of me? (*She runs off to the right, still laughing.*)

(PHILIP *sits in the fire light looking sadly after her, as the curtain falls.*)

ACT II

The scene is the same as the Second Scene of the First Act. The large doors at the back are open showing a luxuriant garden in brilliant sunshine. The baby is in her carriage by the garden door. MARGARET, *in a dainty house dress, is seated in a low chair in the center of the room, mending one of the baby's dresses.* DR. LARKIN, *sitting at the table on the left with his back turned to her, is folding little packages of medicine.* MARGARET *looks happy and contented as she chats with him.*

DOCTOR. You say you have no pain in the eyes?

MARGARET. No pain at all . . . only, once in awhile there is . . . a . . . sort of dimness.

DOCTOR. Yes, a dimness.

MARGARET. As if my eyes were tired.

DOCTOR. Yes!

MARGARET. When I read too long, or . . .

DOCTOR. (*Turning about and looking at her.*) Do you know what would be a good thing for you to do?

MARGARET. What, doctor?

DOCTOR. Wear glasses.

MARGARET. Why, doctor, aren't you dreadful! (*She laughs at him.*) Why, I'd look a sight.

DOCTOR. Well, it would be a good idea, all the same. You should wear glasses when you are reading or sewing, at least.

MARGARET. (*Laughing gaily at him.*) Well, I'll do nothing of the sort. Time enough for me to wear glasses, years and years from now.

DOCTOR. (*Smiling indulgently.*) It would be a good thing to do now. How is "Topsy" this morning?

MARGARET. (*Glancing proudly in the direction of the baby.*) Oh, she's blooming.

DOCTOR. Mrs. Fleming, any time you want to sell that baby, Mrs. Larkin and I will give you ten thousand dollars for her.

MARGARET. (*Laughing and beaming with pride.*) Yes . . . doctor . . . *when* we *want* to sell her. How is Mrs. Larkin?

DOCTOR. She's doing very nicely. I'm going to try to get her up to the mountains this summer. (*He finishes the packages.*) There . . . take one of these powders three times a day. Rest your eyes as much as possible. Don't let anything fret or worry you, and keep out-doors all you can. (*He closes the bag after putting a couple of bottles and a small medicine case in it.*)

MARGARET. Oh, doctor, aren't you going to leave something for Philip?

DOCTOR. (*Giving a dry, little grunt.*) Hum! I forgot about

him. (*Standing by the table, he takes a small case from his satchel removes two large bottles of pellets from it, fills two phials from them and makes a number upon the cork of each with a fountain pen.*) You say he was pretty wet when he came home last night?

MARGARET. Yes, and tired out. He had a very hard day, I think. I never saw him so completely fagged. It seemed to me he had been tramping in the rain for hours. I gave him a good scolding too, I tell you. I doctored him up as well as I could and put him to bed. (*Smiling contentedly.*) He's as bright as a lark this morning, but all the same, I insisted upon his remaining home for a rest.

DOCTOR. You take good care of him, don't you? (*He beams upon her kindly.*)

MARGARET. (*Playfully.*) I've got to . . . he's all I have, and men like Philip are not picked up every day, now, I tell you.

DOCTOR. (*Drily.*) No, men like Philip Fleming are certainly not to be found easily.

MARGARET. I hope there's nothing wrong with him. I was worried last night. You know, he has been working awfully hard lately.

DOCTOR. (*Kindly.*) Now, don't fret about imaginary ills. He's probably a little overworked. It might be a good idea to have him go away for a week or two.

MARGARET. (*Entering into the suggestion.*) Yes . . . a little trip somewhere would help him a lot, I'm sure.

DOCTOR. (*Holding up his finger.*) But you must go with him, though.

(MARGARET, *by this time, is standing up, with the baby's dress tucked under her arm. She takes stitches as she talks.*)

MARGARET. (*Eagerly.*) Of course! I wouldn't let him go alone. Somebody might steal him from me. (*She smiles.*)

DOCTOR. (*Snapping the clasp of his satchel, vehemently murmurs under his breath.*) Hum! They'd bring him back mighty quick, I guess. (*He turns to her.*) Give him these. Tell him to take two alternately every hour.

MARGARET. (*Taking the phials, and nodding her head as if to remember.*) Two every hour—thank you.

(PHILIP *enters from the garden, gaily humming an air. He has a freshly plucked rose in his hand.*)

PHILIP. Good morning, doctor.

DOCTOR. (*Coldly.*) Good morning.

MARGARET. (*Noticing the rose, regretfully.*) Oh, Philip, you plucked that rose.

PHILIP. Yes, isn't it lovely? It's the first of the season. (*He smells it.*)

MARGARET. Yes, and I've been watching it. I wanted it to open yesterday for baby's birthday.

PHILIP. (*Playfully.*) It saved itself for today for baby's mother. (*He puts it on her breast.*)

MARGARET. (*Pleased.*) Well, I'd rather it had bloomed yesterday for her. Excuse me, doctor, I must run into the kitchen. We have a new cook and she needs watching.

PHILIP. (*Gaily.*) And she's a dandy. (*He breaks into a chant.*) Oh, I'm glad we've got a new cookie. I'm glad we've got a new cook. She's . . .

MARGARET. (*Laughing at him.*) Hush! Hush! Philip, stop— be quiet! (*She puts her hand over his mouth. He tries to sing through her fingers.*) She'll hear you. Oh, doctor, isn't he terrible? He's poking fun at her all the time, but she is funny, though. (*She runs off joyously to the right.*)

PHILIP. What a glorious morning, after yesterday.

DOCTOR. (*Eyeing him coldly.*) Yes—it is—you're in high feather this morning, eh?

PHILIP. (*Cheerily.*) Of course I am. What's the good in worrying over things you can't help?

DOCTOR. Have you seen . . . ?

PHILIP. (*Quickly.*) Yes. (*In a low voice.*) I've made arrangements for her to go away as soon as she is well enough.

DOCTOR. *Humph!*

PHILIP. It's a terrible mess. I'll admit I never realized what I was doing, but I shall make things all right for this girl, and her child. (*He sits on the edge of the table to the left. The* DOCTOR *is standing to the right of him.*) Doctor, I'm going to tell my wife this whole, miserable story.

DOCTOR. (*Aghast.*) What?

PHILIP. (*Hastily interrupting.*) Ah, not now—in the future. When we both have grown closer together. When I have shown her by an honest and decent life that I ought to be forgiven—when I feel sure of her faith and confidence— then I shall confess and ask her to forgive me.

DOCTOR. (*Shaking his head.*) That would be a mighty hazardous experiment. You would draw a woman's heart strings closer and closer about you—and then deliberately tear them asunder. Best keep silent·forever.

PHILIP. There would be no hazard. I know Margaret—of course if she found me out now—I admit it—it would be a terrible thing, but—

DOCTOR. (*Abruptly.*) You'd better get Mrs. Fleming away from here for a few weeks.

PHILIP. (*Surprised.*) Away? (*He smiles confidently.*) What need?

DOCTOR. She is threatened with a serious affection of the eyes.

PHILIP. (*His smile fading away, then recovering quickly and laughing lightly.*) Aren't you trying to frighten me, doctor?

DOCTOR. (*Annoyed by his levity.*) I don't care anything about you, but, I tell you, your wife has a tendency to an affection of the eyes called glaucoma.

PHILIP. (*Interested.*) Glaucoma? Affection of the eyes? Why, Margaret has magnificent eyes.

DOCTOR. Yes, she has magnificent eyes, but, her child is the indirect cause of the development of an inherent weakness in them.

PHILIP. In what way?

DOCTOR. Conditions incident to motherhood. Shock. She is showing slight symptoms now that if aggravated would cause very serious consequences.

PHILIP. (*Puzzled.*) I do not understand.

DOCTOR. The eye—like other organs—has its own special secretion, which keeps it nourished and in a healthy state. The inflow and outflow of this secretion is equal. The physician sometimes comes across a patient of apparently sound physique, in whom he will find an abnormal condition of the eye where this natural function is, through some inherent weakness, easily disturbed. When the patient is subject to illness, great physical or mental suffering—the too great emotion of a sudden joy or sorrow—the stimulus of any one of these causes may produce in the eyes a super-abundant influx of this perfectly healthy fluid and the fine outflowing ducts cannot carry it off.

PHILIP. Yes. What then?

DOCTOR. The impact continues—until the result—is—

PHILIP. Yes? What is the result?

DOCTOR. Blindness.

PHILIP. (*Awed.*) Why—that is horrible—is there no remedy?

DOCTOR. Yes. A very delicate operation.

PHILIP. Always successful?

DOCTOR. If performed under proper conditions—yes.

PHILIP. And my wife is in danger of this? (*He walks up and down the room.*)

DOCTOR. There is no danger whatever to Mrs. Fleming, if the serenity of her life is not disturbed. There are slight, but nevertheless serious symptoms that must be remedied at once, with ordinary care. She will outgrow this weakness. Perhaps you will understand now, how necessary it is that she leave Canton for a few weeks.

PHILIP. (*Deeply impressed by the* DOCTOR's *recital.*) Yes, I do. I will set about getting her away at once. I can leave the mill for a while in Foster's hands.

DOCTOR. Yes, he is an honest, capable fellow. Above all things, do not let Mrs. Fleming suspect that there is anything serious the matter. Keep her cheerful.

PHILIP. Ah, Margaret is the sunniest, happiest disposition—nothing troubles her.

DOCTOR. Well, you keep her so.

(PHILIP *takes out his cigar case and offers it to the* DOCTOR. *The latter refuses laconically.*)

Thank you, I have my own.

(*He has taken a cigar from his vest pocket.* PHILIP *strikes a match and offers it to the doctor. At the same time, the* DOCTOR *is lighting his cigar with his own match, ignoring* PHILIP's *attention.* PHILIP *shrugs his shoulders indulgently, lights his cigar and good-naturedly watches the* DOCTOR, *who takes up his satchel and leaves the room hastily with a curt.*)

Good morning.

PHILIP. (*Genially.*) Good morning, Dr. Larkin. (*He sits in the armchair to the right and comfortably contemplates the convolutions of the cigar smoke.*)

(*The closing of the front door is heard.* JOE FLETCHER *appears at the French window, stealthily peering into the room. He sees* PHILIP *and coughs.*)

JOE. Hello, Mr. Fleming!

PHILIP. (*Looking up.*) Hello, Joe—come in.

JOE. (*In a whisper.*) Is it safe?

PHILIP. (*Laughing.*) Yes, I guess so.

JOE. (*Slouching inside.*) Where's Maria?

PHILIP. Gone out.

JOE. (*Relieved.*) Say, that was a damn mean trick you played on me yesterday.

PHILIP. What trick?

JOE. Sending me up here—you knew durn well she'd go fer me.

PHILIP. (*Laughing.*) I didn't know Maria was your wife, honest I didn't.

JOE. Oh, tell that to the marines. I want my sign. (*As* PHILIP *looks puzzled.*) The sample of giant's cement with the plate.

PHILIP. (*Remembering.*) Oh, yes. (*He chuckles to himself, goes to the door at the right and brings back the cracked plate with the big stone hung to it.* JOE *takes it and turns to go.*) Why did you lie to me yesterday?

JOE. I didn't lie to you.

PHILIP. You told me your wife ran away from you.

JOE. So she did.

PHILIP. *She* says you robbed her and left her.

JOE. She's a liar, and I'll tell it to her face.

PHILIP. (*Laughing.*) Come, Joe, you wouldn't dare.

JOE. She's a liar. I'm not afraid of her.

PHILIP. She made you run yesterday.

JOE. (*Holding up the sign.*) Didn't she have this? What chance has a fellow got when a woman has a *weapon* like this?

PHILIP. (*Laughing at him.*) And you were in the war.

JOE. Yes, and I was in the war! The Johnnies didn't fight with things like this.

PHILIP. (*Enjoying the situation.*) Come, Joe, I believe she'd make you run without that.

JOE. She's a liar. I can lick her. (*With conviction.*) I have licked her. (*He grows bolder.*) An' I'll lick her again.

PHILIP. (*Laughing heartily.*) Come, Joe, that'll do. The best way for you to lick 'er is there.

(*He points to the decanter upon the side table.* JOE *gazes upon it tenderly and chuckles with unctuous satisfaction.*)

JOE. That's a great joke, Mr. Fleming. *Kin* I? (*He shuffles over to the decanter.*)

PHILIP. Yes, go ahead.

(JOE *pours the liquor into a glass.* MARIA *walks hastily in through the window and sees* PHILIP.)

MARIA. (*Diffidently.*) Excuse me, Mr. Fleming, I did not

know you vas here. I always come in dot way mit de baby.
(JOE *is in the act of carrying the glass to his lips. He hears*
MARIA's *voice and stands terrified.* MARIA *sees him and
becomes inflamed with indignation. She puts her hands
on her hips and glares at him.*)
Vell, you dom scoundrel!

JOE. (*Soothingly extending a hand to her.*) There now,
Maria, keep cool. Don't lose your temper.

MARIA. (*Mocking him.*) Yah, don't lose my temper. Didn't
I tell you never to darken dis house again? Du Teufel aus
Hölle! (*She makes a lunge at him. He dodges and hops on
tip-toe from side to side in a zig-zag.*)

JOE. Just a minute, Maria! (*He gulps.*) I can—I can explain—
the whole—thing.
(*He makes a desperate bolt, but* MARIA *is on his heels.
He stumbles and falls sprawling upon his hands and face,
with his head to the front, in the center of the room. She
swoops upon him, digs her hands into the loose folds of
his coat between the shoulders and drags him to his feet.
He limps with fright, puffing and spluttering, awkwardly
helping himself and dropping the sign.*)
Maria, for God's sake, don't! I ain't ever done anything
to you.

MARIA. (*Dragging him toward the window.*) Ach, Gott! No,
you have never done nutting to me.

JOE. I'll make it all right with you. Let me go. I want my
sign! Ugh!
(*She throws him through the French window. He stumbles
and staggers out of sight.* MARIA *picks up the sign and
flings it after him. All the time she is scolding and weeping
with anger.*)

MARIA. Don't you dare come here no more to a decent house,
you loafer. You can't explain nutting to me, you tief—you
loafer— (*She sinks into the chair at the right of the table,
leans her arms across the table, buries her face in them
and sobs bitterly. All her fury has vanished and she is
crushed and broken.*)

PHILIP. (*Laughing and calling after* JOE.) Joe, come back!
Joe! (*He goes out through the window.*) Joe!

MARGARET. (*Rushing in and up to the garden door, afraid
some harm has come to the child.*) What on earth is the
matter? An earthquake?

MARIA. (*Sobbing.*) No. Mrs. Fleming. It vas dot miserable husband of me.

MARGARET. What?

MARIA. Yah, I yust came in now, und I find him dere drinking of Mr. Fleming's brandy.

MARGARET. Good gracious—what did you do, Maria?

MARIA. I skipped dot gutter mit him, I bet my life. (*She is still weeping.*)

MARGARET. (*A smile flickering about her lips.*) There, Maria, don't cry. Don't let him trouble you so. How is your sister?

MARIA. Vorse, Mrs. Fleming.

MARGARET. Worse. Oh, I'm so sorry.

MARIA. Yah. I don't tink she vill ever leave dot bed alive. My poor little Lena. Mrs. Fleming, I ask you—mebbe you vill come to see her. She talks about you all de time now.

MARGARET. (*Surprised.*) Talks about me? Why, how does she know me?

MARIA. Vell, she ask about you—a lot—und I tell her of you and your beautiful home und your little baby, und now she says she'd like yust once to look into your face.

MARGARET. (*Hesitating a moment.*) Well, I'll go. If I only could do anything for her, poor girl.

MARIA. Yah, she is a poor girl, Mrs. Fleming. Mebbe she vill tell you the name of dis man vot—

MARGARET. (*With repugnancè.*) Oh, no, no! I don't want to know the brute, or his name.

MARIA. (*Vindictively.*) Oh, Gott! If I vould know it—

MARGARET. (*Breaking in upon her, kindly.*) But, I'll go to see her.

MARIA. Tank you, Mrs. Fleming. You are a goodt lady.

MARGARET. Where did you say she lives?

MARIA. (*Still quietly weeping.*) Forty-two Millbrook Street. By Mrs. Burton's cottage.

MARGARET. Very well.

(PHILIP's *voice is heard outside, laughing.*)

Oh, there's Mr. Fleming. Come, Maria, don't let him see you crying. Come, go to the kitchen and tell Hannah— (*She has urged* MARIA *to her feet and is pressing her toward the door.*)

MARIA. Is dot new girl come?

MARGARET. Yes.

MARIA. Hannah is her name?

MARGARET. (*Pressing her.*) Yes, tell her to make you a nice cup of tea, and then you'd best go back to your sister.

MARIA. Tank you, Mrs. Fleming. I don't want no tea. Mebbe she needs me. I go right back to her. You'll come sure, Mrs. Fleming?

MARGARET. (*Putting her through the door on the right as* PHILIP *comes in through the window on the left.*) Yes, I'll come in a little while.

PHILIP. Oh, Margaret, I wish you'd been here. (*He begins to laugh.*) Such a circus. The funniest thing I ever saw.

MARGARET. Yes, Maria told me. Poor thing. I'm sorry for her. (PHILIP *laughs. She goes to her work basket which is on the center table, and takes out the two phials.* PHILIP *crosses to the right and* MARGARET *goes to him.*)
Here, dear—some medicine Dr. Larkin left for you.

PHILIP. (*Pushing her hand away gently.*) Oh, I don't want any medicine. There's nothing the matter with me. (*He begins to chuckle again.*) If you could—

MARGARET. (*Shaking him by the lapels of his jacket.*) Yes, there is a great deal the matter with you. (*She looks at him seriously and he becomes serious.*) Doctor says you're all run down. You've got to have a rest. Here, now, take two of these pellets, alternating every hour.
(*He takes the phials and puts them in his vest pocket.*)
Take some now!

PHILIP. Oh! Now? Must I?

MARGARET. (*Shaking him.*) Yes, this minute.
(*He takes two pellets and pretends to choke. She shakes him again.*)
Look at your watch. Note the time.

PHILIP. Yes'm.

MARGARET. Well, in an hour, take two from the other phial.

PHILIP. Yes'm. (*He lights a fresh cigar, and* MARGARET *gives a cry of reproval.*)

MARGARET. Philip! What are you doing? (*She rushes at him and takes the cigar from him.*) Don't you know you mustn't smoke when you are taking medicine.

PHILIP. Why not?

MARGARET. It'll kill the effect of it. You may smoke in an hour.

PHILIP. I've got to take more medicine in an hour?

MARGARET. Well, I guess you'll have to give up smoking.

PHILIP. What!

MARGARET. Until you're well.

PHILIP. But, I'm well now.

MARGARET. (*Going through the door on the left.*) *Until you have stopped taking those pellets!*

PHILIP. All right. I'll forget them.

MARGARET. Philip!

PHILIP. (*Going to the baby in the garden doorway.*) The cigars! What are you doing?

MARGARET. Changing my gown. I'm going out.

PHILIP. Where are you going?

MARGARET. Oh, just a little errand.

PHILIP. Well, hurry back.

MARGARET. Yes, I won't be long. (*She gives a little scream.*) Oh!

PHILIP. What's the matter?

MARGARET. Nothing. Stuck a pin into my finger, that's all.

PHILIP. My! You gave me a shock. (*He puts his hand to his heart playfully.*)

MARGARET. (*Laughing.*) Sorry. Did you see my gloves?

PHILIP. Yes.

MARGARET. Where?

PHILIP. On your hands, of course.

MARGARET. Now, don't be silly!

PHILIP. (*Playing with the baby.*) Margaret, you know, baby's eyes are changing.

MARGARET. No.

PHILIP. Yes. They're growing like yours.

MARGARET. Nonsense. She has your eyes.

PHILIP. (*Eyeing the baby critically.*) No, they're exactly like yours. She's got my nose though.

MARGARET. (*Giving a little cry of protest.*) Oh, Philip—don't say that.

PHILIP. Why?

MARGARET. It would be terrible if she had your nose. Just imagine my dainty Lucy with a great big nose like yours.

PHILIP. (*Feeling his nose.*) Why, I think I have a very nice nose.

MARGARET. (*Coming in, laughing.*) Oh, yes, it's a good enough nose—as noses go—but— (*She touches the bell.*)

PHILIP. (*Noticing her gown.*) Your new suit?

MARGARET. (*Gaily.*) Yes. Like it?

PHILIP. It's a dandy. Turn around.

(*She dances over to him and twirls about playfully.*)
Wait, there's a thread. (*He picks it off her skirt.*)
(JANE *enters.*)

MARGARET. Jane, please tell Hannah to come here.

JANE. Yes, ma'am. (*She goes.*)

(PHILIP *begins to chuckle.*)

MARGARET. Now, Philip, I implore you to keep still. Please
don't get me laughing while I'm talking to her.

PHILIP. (*Indignantly.*) I'm not going to say anything.

(HANNAH *appears. She is very large, stout and dignified.*)

MARGARET. (*Hurriedly, in haste to be off.*) Hannah! I'm
going out and I shall not be able to look after the baking
of the bread. When the loaves have raised almost to the
top of the pans put them in the oven.

HANNAH. (*Who has been studying admiringly* MARGARET'S
costume.) Yes, Ma'am. I does always put the bread in
when it's almost up to the top in the pans.

MARGARET. And bake them just one hour.

HANNAH. Ah! Yes, ma'am. I always bakes 'em an hour.

(PHILIP *smothers a laugh in a cough.* MARGARET *stares at
him.*)

MARGARET. And, have luncheon on at half past twelve, please.

HANNAH. Yes, I always has the lunch on at half past twelve,
sharp.

MARGARET. (*Who has been putting on her gloves.*) Thank
you, Hannah, that's all. Well, I'm off. (*To* PHILIP.) Good-
bye, dear. (*She starts off hastily.*)

HANNAH. Good-bye, ma'am. (*She goes out.*)

MARGARET. (*Pausing to look at* PHILIP *as he plays with the
baby in the carriage.*) Oh, how dear you both look there
together.

PHILIP. (*Looking at his watch.*) You'd best hurry if you want
to get back at *half past twelve, sharp.* (*He imitates*
HANNAH.)

MARGARET. (*Rapturously gazing at them.*) Oh, if I could
paint, what a picture I would make of you two!

PHILIP. Are you going?

MARGARET. Yes, I'm going. (*She notices* PHILIP *giving the
baby his watch, and giving a little scream of alarm, she
rushes at him.*) Philip, what are you doing?

PHILIP. That's all right. She won't hurt it.

MARGARET. Suppose she'd swallow it.

PHILIP. Well!

MARGARET. (*Mocking him.*) Well! There, put it in your pocket. And have some sense. (*She picks up the rattle and the big rubber ball and puts them in his hands.*) There, you can play with these. (*They both laugh with the fun of it all.*)

PHILIP. Oh! Go on Margaret, and hurry home.

MARGARET. (*Kissing him and the baby.*) All right. Won't be long. Don't forget your medicine, and please don't smoke when my back is turned. (*She dances out through the French window, over-flowing with fun and animation. This scene must be played rapidly, with a gay, light touch.*)

ACT III

The scene is a neat, plainly furnished sitting-room in MRS. BURTON's *cottage. The walls are covered with old-fashioned wall-paper of a faded green color. Sunlight streams in through two windows at the back. In one there is a small table holding a few pots of geraniums, and in the second, a hanging basket of ivy. A few straggling vines creep about the window-frame. There are doors at the left center, down left and on the right. In the center of the room stands a table with a chair to the right of it, and a few hair-cloth chairs are here and there. A sofa stands against the left wall below the door, and there is a low rocking-chair on the left.*

The room is empty and after a moment the stillness is broken by the wail of an infant. The hushed notes of a woman's voice are heard from the open door on the left, soothing the child. A low knock is heard at the door to the right. The door opens slowly and DOCTOR LARKIN *enters.* MRS. BURTON *emerges from the room on the left with a tiny baby wrapped in a soft white shawl in her arms. She is a motherly woman, large and placid, with a benign immobility of countenance. She speaks with a New England drawl.*

MRS. BURTON. Good morning, doctor. I didn't hear ye knock.

DOCTOR. How is your patient this morning?

MRS. BURTON. Why, ain't yer seen Dr. Taylor? Didn't he tell
ye?

DOCTOR. No. She's—?

MRS. BURTON. (*Nodding her head.*) Yes.

DOCTOR. When did it happen?

MRS. BURTON. About an hour ago. She seemed brighter this
morning. After her sister went out she slept for a while.
When I came in the room she opened her eyes and asked
me for a pencil and paper. I brought 'em to her and she
writ for quite a spell. Then she lay back on the pillow. I
asked her if she wouldn't take a little nourishment. She
smiled and shook her head. Then she gave a long sigh—an'
—an'—that was all there was to it.

DOCTOR. How's the child?

MRS. BURTON. Poor little critter— (*She looks down at it.*) I
can't do nothing for it. I've tried everything. It ought to
have mother's milk—that's all there is to it. Be quiet, you
poor little motherless critter.

DOCTOR. It would be better for it if it had gone with her.

MRS. BURTON. Why, doctor, ain't ye awful?

DOCTOR. Why, what chance has that child got in this world?
I'll send you something for it. (*He turns to go.*)

MRS. BURTON. Don't ye want to see her?

DOCTOR. No! What good can I be to her now, poor devil?
(CHARLEY BURTON, *a sturdy lad of ten, breaks boisterously
into the room from the door on the right, carrying a base-
ball and bat.*)

CHARLEY. Ma! Ma! Here's a woman wants to see Mrs.
Bindley.

MRS. BURTON. (*Reprimanding him.*) Lady! And take your
hat off.
(DOCTOR LARKIN *and* MRS. BURTON *look expectantly toward
the door.* MARGARET *enters slowly, her eyes bent upon her
glove which she is unfastening.* DR. LARKIN *is dumbfounded
at the sight of her. She takes a few steps toward him and
looks up.*)

MARGARET. (*Pleasantly surprised at seeing him.*) Why, doctor! I didn't know that you were on this case.

DOCTOR. (*Confused.*) I'm not. Dr. Taylor—he—called me in
consultation. But, what in the name of all that's wonderful
brings you here?

MARGARET. Maria!

DOCTOR. What Maria? Not—

MARGARET. Yes, our Maria—this sick girl is her sister. (*She removes her hat and places it with her gloves on the table.*)

DOCTOR. (*In consternation.*) Her sister! Then you know?

MARGARET. I know that there is a poor sick girl here who wants—

DOCTOR. (*Going to her, brusquely.*) Mrs. Fleming, you'd best not remain here—the girl is dead. Go home.

MARGARET. (*Pityingly.*) Dead? Poor thing!

DOCTOR. Yes. Does your husband know you are here?

MARGARET. (*Shaking her head.*) Oh, no!

DOCTOR. Come, you must go home! (*He almost pushes her out of the room in his urgency.*)

MARGARET. (*Resisting him gently.*) Ah, no, doctor. Now that I am here, let me stay. I can be of some help, I know.

DOCTOR. No, you can be of no use. Everything has been done.

MARGARET. Well, I'll just say a word to Maria. Where is she?

DOCTOR. I don't know—I don't know anything about Maria.

MRS. BURTON. She's in there. (*She nods toward the door on the left.*)

(*The* DOCTOR *has crowded* MARGARET *almost through the door in his eagerness to have her out of the house. She is reluctantly yielding to him, when* MRS. BURTON'S *voice arrests her. She turns quickly and, looking over the* DOCTOR'S *shoulder, notices the child in* MRS. BURTON'S *arms. She impulsively brushes the* DOCTOR *aside and goes toward her, her face beaming with tender sympathy.*)

MARGARET. Oh, is this the baby?

MRS. BURTON. Yes'm.

MARGARET. (*Going close to her on tip-toes and gazing with maternal solicitude down upon the child.*) Poor little baby! What a dear mite of a thing it is.

MRS. BURTON. Yes'm.

MARGARET. (*Impulsively.*) Doctor, we must take care of this baby.

DOCTOR. (*Impatiently.*) You've got a baby of your *own*, Mrs. Fleming.

MARGARET. Yes, and that's why I pity this one. I suppose, I always did love babies, anyhow. They are such wonderful, mysterious little things, aren't they?

MRS. BURTON. Yes'm.

DOCTOR. (*Spurred by a growing sense of catastrophe.*) Mrs.
Fleming, there is danger to your child in your remaining
here.

MARGARET. (*Alarmed.*) Oh, doctor!

DOCTOR. I hated to tell you this before—but—there is con-
tagion in this atmosphere.

MARGARET. (*Hastily taking her hat from the table.*) Doctor,
why didn't you—
(*She is hurrying away when she is checked by a poignant
moan. She turns a frightened face and sees* MARIA *coming
from the room on the left with a letter in her hand.*
MARIA'S *face is distorted by grief.*)

MARIA. Ah, Mrs. Burton, I have found out who dot man is.
He is— (*She sees* MARGARET *and smiles bitterly upon her.*)
So,—you have come, Mrs. Fleming?

MARGARET. (*Making a movement of sympathy.*) Maria!

MARIA. Vell, you may go back again. You can do nutting for
her now. She is dead. (*Perversely.*) But, ven you do go,
you vill take dot baby back mit you. He shall now have
two babies instead of one.

MARGARET. (*Smiling.*) What do you mean, Maria? Who shall
have two babies?

MARIA. (*Fiercely.*) Philip Fleming—dot's who.
(MARGARET *stares at her, only comprehending half what*
MARIA *means.* DR. LARKIN *goes quickly to her.*)

DOCTOR. Come away, Mrs. Fleming—the woman is crazy.
(*He tries to draw her away.*)

MARIA. (*Contemptuously.*) No, I ain't crazy! (*She shakes
the letter at* MARGARET.) You read dot letter and see if I
vas crazy!
(MARGARET, *in a dazed way, reaches for the letter, and
tries to read it, turning it different ways.*)

MARGARET. I cannot make it out. (*She hands it to the doctor,
and says helplessly.*) Read it—to me—doctor—please.

DOCTOR. (*Beside himself and snatching the letter.*) No, nor
shall you. (*He makes a motion to tear the letter.*)

MARIA. (*Threateningly.*) Don't you tear dot letter, doctor.

MARGARET. (*Putting her hand out gently.*) You must not
destroy that letter, doctor. Give it back to me. (DR. LARKIN
returns the letter reluctantly. MARGARET *attempts to read
it, fails, becomes impatient, and hands it to* MARIA, *helplessly.*) You read it to me, Maria.

(MARIA, *whose passion has subsided, takes the letter in an awed manner and begins to read it. The* DOCTOR *is in a daze.* MARGARET *sinks into the chair to the right of the table. She has recovered her calm poise, but does not seem to be at all the same* MARGARET.)

MARIA. (*Reading in a simple, unaffected manner.*)

Canton, June 10,

DEAR MR. FLEMING:

You was good to come to see me, and I thank you. I will not trouble you no more. I am sorry for what has happened. I know you never loved me and I never asked you to, but I loved you. It was all my fault. I will never trouble you no more. You can do what you like with the baby. I do not care. Do not be afraid, I shall never tell. They tried to get me to but I never shall. Nobody will ever know. No more at present, from your obedient servant,

LENA SCHMIDT.

MARGARET. (*Turning to the* DOCTOR, *who is standing close to her chair.*) Did you know—anything of this—doctor?

DOCTOR. (*Evasively.*) Well—I knew—something of it—but, this girl may be lying. Such as she is—will say anything sometimes.

MARIA. (*Fiercely.*) Don't you say dot, doctor. She would not tell nutting to hurt him, not to save her soul.

DOCTOR. (*With finality.*) Well, now that you know the worst, come away from here—come home.

MARIA. (*Bitterly.*) Oh! Ya! She can go home. She have alvays got a home und a husband und fine clothes, because she is his vife, but my poor sister don't have any of dese tings, because she is only de poor mistress. But, by Gott, she shall not go home unless she takes dot baby back mit her.

DOCTOR. She shall do nothing of the sort.

MARIA. Vell, den, I vill take it, und fling it in his face.

MARGARET. (*Calmly, and rising from the chair.*) You shall not go near him. You shall not say—one word to him!

MARIA. Von't I? Who is going to stop me? I vould yust like to know dot?

MARGARET. (*Quite calmly.*) I am!

MARIA. (*Mockingly.*) You—you vill take his part, because

you are his vife! (*Fiercely.*) Vell! (*She draws a pistol from her dress pocket.*) Do you see dot gun? Vell, I buy dot gun, und I swore dot ven I find out dot man I vill have his life. Und, if you try to stop me, I vill lay you stiff und cold beside her.

MARGARET. (*Calmly, pityingly, holding out her hand as though to quiet her.*) Maria! Stop! How dare you talk like that to me? Give me that pistol.

(MARIA, *awed by* MARGARET'S *spirit, meekly hands her the weapon.*)

You think—I—am happy—because I am his wife? Why, you poor fool, that girl (*She points to the door on the left*) never in all her life suffered one thousandth part what I have suffered in these past five minutes. Do you dare to compare her to me? I have not uttered one word of re-proach, even against her, and yet she has done me a wrong, that not all the death-bed letters that were ever written can undo. I wonder what I have ever done to deserve this! (*She loses control of herself and sinks sob-bing, into the chair, her arms upon the table, and her head dropping upon them.*)

DOCTOR. (*Overcome by the situation, throws his arms about her and tries to draw her to her feet.*) For God's sake, Mrs. Fleming, let me take you out of this hell.

MARGARET. (*Gently resisting him.*) Ah, doctor, you cannot take *this hell* out of my breast. (*Suddenly her manner changes. She says with quick decision.*) Maria, get me a sheet of writing paper. Doctor, give me a pencil.

(DOCTOR LARKIN *puts his hand into his vest pocket.* MARIA, *who seems dazed, looks helplessly about as though the paper might be within reach. Then suddenly thinking of the letter in her hand, she tears off the blank half of it and quickly lays it on the table before* MARGARET.)

DOCTOR. (*Giving her the pencil.*) What are you going to do?

MARGARET. Send—for *him!*

DOCTOR. No—not here!

MARGARET. Yes—here— (*She writes nervously, mumbling what she writes.*) "Philip: I am waiting for you, here. That girl is *dead.*" (*She folds the letter.*) Where's that boy?

(MARIA *and* MRS. BURTON *both make a movement in search of* CHARLEY.)

MARIA. Charley! (*She goes to the door at the back and calls again in a hushed voice.*) Charley! (CHARLEY *enters. She*

whispers to him that the lady wants him.) You, go quick!
(CHARLEY *goes to* MARGARET.)

MARGARET. (*In tense nervousness.*) Charley, do you know
Mr. Fleming?

CHARLEY. Yes'm.

MARGARET. Do you know where he lives?

CHARLEY. Yes'm—on Canton Street.

MARGARET. Yes—go there—don't ring the bell—go through the
garden—you will find him there, playing with the baby.
Give him this.

CHARLEY. Any answer?

MARGARET. (*At nervous tension.*) No! Go quick! Quick! (*She
springs to her feet.*) Now, doctor—I want you to leave me!

DOCTOR. Mrs. Fleming, for God's sake don't see him here.

MARGARET. Yes, here—and—alone! Please go. (*The* DOCTOR
does not respond.) I don't want you or any other living
being to hear what passes between him and me, and,
(*She points to the room.*) *that dead girl.* Please go!

DOCTOR. Mrs. Fleming, as your physician, I order you to
leave this place at once.

MARGARET. No, doctor—I must see him, *here.*

DOCTOR. (*With gentle persuasion.*) Mrs. Fleming, you have
no right to do this. Think of your child.

MARGARET. (*Remembering.*) My baby! My poor, little innocent baby! Oh, I wish to God that she were dead. (*She
is beside herself and not realizing what she says. She
crosses to the left.*)

DOCTOR. (*Following her.*) Mrs. Fleming, in God's name, calm
yourself! I have tried to keep it from you, but, I am forced
to tell you— (*He is so deeply moved that he is almost
incoherent.*) If you continue in this way, dear lady, you
are exposing yourself to a terrible affliction—this trouble—
with your eyes. You are threatened with—if you keep up
this strain—a sudden blindness may fall upon you.

MARGARET. (*Appalled.*) Blind! Blind! (*She speaks in a low
terrified voice.*) Oh, no doctor, not *that*—not *now*—not until
after I've seen him.

DOCTOR. Not only that, but if you keep up this strain much
longer, it may cost you your life.

MARGARET. I don't care—what happens to me, only, let me
see him, and then, the sooner it all comes the better. (*She
crosses to the left with the* DOCTOR *following her.*)

DOCTOR. (*Growing desperate, and throwing his arms about*

her.) Mrs. Fleming, you must leave this place! Come home.

MARGARET. No. Doctor, please leave me alone. (*She draws herself from him.*) I tell you I've got to see him here. (*Then with a sweet intimacy, she goes to him.*) A woman has a strange feeling for the physician who brings her child into the world—I love you—I have always obeyed your orders, haven't I? (*She speaks brokenly.*)

DOCTOR. (*Quietly.*) Always.

MARGARET. Then, let me be the doctor now, and I order you to leave this house at once.

DOCTOR. (*Hopelessly.*) You are determined to do this thing?

MARGARET. (*With finality.*) Yes.

DOCTOR. Very well then—good-bye. (*He holds out his hand, which she takes mechanically. He holds her hand warmly for a moment. She clings to him as though afraid to let him go, then slowly draws away.*)

MARGARET. Good-bye!

(*The* DOCTOR *leaves the room quickly.* MARGARET *takes a step after him until she touches the left side of the table in the center. She stands there gazing into space, the calmness of death upon her face. The sunlight streaming through the window falls upon her.* MRS. BURTON *is sitting in a rocking-chair in the corner of the room.* MARIA *is sitting on the sofa at the left, weeping silently, with clasped hands, her arms lying in her lap, her body bent. She makes a plaintive moan before she speaks.*)

MARIA. Ah—Mrs. Fleming, you must not do dis ting. Vat vas I—vot was she, I'd like to know—dot ve should make dis trouble for you? You come here, like an angel to help us, und I have stung you like a snake in dot grass. (*She goes to* MARGARET *and falls upon her knees beside her.*) Oh, Mrs. Fleming, on my knees I ask you to forgive me.

(MARGARET *stands immobile at the table, her right hand resting upon its edge—her left hand partly against her cheek. She is lost in spiritual contemplation of the torment she is suffering. She shows impatience at the sound of* MARIA's *voice as though loath to be disturbed. She replies wearily.*)

MARGARET. I have nothing to forgive. Get up, Maria. You have done nothing to me—go away!

MARIA. (*In a paroxysm of contrition.*) Oh, I beg, Mrs. Fleming, dot you vill take dot gun and blow my brains out.

MARGARET. Don't go on like that, Maria! (MARIA's *weeping irritates her.*) Get up! Please go away. Go away, I say!
(MARIA *slinks away quietly into the back room.* MARGARET *takes a long, sobbing breath, which ends in a sigh. She stares into space and a blank look comes into her face as though she were gazing at things beyond her comprehension. Presently the silence is broken by a low wail from the infant. It half arouses her.*)

MARGARET. What is the matter with that child? (*Her voice seems remote. Her expression remains fixed.*) Why don't you keep it quiet?

MRS. BURTON. (*In a hushed voice.*) It's hungry.

MARGARET. (*In the same mood, but her voice is a little querulous.*) Well, then, why don't you feed it?

MRS. BURTON. I can't get nothing fit for it. I've tried everything I could think of, but it's no use. (*She gets up and places the child upon the sofa to the left.*) There, be still, you poor little critter, an' I'll see what I ken get fer ye. (*As she goes to the door at the back,* MARGARET *speaks wearily.*)

MARGARET. Bring a lamp—it's getting dark here. (*She is still in the same attitude by the table. There is a silence, then the child's wail arouses her. She half turns her head in its direction—and tries to quiet it.*) Hush—child—hush— (*Then she reaches out her hand as if to pat it.*) There—there— poor little thing. Don't fret—it's no use to fret, child—be quiet now—there—there, now. (*She turns and slowly gropes her way to the sofa, sits on the edge of it, and feels for the child and gently pats it. She murmurs softly.*) Hush—baby —go to sleep.
(*There is a silence while a soft flood of sunshine plays about her. A pitying half smile flits across her face. She utters a faint sigh and again drifts away into that inner consciousness where she evidently finds peace. Again the child is restless—it arouses her and, hopeless of comforting it, she takes it in her arms. After a moment, she rises to her feet and stumbles toward the table. She knocks against the low chair. At the same moment,* PHILIP FLEMING *dashes breathlessly into the room through the door on the right. He pauses in horror as* MARGARET *raises her head, her eyes wide open, staring into his—her face calm and remote. She hushes the child softly, and sits in the low chair.* PHILIP *stands in dumb amazement watching her. The child begins*

*to fret her again. She seems hopeless of comforting it. Then
scarcely conscious of what she is doing, suddenly with an
impatient, swift movement she unbuttons her dress to give
nourishment to the child, when the picture fades away into
darkness.*)

ACT IV

*The scene is the same as the Second Act. The doors and
window leading into the garden are open.*

MARIA *is seated close to the open door, sewing. She occasionally looks into the garden as if guarding something.
She is neatly dressed, fresh and orderly looking. Her
manner is subdued. A bell rings and a closing door is heard.
Then* DOCTOR LARKIN *enters.* MARIA *goes to meet him and
scans his face anxiously.*

MARIA. Goot morning, doctor.

DOCTOR. Good morning. Well! Any news?

MARIA. (*Losing interest and shaking her head sadly.*) No,
doctor. No vord from him yet. It is seven days now—I
hoped—mebbe you might have some.

DOCTOR. No—nothing. How is Mrs. Fleming?

(MARIA *sits down to the left of the center of the room and
the doctor to the right.*)

MARIA. Yust the same as yesterday, und the day before, und
all the udder days. Ach, so bright, und so cheerful, but I
tink all the same she is breaking her heart. Ach, ven I look
into her sad eyes—vot cannot see me—I am ashamed to
hold my head up. (*She brushes away the tears.*)

DOCTOR. Does she talk about him at all?

MARIA. No, she never speaks his name.

DOCTOR. How is the child?

MARIA. (*Brightening.*) She is fine. Dot little tooth came
trough dis morning und she don't fret no more now.

DOCTOR. And, the *other* one?

MARIA. (*Indifferently.*) Oh, he's all right. I put him beside
Lucy in her crib dis morning und she laughs and pulls at
him und plays mit him yust like he vas a little kitten. Dis
is no place for him, doctor. Ven Mr. Fleming comes home

he vill fix tings, und I vill take him away by myself—vere
she no more can be troubled mit him.

DOCTOR. Things will come out all right. You'd best keep quiet.
Have nothing whatever to say in this matter.

MARIA. Ya. I make enough trouble already mit my tongue.
You bet I keep it shut in my head now. Shall I call Mrs.
Fleming? She is in the garden.

DOCTOR. She's there a great deal now, isn't she?

MARIA. Ya, she is always dere by the blossoms, und the
babies. (*She goes to the door and says in slow, deferential
voice.*) Mrs. Fleming, Doctor Larkin is here.

MARGARET. (*Outside.*) Yes, I'll come. (*She slowly emerges
from the garden into the doorway, her arms filled with
flowers. She is daintily dressed and there is a subtle dignity
and reserve about her. She smiles cheerily.*) Good morning, doctor. Maria, there are some daffodils out by the
yellow bed. Bring them, please. (*She slowly enters the
room.*)

(*The* DOCTOR *goes to her and gently leads her to the table
on the right where she puts the flowers, after carefully
locating a place to lay them.*)

DOCTOR. Well, well, where did you get such a lot of roses?
I couldn't gather so many in a month from my scrubby
bushes. The bugs eat 'em all up.

MARGARET. Why don't you spray them? (MARIA *brings a
large loose bunch of daffodils.*) Bring some jars, Maria.

DOCTOR. I did spray them.

MARGARET. When?

DOCTOR. When I saw the rose bugs.

MARGARET. (*Smiling.*) That's a fine time to spray bushes.
Don't you know that the time to prevent trouble is to look
ahead? From potatoes to roses, spray before anything
happens—*then* nothing *will* happen.

DOCTOR. (*Laughing.*) Yes, of course, I know, but I forgot to
do it until I saw two big, yellow bugs in the heart of
every rose and all the foliage chewed up.

MARGARET. There's no use in it now. You are just wasting
time. Start early next year before the leaves open.

DOCTOR. (*Admiringly.*) What a brave, cheery little woman
you are.

MARGARET. What's the use in being anything else? I don't see
any good in living in this world, unless you can live right.

DOCTOR. And this world needs just such women as you.

MARGARET. What does the world know or care about me?
(*The bell rings and the door opens and shuts.*)

DOCTOR. Very little, but it's got to feel your influence. (*He pats her hand.*)

(*The* MAID *enters.*)

MAID. Mr. Foster wishes to see you for a moment, Mrs. Fleming.

MARGARET. Tell him to come in.

(*The* MAID *goes out. In a moment* FOSTER *enters, flurried and embarrassed.*)

Good morning, Mr. Foster. (*She holds out her hands to him.*) Anything wrong at the mill?

FOSTER. Good morning, Mrs. Fleming. Oh, no—not at all, not at all. How do you do, doctor? (*He shakes hands with the* DOCTOR *with unusual warmth.*)

DOCTOR. (*Somewhat surprised and looking at him quizzically.*). Hello, Foster.

MARGARET. Will you sit down, Mr. Foster?

FOSTER. Thank you—yes, I will. What beautiful flowers. Mother says you have the loveliest garden in Canton.

MARGARET. (*Pleased.*) That's awfully nice of her. I had a delightful visit with her yesterday.

FOSTER. (*Nervously.*) Yes, she told me so.

MARGARET. We sat in the garden. What a sweet, happy soul she is.

FOSTER. (*Fussing with his hat and getting up and moving his chair close to the* DOCTOR's.) Yes. Mother always sees the bright side of the worst things.

MARGARET. She's very proud of you.

FOSTER. (*Laughing foolishly.*) Oh, yes, she is happy over anything I do. (*He looks at* MARGARET *furtively, then at the doctor. He evidently has something to say. Suddenly in a tense whisper he speaks to the doctor.*) Mr. Fleming has come back.

DOCTOR. Hush! Where is he? At the mill?

FOSTER. No. Here—outside.

DOCTOR. How does he look?

FOSTER. He's a wreck. He wants to see her.

DOCTOR. Well, tell her—I'll go— (*He rises.*)

FOSTER. No! (*He grabs him by the coat.*) For God's sake don't go. You tell her—you're her doctor.

(MARGARET *who has been busy with the flowers, becomes suddenly interested.*)

MARGARET. What are you two whispering about?

FOSTER. (*Laughing nervously.*) Oh, just a little advice, that's all. (*He goes to* MARGARET.) I'll say good morning, Mrs. Fleming. Glad to see you—er—looking—ah—so well. (*He shakes hands and rushes out.*)

(MARGARET *stands a little mystified. The* DOCTOR *approaches her gently.*)

DOCTOR. (*Very tenderly.*) Mrs. Fleming—I have something to say to you.

MARGARET. (*Standing tense and with ominous conviction.*) Philip is dead!

DOCTOR. No. He is not dead.

MARGARET. Where is he?

DOCTOR. *Outside.*

MARGARET. Why doesn't he come in?

DOCTOR. He's ashamed—afraid.

MARGARET. This is his home. Why should he be afraid to enter it? I will go to him. (*She starts toward the door, and then staggers. The* DOCTOR *puts an arm around her.*)

DOCTOR. There now. Keep up your courage. Don't forget, everything depends upon you.

MARGARET. (*Brokenly.*) I'm brave, doctor. I—perhaps it's best for you to tell him to come here.

DOCTOR. (*Patting her on the shoulder.*) Remember, you are very precious to us all. We cannot afford to lose *you*.

(MARGARET *stands by the table, calm and tense.* PHILIP *comes in from the right, carrying his cap in his hands. He looks weary and broken. He crosses behind* MARGARET *to the center of the stage and standing humbly before her, murmurs her name softly.*)

PHILIP. Margaret!

MARGARET. Well, Philip. (*After a slight pause.*) You have come back.

PHILIP. (*Humbly.*) Yes.

MARGARET. (*Gently.*) Why did you go away?

PHILIP. (*Overwhelmed with shame.*) I couldn't face you. I wanted to get away somewhere, and hide forever. (*He looks sharply at her.*) Can't you see me, Margaret?

MARGARET. (*Shaking her head.*) No!

PHILIP. (*Awed.*) You are blind! Oh!

(MARGARET *sits down in a chair by the table.* PHILIP *remains standing.*)

MARGARET. Don't mind. I shall be cured. Doctor Norton sees

me every day. He will operate as soon as he finds me normal.

PHILIP. You have been suffering?

MARGARET. Oh, no. (*After a pause.*) Philip, do you think that was right? To run away and hide?

PHILIP. I did not consider whether it was right or wrong. (*He speaks bitterly.*) I did not know the meaning of those words. I never have.

MARGARET. Oh, you are a man—people will soon forget.

PHILIP. (*Fiercely.*) I do not care about others. It is you, Margaret—will you ever forget? Will you ever forgive?

MARGARET. (*Shaking her head and smiling sadly.*) There is nothing to forgive. And, I want to forget.

PHILIP. (*Bewildered by her magnanimity, but full of hope.*) Then you will let me come back to you? You will help me to be a better—a wiser man?

MARGARET. (*Smilingly gently.*) Yes, Philip.
(*A quick joy takes hold of* PHILIP. *He makes a warm movement to go to her, then checks himself, and approaches her slowly while speaking, overcome by the wonder and beauty of her kindness.*)

PHILIP. All my life, Margaret, I will make amends for what I have done. I will atone for my ignorance—Oh, my wife— my dear, dear wife. (*He hangs over her tenderly, not daring to touch her.*)
(*At the word "wife"* MARGARET *rises, shrinking from him as though some dead thing was near her. A look of agony flits across her face.*)

MARGARET. No! Philip, not that! No! (*She puts out her hands to ward him off.*)

PHILIP. (*Beseechingly.*) Margaret!

MARGARET. (*Her face poignant with suppressed emotion, she confesses, brokenly.*) The wife-heart has gone out of me.

PHILIP. Don't—don't say that, Margaret.

MARGARET. I must. Ah, Philip, how I worshipped you. You were my idol. Is it my fault that you lie broken at my feet?

PHILIP. (*With urgency.*) You say you want to forget—that you forgive! Will you—?

MARGARET. Can't you understand? It is not a question of for-getting, or of forgiving— (*For an instant she is at a loss how to convince him.*) Can't you understand? Philip! (*Then suddenly.*) Suppose—I—had been unfaithful to you?

PHILIP. (*With a cry of repugnance.*) Oh, Margaret!

MARGARET. (*Brokenly.*) There! You see! You are a man, and you have your ideals of—the—sanctity—of—the thing you love. Well, I am a woman—and perhaps—I, too, have the same ideals. I don't know. But, I, too, cry "pollution." (*She is deeply moved.*)

PHILIP. (*Abashed.*) I did not know. I never realized before, the iniquity—of my—behavior. Oh, if I only had my life to live over again. Men, as a rule, do not consider others when urged on by their desires. How you must hate me.

MARGARET. No, I don't—I love you—I pity you.

PHILIP. Dear, not now—but in the future—some time—away in the future—perhaps, the old Margaret—

MARGARET. Ah, Philip, the old Margaret is dead. The truth killed her.

PHILIP. Then—there is no hope for me?

(*There is a dignity and a growing manliness in his demeanor as the scene progresses.*)

MARGARET. (*Warmly.*) Yes. Every hope.

PHILIP. Well, what do you want me to do? Shall I go away?

MARGARET. No. Your place is here. You cannot shirk your responsibilities now.

PHILIP. I do not want to shirk my responsibilities, Margaret. I want to do whatever you think is best.

MARGARET. Very well. It is best for us both to remain here, and take up the old life together. It will be a little hard for you, but you are a man—you will soon live it down.

PHILIP. Yes—I *will* live it down.

MARGARET. Go to the mill tomorrow morning and take up your work again, as though this thing had never happened.

PHILIP. Yes. All right. I'll do that.

MARGARET. Mr. Foster, you know, you have an unusually capable man there?

PHILIP. Yes, I appreciate Foster. He's a nice chap, too.

MARGARET. He has carried through a very critical week at the mill.

PHILIP. Don't worry, Margaret, everything will be all right there now. I will put my whole heart and soul into the work.

MARGARET. Then, you must do something for your child.

PHILIP. Yes, our dear child.

MARGARET. No, not our child—not Lucy. Your son.

PHILIP. My son?

MARGARET. Yes.

PHILIP. Where is he?

MARGARET. Here.

PHILIP. (*Resentfully.*) Who brought him here?

MARGARET. I did.

PHILIP. (*Amazed.*) You brought that child here?

MARGARET. Yes, where else should he go?

PHILIP. You have done that?

MARGARET. What other thing was there for me to do? Surely
if he was good enough to bring into the world, he is good
enough to find a shelter under your roof.

PHILIP. (*Moved by her magnanimity.*) I never dreamed that
you would do that, Margaret.

MARGARET. Well, he is here. Now, what are you going to do
with him?

PHILIP. (*Helplessly.*) What can I do?

MARGARET. Give him a name, educate him. Try to make
atonement for the wrong you did his mother. You must
teach him never to be ashamed of her, to love her memory—motherhood is a divine thing—remember that, Philip,
no matter when, or how. You can do fine things for this
unfortunate child.

PHILIP. (*Contemptuously.*) Fine things for him! I am not
fit to guide a young life. A fine thing I have made of my
own.

MARGARET. There is no use now lamenting what was done
yesterday. That's finished. Tomorrow? What are you going
to do with that?

PHILIP. There does not seem any "tomorrow" worth while
for me. The past—

MARGARET. The past is dead. We must face the living future.
Now, Philip, there are big things ahead for you, if you
will only look for them. They certainly will not *come* to
you. I will help you—we will fight this together.

PHILIP. Forgive me, please. I'll not talk like that any more.

MARGARET. Of course, there will be a lot of talk—mean talk—
but they will get tired of that in the end. Where have you
been all this time?

PHILIP. In Boston.

MARGARET. What have you been doing?

PHILIP. Nothing—I've been—in the hospital.

MARGARET. (*Stretching out her arms to him with an infinite tenderness.*) Ah, Philip, you have been ill?

PHILIP. No!

MARGARET. What was it. (*He is silent.*) Please tell me.

PHILIP. (*Rather reluctantly reciting his story.*) I was walking across the bridge over the Charles river one night—I was sick of myself—the whole world—I believed I should never see your face again. The water looked so quiet, it fascinated me. I just dropped into it and went down. It seemed like going to sleep. Then I woke up and I was in a narrow bed in a big room.

MARGARET. (*Breathless.*) The hospital?

PHILIP. Yes.

MARGARET. Oh, that was a cruel thing to do. Were they kind to you there?

PHILIP. Yes. There was an old nurse there—she was sharp. She told me not to be a fool, but to go back to my wife. She said—"If she's any good, she will forgive you." (*He smiles whimsically.*) Margaret, some day I am going to earn your respect, and then—I know, I shall be able to win you back to me all over again.

MARGARET. (*Smiling sadly.*) I don't know. That would be a wonderful thing. (*She weeps silently.*) A very wonderful thing. (*Then suddenly she springs to her feet.*) Ah, dreams! Philip! Dreams! And we must get to work.

(PHILIP *is inspired by her manner, and there is a quickening of his spirit, a response to her in the new vibration in his voice.*)

PHILIP. Work! Yes—I'll not wait until tomorrow. I'll go to the mill now.

MARGARET. That's fine. Do it.

PHILIP. Yes, I'll take a bath and get into some fresh clothing first.

MARGARET. Do. You must look pretty shabby knocking about for a week without a home.

PHILIP. Oh, I'll be all right. I'd like to see Lucy. (*He looks about.*) Where is she?

(MARGARET *is at the table occupied with the flowers.*)

MARGARET. They are both out there. (*She indicates with a turn of her head.*) In the garden.

(PHILIP *goes quickly to the door opening upon the garden and gazes out eagerly.* MARGARET, *at the table, pauses in in her work, gives a long sigh of relief and contentment. Her eyes look into the darkness and a serene joy illuminates her face. The picture slowly fades out as* PHILIP *steps buoyantly into the garden.*)

SELECTIVE BIBLIOGRAPHY

Anderson, John. *The American Theatre* (New York, 1938).

Clark, Barrett H., ed. *America's Lost Plays*, 20 vol. (Princeton, 1940–41; Bloomington, Indiana, 1963–65).

*Hartman, John Geoffrey. *The Development of American Social Comedy from 1787 to 1936* (Philadelphia, 1939).

*Hewitt, Barnard. *Theatre U.S.A. 1668–1957* (New York, 1959).

Hornblow, Arthur. *A History of the Theatre in America: From Its Beginnings to the Present Time*, 2 vol. (Philadelphia and London, 1919).

Hughes, Glenn. *A History of the American Theatre 1700–1950* (New York, 1951).

Hutton, Laurence. *Curiosities of the American Stage* (New York, 1891).

*Moody, Richard. *America Takes the Stage: Romanticism in American Drama and Theatre, 1750–1900* (Bloomington, 1955).

Morris, Lloyd. *Curtain Time: The Story of the American Theatre* (New York, 1953).

Moses, Montrose J. *The American Dramatist* (Boston, 1925).

————— and John Mason Brown. *The American Theatre as Seen by Its Critics, 1752–1934* (New York, 1934).

Odell, George C.D. *Annals of the New York Stage*, 15 vol. (New York, 1927–49).

*Quinn, Arthur H. *A History of the American Drama from the Beginning to the Civil War* (New York, 1923 and 1943).

*—————. *A History of the American Drama from the Civil War to the Present Day*, 2 vol. (New York, 1927, 1937, and 1943).

Smith, Cecil. *Musical Comedy in America* (New York, 1950).

Taubman, Howard. *The Making of the American Theatre* (New York, 1965).

* Comprehensive bibliographies may be found in these volumes and in Richard Moody's extensive collection, *Dramas from the American Theatre 1762–1909* (Cleveland and New York, 1966).

Myron Matlaw, Professor of English at Queens College of the City University of New York, is the author of *Modern World Drama: An Encyclopedia*, the co-author of *Pro and Con*, and the editor of *Story and Critic* and *American Popular Entertainment*. His articles on literature and the theatre have appeared in numerous magazines and scholarly journals, and his studies of early American vaudeville won an award from the American Council of Learned Societies. Dr. Matlaw is currently writing a biography of James O'Neill.

"FIVE SPLENDID PLAYS... ENJOYABLE TO READ AND AS TIMELY TO PRODUCE.*"

**Plays by American Women
Edited and with an introduction
by Judith E. Barlow**

*"Barlow's introduction not only offers a description and analysis of the five playwrights but also sets them in an historical context."

—Booklist

A MAN'S WORLD
by Rachel Crothers
TRIFLES
by Susan Glaspell
MISS LULU BETT
by Zona Gale
PLUMES
by Georgia Douglas Johnson
MACHINAL
by Sophie Treadwell

These important dramatists did more than write significant new plays; they introduced to the American stage a new and vital character; the modern American woman in her quest for a forceful role in a changing American scene. It will be hard to remember that these women playwrights were ever forgotten.

APPLAUSE
THEATRE BOOK PUBLISHERS
100 West 67 St •New York, N.Y. 10023•(212)595 4735

"INDISPENSABLE!"

—Robert Brustein
Director, Loeb Drama
Center
Harvard University

The Brute and Other Farces
by Anton Chekhov
Edited by Eric Bentley

"A truly delightful collection!"
—Lloyd Richards
 Dean
 Yale School of Drama

All the farces of Russia's greatest dramatist are rendered here in the classic
lively translations which audiences
and scholars alike applaud on the stage
and in the classroom.

The blustering, stuttering eloquence of
Chekhov's unlikely heroes has en-
dured to shape the voice of contemporary theatre. This volume presents
seven minor masterpieces:

HARMFULNESS OF TOBACCO
SWAN SONG
THE BRUTE
MARRIAGE PROPOSAL
SUMMER IN THE COUNTRY
A WEDDING
THE CELEBRATION

APPLAUSE
THEATRE BOOK PUBLISHERS
100 West 67 St •New York, N.Y. 10023•(212)595 4735